For Reference

Not to be taken

from this library

D1404602

Endangered Wildlife and Plants of the World

Volume 4
DEE–FOX

Marshall Cavendish
New York • London • Toronto • Sydney

Marshall Cavendish Corporation
99 White Plains Road
Tarrytown, NY 10591-9001

Created by Brown Partworks Ltd.
Project Editor: Anne Hildyard
Associate Editors: Paul Thompson, Amy Prior
Managing Editor: Tim Cooke
Design: Whitelight
Picture Research: Helen Simm
Index Editor: Kay Ollerenshaw
Production Editor: Matt Weyland
Illustrations: Barbara Emmons, Jackie Harland, Tracy Williamson

Library of Congress Cataloging-in-Publication Data

Endangered wildlife and plants of the world
p.cm.
Includes bibliographical references (p.).
ISBN 0-7614-7194-4 (set)
ISBN 0-7614-7198-7 (vol. 4)
1. Endangered species--Encyclopedias. I. Marshall Cavendish Corporation.

QH75.E68 2001
333.95'22'03--dc21
99-086194

Printed in Malaysia
Bound in the United States of America
07 06 05 04 03 02 01 00 7 6 5 4 3 2 1

TABLE OF CONTENTS/VOLUME 4

ESA and IUCN

In this set of endangered animals and plants, each species, where appropriate, is given an ESA status and an IUCN status. The sources consulted to determine the status of each species are the Endangered Species List maintained by the U.S. Fish and Wildlife Service and the Red Lists compiled by IUCN–The World Conservation Union, which is a worldwide organization based in Switzerland.

ENDANGERED SPECIES ACT

The Endangered Species Act (ESA) was initially passed by the U.S. Congress in 1973, and reauthorized in 1988. The aim of the ESA is to rescue species that are in danger of extinction due to human action and to conserve the species and their ecosystems. Endangered plants and animals are listed by the U.S. Fish and Wildlife Service (USFWS), which is part of the Department of Interior. Once a species is listed, the USFWS is required to develop recovery plans, and ensure that the threatened species is not further harmed by any actions of the U.S. government or U.S. citizens. The act specifically forbids the buying, selling, transporting, importing, or exporting of any listed species. It also bans the taking of any listed species in the U.S. and its territories, on both private and public lands. Violators can face heavy fines or imprisonment. However, the ESA requires that the protection of the species is balanced with economic factors.

The ESA recognizes two categories of risk for species:

Endangered: A species that is in danger of extinction throughout all or a significant part of its range.

Threatened: A species that is likely to become endangered in the foreseeable future.

RECOVERY

Recovery takes place when the decline of the endangered or threatened species is halted or reversed, and the circumstances that caused the threat have been removed. The ultimate aim is the recovery of the species to the point where it no longer requires protection under the act.

Recovery can take a long time. Because the decline of the species may have occurred over centuries, the loss cannot be reversed overnight. There are many factors involved: the number of individuals of the species that remain in the wild, how long it takes the species to mature and reproduce, how much habitat is remaining, and whether the reasons for the decline are clear cut and understood. Recovery plans employ a wide range of strategies that involve the following: reintroduction of species into formerly occupied habitat, land aquisition and management, captive breeding, habitat protection, research, population counts, public education projects, and assistance for private landowners.

SUCCESS STORIES

Despite the difficulties, recovery programs do work, and the joint efforts of the USFWS, other federal and state agencies, tribal governments, and private landowners have not been in vain. Only seven species, less than 1 percent of all the species listed between 1968 and 1993, are now known to be extinct. The other 99 percent of listed species have not been lost to extinction, and this confirms the success of the act.

There are some good examples of successful recovery plans. In 1999, the peregrine falcon, the bald eagle, and the Aleutian goose were removed from the endangered species list. The falcon's numbers have risen dramatically. In 1970, there were only 39 pairs of falcons in the United States. By 1999, the number had risen to 1,650 pairs. The credit for the recovery goes to the late Rachel

Carson, who highlighted the dangers of DDT, and also to the Endangered Species Act, which enabled the federal government to breed falcons in captivity, and took steps to protect their habitat.

Young bald eagles were also successfully translocated into habitat that they formerly occupied, and the Aleutian Canada goose has improved due to restoration of its habitat and reintroduction into former habitat.

IUCN—THE WORLD CONSERVATION UNION

The IUCN (International Union for Conservation of Nature) was established in 1947. It is an alliance of governments, governmental agencies, and nongovernmental agencies. The aim of the IUCN is to help and encourage nations to conserve wildlife and natural resources. Organizations such as the Species Survival Commission is one of several IUCN commissions that assesses the conservation status of species and subspecies globally. Taxa that are threatened with extinction are noted and steps are taken for their conservation by programs designed to save, restore, and manage species and their habitats. The Survival Commission is committed to providing objective information on the status of globally threatened species, and produces two publications: the *IUCN Red List of Threatened Animals*, and the *IUCN Red List of Threatened Plants*. They are compiled from scientific data and provide the status of threatened species, depending on their existence in the wild and threats that undermine that existence. The lists for plants and animals differ slightly.

The categories from the *IUCN Red List of Threatened Animals* used in *Endangered Wildlife and Plants of the World* are as follows:

Extinct: A species is extinct when there is no reasonable doubt that the last individual has died.

Extinct in the wild: A species that is known only to survive in captivity, well outside its natural range.

Critically endangered: A species that is facing an extremely high risk of extinction in the wild in the immediate future.

Endangered: A species that is facing a very high risk of extinction in the wild in the near future.

Vulnerable: A species that is facing a high risk of extinction in the wild in the medium-term future.

Lower risk: A species that does not satisfy the criteria for designation as critically endangered, endangered, or vulnerable. Species included in the lower risk category can be separated into three subcategories:

Conservation dependent: A species that is part of a conservation program. Without the program, the species would qualify for one of the threatened categories within five years.

Near threatened: A species that does not qualify for conservation dependent, but is close to qualifying as vulnerable.

Least concern: A species that does not qualify for conservation dependent or near threatened.

Data deficient: A species on which there is inadequate information to make an asssessment of risk of extinction. Because there is a possibility that future research will show that the species is threatened, more information is required.

The categories from the *IUCN Red List of Threatened Plants*, used in *Endangered Wildlife and Plants of the World*, are as follows:

Extinct: A species that has not definitely been located in the wild during the last 50 years.

Endangered: A species whose survival is unlikely if the factors that threaten it continue. Included are species whose numbers have been reduced to a critical level, or whose habitats have been so drastically reduced that they are deemed to be in immediate danger of extinction. Also included in this category are species that may be extinct but have definitely been seen in the wild in the past 50 years.

Vulnerable: A species that is thought likely to move into the endangered category in the near future if the factors that threaten it remain.

Rare: A species with small world populations that are not at present endangered or vulnerable, but are at risk. These species are usually in restricted areas or are thinly spread over a larger range.

Cedros Island Mule Deer

(Odocoileus hemionus cerrosensis)

ESA: Endangered

IUCN: Endangered

Weight: 176–220 lb. (80–100 kg)
Shoulder height: 35½-39 in. (90–100 cm)
Diet: Grasses, leaves, and twigs
Gestation period: 195–210 days
Longevity: 15 years
Habitat: Scrub bush to forest
Range: Cedros (Cerros) Island, Baja California

THE CEDROS ISLAND mule deer is part of a larger group of North American mule deer (*Odocoileus hemionus*). The other dominant group of deer in North America are the white-tailed deer (*Odocoileus virginianus*). These two groups dominate the mainland of North America. The white-tailed deer is found mostly in the eastern United States, while the mule deer is found in the western part; however, there are areas of overlap.

There are some island populations, and island populations are vulnerable because they have nowhere to go if their habitat is altered. Poaching and habitat destruction jeopardize their survival. One such island population, the Cedros Island mule deer, is found off the coast of Baja California. The population was estimated to be stable at around 275 animals in 1985, however local reports in 1996 indicated that domestic and perhaps feral dogs were hunting the deer. Although protected under Mexican law, this deer is also hunted by local people for sport and subsistence. There are no captive populations for this deer to fall back on, only the population of about 50 individuals remaining on the island.

This deer is similar to other mule deer. The males and females live apart except during the rutting season in the fall. They have the same cycle of antler growth as mainland deer. They are grazers, and eat any available vegetation.

Columbian White-tailed Deer

(Odocoileus virginianus leucurus)

ESA: Endangered

IUCN: Lower risk

Weight: 176–265 lb. (80–120 kg)
Shoulder height: 31½–39 in. (80–100 cm)
Diet: Leaves, shoots, twigs, and grasses
Gestation period: 195–210 days
Longevity: 15 years
Habitat: Forests to scrub grass
Range: Western Oregon, Washington

THE COLUMBIAN white-tailed deer is a member of the subfamily known as roe or New World deer, commonly found in the eastern United States.

This species, however, is an exception, ranging in a small area along the lower Columbia River. The Columbian is a medium-sized white-tailed deer, and in its habits is very much like other white-tailed deer, except that it prefers living along streams and rivers. The males tend to be solitary or live in small groups of bucks; they remain apart from the females except during the rutting season in the fall.

The primary cause of their decline was due to the conversion of prairie and forest habitat into crops and pasture land. Flooding, vehicle traffic, and residential development have also taken their toll. Today, the Columbian white-tailed deer survives in two populations, with one in Douglas County, Oregon estimated at 3,000 to 4,000, and one in the lower Columbia River area, with 800 to 1,000 animals. Both populations are believed to be stable, and this deer is considered to be on the road to recovery. At present there is no captive population.

Corsican Red Deer

(Cervus elaphus corsicanus)

ESA: Endangered

IUCN: Endangered

Weight: 165–176 lb. (75–80 kg)
Shoulder height: 33½–39 in. (85–100 cm)
Diet: Leaves, twigs, and grasses
Gestation period: 230–240 days
Longevity: 15–18 years
Habitat: Scrub forest
Range: Southern Sardinia

THE CORSICAN red deer gets its name from the island of Corsica in the Mediterranean Sea. Ironically, this deer became extinct on

Corsica around 1970. It now survives only on the island of Sardinia, due south. The *Cervus* genus to which it belongs is a red deer group that ranges throughout Europe and Asia. The Corsican deer is one of the smallest specimens of this group, which is not surprising among island forms.

Because the Corsican red deer lives only on an island, its territory is limited. Sardinia has a substantial human population, and because of poaching and habitat disturbance, the deer are now found only in the southern part of the island. In 1986 their numbers were estimated at 240 to 330 individuals living in three separate areas. Two pairs were reintroduced to Corsica in 1985 into a fenced national park, and their number has since increased to some 300. This species has the typical red deer mating cycle in which the sexes live apart except during the rutting season, which takes place in the fall. The fawns are born in the spring.

There is no captive population of Corsican red deer. Individuals in the wild have legal protection; however, that does not stop the competition with domestic sheep and goats for good grazing land.

Hangul (Kashmir) Deer

(Cervus elaphus hanglu)

IUCN: Endangered

Class: Mammalia
Order: Artiodactyla
Family: Cervidae
Subfamily: Cervinae
Weight: 330–397 lb. (150–180 kg)
Shoulder height: 48–53 in. (122–135 cm)
Diet: Leaves, twigs, and grasses
Gestation period: 225–245 days
Longevity: 15–18 years
Habitat: Open forest to bush
Range: India-Kashmir

THE HANGUL, or Kashmir deer, used to be numerous in the region known as the vale of Kashmir, in riverine and upland forest. Now its population has been decimated, from a population that once numbered around 3,000 to 4,000 to no more than 200. The only viable population left is in the Dachigam Sanctuary, which was set aside nearly 50 years ago as a refuge for the hangul. Unfortunately the protections were not really enforced until about 1951, and even after that great quantities of sheep and water buffalo grazed in the area and degraded the environment. Poaching, too, has been a problem as an organized operation in the past, with hunters working in groups and preying upon the hangul and other fauna.

Poaching has finally come under control and there seems to be a reasonable amount of protection given now to the hangul. The range left for the hangul

N

CORSICAN RED DEER
Europe

deer's existence is very limited, and there is now no territory remaining for it to expand.

The hangul is a handsome member of the red deer species. It is fairly large, standing up to four feet (1.2 meters) tall.

The hangul breeds according to a seasonal cycle: the mating, or rut, takes place in autumn, and the young are born in the spring.

There may be a few individuals in some of the more remote areas of its range, but the only viable population is in the Dachigam sanctuary. At the last population count, there were approximately 800 animals left, and there is no breeding group in captivity to replace the wild population. The solution is to relocate the existing wild population to safe areas resembling their habitat.

No plans have yet been made to accomplish this, and the hangul is considered to be endangered.

Key Deer
(Odocoileus virginianus clavium)

ESA: Endangered

IUCN: Endangered

Weight: 55–88 lb. (25–40 kg)
Shoulder height: 24–29½ in. (60–75 cm)
Diet: Leaves, twigs, and grasses
Gestation period: 290–310 days
Longevity: 15–18 years
Habitat: Palmetto palm scrub
Range: Florida Keys

THE KEY DEER is another member of the white-tailed deer subfamily that ranges in the eastern portion of the United States. There are also a number of white-tailed populations found on adjacent islands off the eastern and southern coast. Perhaps

the best-known is the Florida Key deer, named for the chain of islands that extends off the tip of Florida to the Gulf of Mexico.

This deer lived on the Keys long before the islands were populated by people, which means their population has been isolated from the mainland for so long that there are some dramatic differences between the Florida Key deer and other mainland white-tailed deer.

Key deer have similar reproductive and behavioral patterns to those of their mainland cousins, but they do manage to feed off much coarser vegetation. Because of their seaside habitat, they have grown to be much more tolerant of salt. They can subsist on brackish water, something other deer would resist. The key deer have been severely limited by the available land area and food supply, so

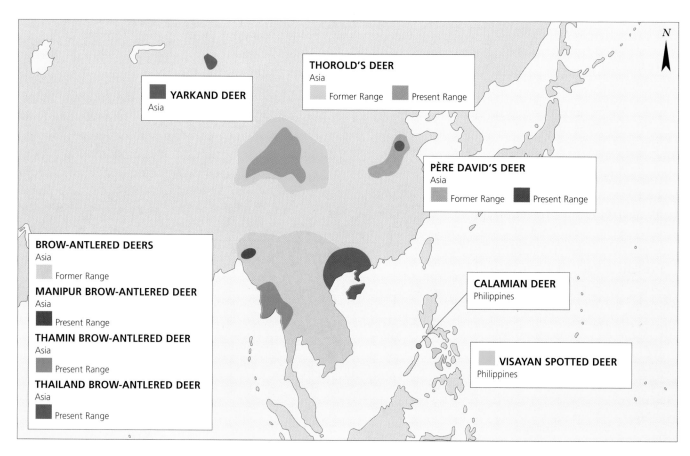

their reproductive rate is considerably lower than that of mainland deer.

Probably the most unusual difference between the Key deer and mainland deer is the Key deer's tiny size. A newborn fawn footprint is about the same size as a human thumbnail. Even adults don't weigh much over 40 kilograms (88 pounds). Since their size is very small, their food requirements are far less than for mainland deer.

Some of these animals have been kept in captive populations on the mainland. When their food is restricted to nearly the same type and amount that they would obtain in the Keys, they grow to normal size. However, in some feeding experiments in which these deer were given a higher quality of food over a period of time, each generation tended to increase in size.

With each generation, these Florida Key deer began to resemble their larger mainland relatives. Their larger size, however, would have been a threat to their survival on the Keys.

Threats

Since the appearance of people and the growth of the tourist industry in the Florida Keys, many deer have been killed each year by automobiles while they were crossing the main highway.

Present threats include habitat loss due to development, reduction of surface fresh water, road kills, and predation by domestic dogs. As the population probably numbers only 250 to 300 animals, its long-term viability is also considered susceptible to environmental catastrophes such as hurricanes.

Manipur Brow-antlered Deer

(Cervus eldi eldi)

ESA: Endangered

IUCN: Critically endangered

Thailand Brow-antlered Deer

(Cervus eldi siamensis)

IUCN: Data deficient

Weight: 210–265 lb. (95–120 kg)
Shoulder height: 43–47 in. (110–120 cm)
Diet: Leaves, twigs, and grasses
Gestation period: 225–240 days
Longevity: 15–18 years
Habitat: Forest, swamp, grassland near water
Range: India (Manipur subspecies); Southeast Asia, Hainan Islands (Thailand subspecies)

THIS DEER is commonly called Eld's deer and has adapted to swampy habitats. It prefers open grassy plains and deciduous forests adjacent to swampy areas, although the brow-antlered deer is extremely well adapted to a wet environment, having relatively broad hooves that allow it to move through muddy, swampy ground with ease.

There are actually three kinds of Eld's deer. The form found in India is called the Manipur brow-

antlered deer. There is also the thamin (*Cervus eldi thamin*) subspecies found in Myanmar and Thailand, and the third subspecies is called the Thailand brow-antlered deer, found over much of Southeast Asia, particularly in Indochina. All of the Eld's deer subspecies are in trouble, but the Manipur brow-antlered deer has the worst problems because it is critically endangered.

Predation and habitat loss

The Manipur brow-antlered deer is now found only in a single population at the southern end of Loktak Lake in Manipur, India, in Keibul Lamjao National Park. The population increased to 127 by the mid-1990s, compared to only 14 animals in the 1970s. However, only 42 animals were counted in a subsequent aerial survey. They are preyed upon by tigers and leopards, occasionally by wild dogs (dholes), and by crocodiles, which also inhabit the deer's swampy habitat.

The most disastrous problems, however, have been caused by the destruction of their habitat and poaching by humans.

While a survey has been undertaken to assess the potential for reintroductions, the captive population of Manipur brow-antlered deer in the major Indian zoos has many problems. Not only are the animals from a narrow gene pool—and show many signs of inbreeding—but they have also been plagued by outbreaks of tuberculosis.

By 1994, 14 zoos held 107 animals, an increase from 97 animals held in 1992. However, considering that less than 100 of these animals are left in one isolated part of India, the Manipur

441

The Thailand brow-antlered deer has been preyed upon by other animals, such as tigers and leopards. The greatest damage to the population, however, has been brought about by humans. Destruction of habitat and poaching have seriously reduced the numbers of this unusual deer throughout Southeast Asia.

is surely one of the most severely endangered deer species in the world. This deer has now been banned from international commercial trade under the Convention on International Trade in Endangered Species of Wild Fauna and Flora (CITES).

Indochina population

The Thailand brow-antlered deer is found in parts of Laos, Kampuchea, Vietnam, and over into the Hainan Islands.

It is believed extinct in the country for which it is named, Thailand. Elsewhere, this deer has

The Manipur brow-antlered deer (*Cervus eldi eldi*) is one of three subspecies of Eld's deer. There are very few remaining of this particular subspecies and they occur only near Loktak Lake in the Manipur area of Assam, in India.

also suffered decline due to severe habitat destruction and poaching.

In habits it is very much like the other brow-antlered deer, the Manipur and the thamin. The males live separately from the small groups of females, and the two groups only appear to come together during the breeding season between March and May.

Brow-antlered deer eat whatever vegetation is available, including twigs and grasses. Not only are the deer preyed on by humans, but they are also taken by tigers, leopards, Asiatic wild dogs (dholes), and crocodiles.

Bleak future

The range of the Thailand brow-antlered deer is broad, but there is no information about its endangerment status, in fact there is insufficient data available to accurately assess its status at this time. Unfortunately there is virtually no captive population. In the late 1980s only three captive deer were noted in Bangkok, and five in Paris, France.

Père David's Deer
(Elaphurus davidianus)

IUCN: Critically endangered

Weight: 440–606 lb. (200–275 kg)
Shoulder height: 39–79 in. (100–200 cm)
Diet: Leaves, twigs, and grasses
Gestation period: 270–300 days
Longevity: 20 years
Habitat: Swampy lowlands
Range: Northern China

THE PÈRE, or Father David's deer, have never been known to live in the wild in historic times.

A French missionary named Armand David (Père David) worked in China in the 19th century, and was an amateur naturalist. Père David was allowed to enter the Imperial Hunting Park, a preserve established centuries before. He saw

there an unusual deer. It had huge broad feet, akin to those of cattle, and a long flowing tail like that of a horse. This deer had a long face, and the male's antlers were different from those of any other species: they were turned 180 degrees, as if they were pointing backward.

Père David obtained a skull and skin, which he sent back to Paris. The proof was undeniable, and the deer was named after him (*Elaphurus davidianus*).

The deer probably existed very early in north central China, where there once was a large population of these animals. Individuals were taken from the wild and preserved in the Imperial Hunting Park for many centuries. There are no records of it in the wild. Not only does this deer have the strange traits described by Père David, but it has leg tendons unlike those of any other member of the deer family. They produce a snapping or clicking sound when they walk. Only reindeer, caribou, and this deer share the characteristic.

Over several years a number of live animals were caught and sent to Europe. A trio went to the Berlin Zoo and some went to Paris and London. Good records were not kept, and it is not known which individuals bred. However, over a period of time, many of the animals disappeared, while others were bred in zoos.

The Berlin Zoo had the best breeding success with one male and two females, but no regular groups of Père David's deer were established until the Duke of Bedford gathered up every Père David's deer in Europe and took them to his estate at Woburn Abbey in England. He bred them

into a substantial population, and all Père David's deer in zoos today are descended from this stock.

The Chinese population

Although individual deer were pulled out of the Imperial Hunting Park and sent to Europe, the remaining population lived as they had for centuries, until the mid-1890s. Then a flood caused part of a wall to collapse, and half of the deer escaped. As it was a time of famine, they were eaten by starving people. The wall was repaired, and the animals left inside began breeding back.

The next tragedy was the Boxer Rebellion at the turn of the century. The allied armies occupied Peking and the Imperial Hunting Park, where soldiers shot most of the deer. The last ones died in the 1920s. Since then Père David's

The Père David's deer looks very different from other species, probably because it was isolated in the Imperial Hunting Park of China for centuries.

deer has been extinct in China. Père David's deer have since been sent back to China. They were reintroduced into a wild swampy preserve where they may have originated, and seem to flourish. A census in December, 1999 estimated the population as 364.

Considering all the time they spent in captivity and their narrow gene pool, the deer have remained healthy and have defeated many typical problems of inbreeding. The captive populations have increased. There are some infertile males and birth defects, such as undershot jaws, and cleft palates are common. Nonetheless this deer remains a success story in captive breeding.

Persian Fallow Deer

(Dama dama mesopotamica)

ESA: Endangered

IUCN: Endangered

Weight: 220–331 lb. (100–150 kg)
Shoulder height: 35½–55 in. (90–140 cm)
Diet: Primarily leaves and twigs, some grasses
Gestation period: 225 days
Longevity: 20 years
Habitat: Open forest to scrub
Range: Iran

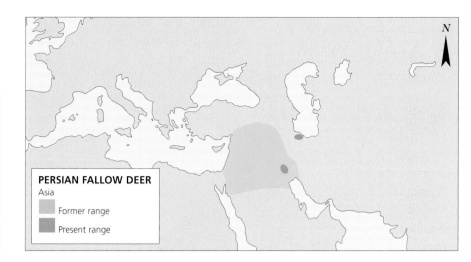

PERSIAN FALLOW DEER
Asia
Former range
Present range

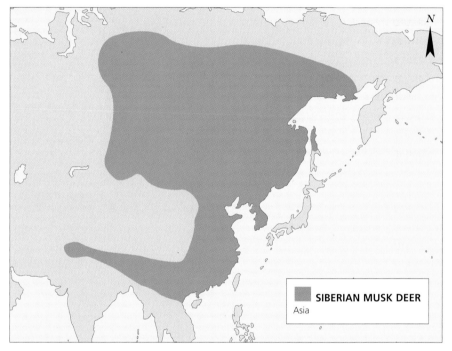

SIBERIAN MUSK DEER
Asia

THIS ANIMAL used to be found over a large area of the Middle East, in habitats ranging from open forest to heavy scrub thickets. At one point in the last 30 years it was thought to be extinct. However, a remnant population was found on the border between Iran and Iraq.

Its habits are similar to other fallow deer. It has been known in the past to be fairly sociable, but due to habitat destruction and heavy poaching it is now much more secretive. This species is endangered due to competition from domestic cattle in their small remaining habitat.

Fallow deer are primarily browsers. The sexes stay separate until rutting season, around the end of August. In addition to people, these deer are preyed on by hyenas, wolves, and wild dogs.

The Persian or Mesopotamian fallow deer is slightly larger in body form and bulk than the common fallow. It is a uniformly dark fawn color on its back,

which becomes even darker in the winter, and fades into a lighter fawn color on the belly and underneath the neck. It has considerable white spotting over the back, with one line of spots that continues down the flank and sides, giving the appearance of a striped marking.

The antlers are palmate, or broadened, but they are not nearly as large as the antlers of the common fallow. While the Persian fallow deer's antlers may not be imposing, the rest of its body is, weighing around 300 pounds (136 kilograms).

There are believed to be only two remaining wild populations of Persian fallow deer, one at Dez River Wildlife Sanctuary with fewer than 15 animals and another with perhaps only five animals at Karkeh River Wildlife Sanctuary. There have also been a number of reintroductions, although some of these animals have died.

The present population, including captive animals, is thought not to exceed 250 and the captive population is probably a mix of purebred and hybrid fallow deer.

Siberian Musk Deer

(Moschus moschiferus linnaeus)

ESA: Endangered

IUCN: Vulnerable

Weight: 20–40 lb. (9–18 kg)
Shoulder height: 22–26 in. (55–65 cm)
Diet: Leaves, grasses, bark, and lichen
Gestation period: 150–180 days
Longevity: 13 years (captivity)
Habitat: Open sub-alpine forest
Range: East and Central Siberia to Mongolia, East and Central China, Tibet, Himalayas to Northern Burma, Assam, Thailand, and Northern Vietnam

THIS ANIMAL is not a true deer. It has no antlers (all other deer possess antlers, with the exception of the water deer), no gall bladder, and the male has a unique organ known as a musk gland on its abdomen near the umbilicus. This musk gland is essential to its lifestyle. This small, hoofed animal has longish hair which is very bristly, dark brown in color and speckled with gray. It has a pointed face, large ears and a very small tail that is hidden in the hair of its rump. Male musk deer are solitary, except during the breeding season. The breeding season appears to be in December or January. In May or June a single fawn is born; occasionally there may be twins.

This deer's diet consists of the available vegetation. It is fond of lichens and moss. It is preyed upon by humans and also by the dominant predators in its range.

These are wolves, dholes, and leopards. The males are armed with very long canine teeth that protrude and can be up to almost 3½ inches in length (9 centimeters).

The musk gland is used by the males for the social marking of their territory as well as during the breeding season. The musk gland produces a waxy exudate (secretion) that is commercially valued for use in expensive perfumes, and is also used in folk medicines, including its questionable use as an aphrodisiac. After the animal is killed, the gland is removed and sun-dried. It is extracted in the form of a self-contained pod. Only a small amount is removed from each pod. It is estimated that 200 male musk deer are killed to obtain one kilogram (2.2 pounds) of musk. It is one of the most expensive products to buy in its pure form. In the early 1980s it sold for between $40,000 and $60,000 for 2.2 pounds (1 kilogram) on the international market, and the cost has escalated. Demand for musk has caused the animal to become endangered. The musk deer has a very large range, but its numbers have been so reduced that it is now represented by fragmented populations. It is now thought that over its extensive range there are only about 40,000 animals. The irony is that the animal does not have to be destroyed to obtain the musk. When captured young, the deer become docile and easily handled and can be milked twice a year starting from the age of one year. There are some places in China where this is the method by which the musk is obtained; however, the demand for its musk is so high, and the rewards so lucrative,

that the destruction of the wild musk deer population continues nearly unabated. Most countries within the animal's range have protective regulations but there is little enforcement, and since so much value is placed on the musk, there are many ways to circumvent the laws. As long as the musk is so valued, the future for the musk deer is tenuous at best.

Swamp Deer (Barasingha)

(Cervus duvauceli)

ESA: Endangered

IUCN: Vulnerable

Weight: 385–617 lb. (175–280 kg)
Shoulder height: 45–49 in. (115–125 cm)
Diet: Primarily grasses
Gestation period: 225 days
Longevity: 18–20 years
Habitat: Open forest near water, swampy grasslands
Range: India, Nepal

THE BARASINGHA is a Hindi name that refers to six tines—the number of points an adult male swamp deer has on its antlers. The barasingha is found in northern and central India and in one area of Nepal.

There are three different subspecies of this deer. *Cervus duvauceli duvauceli* is found in northern India and Nepal and has the largest population, with 3,500 to 4,000 in India and more than 1,800 in Nepal. The most endangered is the peninsular form, *Cervus duvauceli branderi,* which is restricted to a single population in central India and is believed to number only about 500. A third subspecies, *Cervus duvauceli ranjitsinhi*, is restricted to a single population of 350 to 500 in Kaziranga National Park in eastern India. Swamp deer have similar habits. They are found from open grasslands and forest to large swampy areas. The males live apart from the females except for the rutting season in late December. They are active during the day and graze on plants and grasses. Often the males will violently attack the vegetation around them with their hard antlers, and large quantities of twigs and brush as well as grass get caught in their antlers. This is simply part of their male behavior.

Seasonal color change

In many of these deer there is a marked color change from winter to summer. In winter they become quite darkish brown in color and there is little evidence of spotting or striping. However, in the summer their coat is a bright golden fawn color and there are often white spots running down their back as well as a darkish stripe.

Swamp deer are preyed upon by humans; however, leopards and tigers also take their toll. Leopards will attack the younger animals. Tigers, if pressed by hunger, will take on some of the adults despite their size. In some areas the deer are prized by hunters for their meat, which is said to taste very much like veal.

Most swamp deer are found in protected reserves. Their downfall is mainly the result of habitat destruction, but it is also due to illegal hunting and competition for habitat from other deer. Efforts to help the swamp deer to recover focus on protecting the grasslands within the deer's range. The deer is banned from international commercial trade under CITES. In North America and Europe there is a very stable population in captivity, with approximately 250 individuals in 38 zoos as of 1989. However, the gene pool is narrow. It is believed to have originated from only three animals imported over 100 years ago.

These swamp deer have done well in captivity because they are a hardy species that will acclimatize fairly readily to a wide variety of climatic conditions.

Although they prefer wet, soggy areas, in the United States they have been introduced with success in the high, dry lands of Texas and Oklahoma. A concerted effort needs to be made to broaden the gene pool.

In India there were 74 *Cervus duvauceli duvauceli* in 10 Indian zoos in 1995. They are all descendants of three deer.

The barasingha, or swamp deer, does well in captivity. In India alone there are more than 120 individuals of one subspecies in captivity.

Thorold's Deer
(Cervus albirostris)

IUCN: Vulnerable

Weight: 287–331 lb. (130–150 kg)
Shoulder height: 47–51 in. (120–130 cm)
Diet: Leaves, twigs, and grasses
Gestation period: 240–270 days
Longevity: 15 years
Habitat: High-altitude pine forest and meadows
Range: China

THIS IS ALSO KNOWN as the white-lipped deer. It is a distant relation to the Asiatic form called the wapiti (*Cervus canadensis*). The antlers and habits of the two forms are similar. It is found from the forest edges to open grassland in the highlands of the Tibetan plateau.

Although Thorold's deer has been hunted extensively and its range has diminished, it still exists in high numbers. Some recent estimates, including captive animals, range from 30,000 to 50,000. However, the wild population is scattered and is believed to number only about 6,000. In addition, while very large groups were once maintained on reserves for breeding for their antlers used in traditional Chinese medicine, many government deer farms were closed by the end of the 1980s due to overproduction by farms in New Zealand and elsewhere. The current population of this deer is unknown.

This large deer gets its other name from its white lip. The area around the muzzle is white and extends a short distance down the throat. The deer's winter coat is particularly striking, and there is a peculiar reversal of the hairs on their withers (they face forward instead of back toward the tail) so that they appear to have a slight hump or saddle.

While Thorold's deer is legally protected in China, hunting for its antlers as well as meat and other organs poses a major threat to wild populations. Competition with livestock and habitat conversion are also problems, with the latter fragmenting populations, particularly in the Qinghai and Xizang provinces.

Visayan Spotted Deer
(Cervus alfredi)

ESA: Endangered

IUCN: Endangered

Weight: 82–132 lb. (37–60 kg)
Shoulder height: 47–51 in. (120–130 cm)
Diet: Leaves, twigs, and grasses
Gestation period: Unknown
Longevity: Unknown
Habitat: Open forest to dense thickets
Range: Visayan Islands, Philippines

THIS HANDSOME deer comes only from the Visayan Islands, part of the Philippine Archipelago. One of its distant relatives, the sambar deer (*Cervus unicolor*), is one of the most dominant forms of deer in tropical Asia. The Visayan spotted deer have been listed as a subspecies of both the sambar and the Philippine sambar (*Cervus mariannus*); however, it is now considered to be an entirely separate species. The Visayan spotted deer is also known as the Prince Alfred's deer. Population in the wild is estimated at fewer than 300.

Like the sambar deer, the Visayan spotted deer is found in open forest and dense thickets and feeds on any and all vegetation. It has a beautiful dark coat with a white underpart and spotting that sometimes merges to give the appearance of lines. Unlike the rest of the sambar group, the antlers of the Visayan spotted deer are not particularly prominent.

Captivity
A handful of the Visayan spotted deer have been kept in captivity on the Philippine islands. In 1990 breeding groups of the species were established on Panay and Negros Islands as well as in Europe. In total some 30 animals are now held in captivity in the Philippines Islands, 11 at the Mulhouse Zoo in France, and two at the West Berlin Zoo in Germany.

If the breeding groups are successful, their combined efforts may well offer a healthy captive population as a protective measure against disaster in the wild. It is too early to predict how successful such captive-breeding programs will be.

The current numbers of Visayan spotted deer in the wild are estimated to be at less than 100 individuals. With the continued deforestation, disruption of habitat, and poaching, this tiny wild population is now in great jeopardy.

Yarkand Deer
(Cervus elaphus yarkandensis)

ESA: Endangered	
IUCN: Endangered	

Weight: 441–772 lb. (200–350 kg)
Shoulder height: 53–55 in. (135–140 cm)
Diet: Leaves, twigs, and grasses
Gestation period: 230–240 days
Longevity: 18–20 years
Habitat: Open and scrub forest
Range: Western China, Xinjiang

THE YARKAND deer is part of the red deer group or Cervinae subfamily. It is found in China in open forest, scrub forest, scrub thickets, and open grassy areas.

The females live apart from the males except during the rutting season between September and October. They used to be preyed upon by wolves, and are now hunted for their meat and hides, and also for their antlers, which are used in Chinese folk medicine.

This fairly large deer has only rarely come into captivity, although many are kept on deer farms where the antlers are harvested. Their problems are due to a shrinking habitat that has been disturbed by agriculture. They compete with people for what is left of their habitat.

With more than 1.1 billion people, China is the most populous nation on earth. Its land area is roughly the same size as the United States, yet less than one percent of its land is protected (nine percent is set aside in the United States). Air pollution from factories and automobiles is unchecked. China is increasingly dependent upon imported wood as it cuts down its remaining 300 million acres of timber land. Soil erosion is choking China's great rivers to the point where many species of fish will be lost forever.

All of this environmental abuse takes its toll on plant and animal species alike. The plants disappear, followed by the animals that eat them. The Chinese have given the yarkand deer protection, but it is subject to poaching for its antlers, tendons, reproductive organs, and other parts for use in Chinese medicine. The population is diminishing and it now numbers only 4,000 to 5,000, scattered along the Tarim and Karakax Rivers.

Warren D. Thomas

DESMANS

Class: Mammalia
Order: Insectivora
Family: Talpidae

Desmans are part of the same family as moles and shrew moles. Some 32 species are found in the Northern Hemisphere, with features distinguishing the Old World or Eurasian varieties from the North American ones.

The Russian desman is the largest of the family Talpidae. Moles and desmans have long, cylindrical-shaped bodies and the long snouts that are typical of insectivores who burrow tunnels. They use their snout to push soil out of the way, thus producing the molehill that is the bane of gardeners. These creatures spend most of their lives underground.

Pyrenean Desman
(Galemys pyrenaicus)

IUCN: Vulnerable	

Weight: 1¼–2¾ oz. (35–80 g)
Head-body length: 4½–6 in. (110–156 mm)
Diet: Carnivorous
Gestation period: 30 days
Longevity: 3½ years
Habitat: Swift-flowing mountain streams
Range: Southern France, northern Spain, and northern Portugal

AMID THE fast-flowing mountain streams in northern Spain and southern France lives a small furry creature that will suddenly bob to the surface like a cork in order to take a breath of fresh air. It then dives and probes the stream bottom in search of food. This is a feeding foray by the Pyrenean, or Iberian, desman. Once relatively common in the mountain streams of this region, a number of factors have resulted in the steady decline of the desman. Pollution, persecution, and overzealous collection are the usual culprits. Today, the species is threatened and may soon become endangered if these problems remain unchanged.

A funny nose
The Pyrenean desman (named for the mountain range that divides Spain and France) has dark brown fur on its back, while its underparts are a pale gray. The naked tail is also pale,

Desmans are active by day and night, when they feed on worms, insect larvae, and other invertebrates. This Pyrenean desman is found in southern France, northern Spain, and Portugal.

almost whitish; the small front feet, the large hind feet, and the nose are black. The nose, or more correctly the muzzle, is the most unique characteristic of this animal, which looks like it was constructed out of spare parts. Its muzzle is nearly 1 inch (2.5 centimeters) long or about one-fifth of the desman's total body length. Unlike the rest of the body, the muzzle is not covered with fur, instead it has shorter, coarser hairs known as vibrissae.

Vibrissae are specialized hairs with roots that are surrounded by touch-receptor cells. These structures allow the desman to detect even the slightest movement of potential prey when it sticks its long snout into the mud or into cracks and crevices. Its prey includes small fish, aquatic insects, worms, and crustaceans.

The desman is an accomplished underwater swimmer and, using its large hind feet to propel it through the water, may capture and consume up to two-thirds its body weight each day.

Nocturnal eater

The desman feeds primarily at night, using its keen sense of smell as well as its sense of touch for recognition of close objects. The desman's eyes are not very large, leading some experts to speculate about how the animal is able to navigate swiftly flowing streams at night.

Research has produced evidence that the desman uses echolocation (the process of emitting sound waves that bounce off objects and return to the sender) to find its way around its home range, much like bats and dolphins do.

Not too friendly

While the Russian desman (*Desmana moschata*) is known to be social and often shares its den with several other adults, the Pyrenean desman is extremely aggressive toward others of its kind, with the exception of its mate. For this reason, each den is believed to contain only one adult pair, possibly with their juvenile offspring from the previous breeding season. While the male of a pair has a slightly larger home range and territory than the female, animals of both sexes share the task of scent-marking and defending their territory.

There is little aggression among desmans in the wild because they practice mutual avoidance by paying attention to scent markings. Studies of captive individuals reveal that close confinement leads to fights, usually resulting in death for one of the combatants.

PYRENEAN DESMAN
Europe

N

RUSSIAN DESMAN
Asia

Russian Desman
(Desmana moschata)

IUCN: Vulnerable

Weight : About 5 oz. (140 g)
Head-body length: 7–8½ in.
(180–220 mm)
Diet: Carnivorous
Gestation period: Unknown
Longevity: Unknown
Habitat: Banks of streams,
ponds, and lakes
Range: Eastern Europe and
central Asia

Female desmans enter estrus in January, and gestation lasts a mere 30 days. Pregnant females observed from February until the end of June suggest that there may be several breeding periods during each breeding season. Since litter size ranges from one to five (averaging nearly four), the desman population—if given protection—may be able to rebound relatively quickly.

Grooming for survival

Desmans observed in captivity are known to groom their fur every time they come out of the water. This helps to spread skin oils through the fur and is critical to the animal's survival. When unable to keep the fur waterproofed, the desman is not insulated from cold streams and can die quickly from hypothermia. Therefore, pollution of streams is a double-edged sword for the desman. First the pollution enters the food chain and is ingested by the desman when eating prey. Second, some of the pollutants act as surfac-

tants, or soaps that strip the vital waterproofing oils from the desman's fur.

Other threats

While it is important that pollution levels be reduced, this alone will not ensure the Pyrenean desman's continued existence. There are a number of other phenomena that threaten this animal as well. As with wildlife around the world, this desman's habitat is being fragmented by human activities along watercourses. Fishers persecute the desman because they believe it competes with them for fish. Some populations have also suffered at the hands of overly enthusiastic scientific collectors.

Finally, mink that have escaped from fur farms have established themselves in the wild. Unfortunately, these aggressive animals are often competing with, and displacing, desmans. To ensure the continued existence of this peculiar aquatic carnivore, all these problems will need to be corrected.

THE RUSSIAN DESMAN appears to be part shrew and part mole. It lives mainly in water, similar to a beaver. It is found in slowly flowing or still bodies of water in the Ural and Volga River basins, which empty into the Caspian Sea, and in the Don River basin, which empties into the Black Sea. This species has suffered population declines and is listed as a threatened species by Russian experts and by the IUCN.

The fur is a reddish brown fading to gray underneath and is a plush, dense undercoat protected by longer, coarser hairs. The tail is flattened from side to side and, with the four webbed feet, propels the animal through the water.

The animal's most unique trait is its flexible, grooved snout, which appears flattened above and below and is used to search in crevices for food. Desmans feed on insects, mollusks, crustaceans, fish, and amphibians.

An unusual den

Russian desmans construct their dens in the banks along the waterways where they live. These dens can have several chambers near the surface. The dens are often built under the roots of a woody plant, to allow the passage of air into the chambers. This is essential because the entrance(s) to the den are underwater and are connected by tunnels to the sleeping and eating chambers. The desman usually spends its days in a nest of leaves or moss in the sleeping chamber, coming out at night to forage.

The rare exceptions to this nocturnal lifestyle occur during the spring and are most probably associated with breeding.

Desmans are social, with as many as eight adults sharing a den. Little is known of their breeding biology, but there are indications of two birth periods—one in early June and the other in early November. Desman litters consist of three to five young.

Victims of vanity

While the desman was common in the mid-19th century, hunting and trapping for the musk gland and the pelt began to take its toll. The musk is used to make perfume, and the pelt is used for hats, mittens, and collar trims. By the beginning of the 20th century as many as 20,000 pelts were sold annually, and the species was nearly beyond recovery.

Also the Russian desman's habitat was being destroyed by human development, and water pollution was becoming a dangerous threat. Exotic mammals such as the muskrat (*Ondatra zibethicus*) and the nutria (*Myocastor coypus*), brought to Russia from North and South America respectively, were introduced into the desman's range, and competed for both food and nest sites.

Since 1920 the species has been protected by the former government of the Soviet Union. An active recovery program introduced these animals into new habitat, including two new river basins: the Dnieper and the upper Ob. This stabilized the population slide, and the numbers are now increasing. Population estimates range from 37,000 to 40,700, with the largest number found in the Volga River basin. If humans can eliminate the destructive development in vital desman habitat, reduce water pollution, and lessen the competition from muskrats and nutria, this species could be saved from extinction. Captive breeding and reintroductions have been successful and there are now five nature reserves and 80 refuges for the Russian Desman.

Terry Tompkins

Dhole

(Cuon alpinus)

ESA: Endangered

IUCN: Vulnerable

Class: Mammalia
Order: Carnivora
Family: Canidae
Weight: 22–46 lb. (10–21 kg)
Shoulder height: 16.5–21½ in. (420–550 mm)
Diet: Carnivorous
Gestation period: 60–62 days
Longevity: 15–16 years in captivity
Habitat: Forest and scrub
Range: Southern Siberia, central Asia, India, and Indochina reservoirs

THROUGHOUT THE Asian countryside the eerie whistling sound of the dhole, or Asiatic wild dog, is not heard as often today as it was in the past. This whistling, a means of communication for a pack of dhole regrouping after an unsuccessful hunt, inspired the other common name of this species—the whistling dog. The dhole's decline, although welcomed by many people who live within its range, is unfortunate. Its disappearance could be detrimental for many of the biological communities where it is an important predator.

Although there are some differences in coloration because of its wide range, dhole are generally a rusty red color above, with paler fur on the chin, chest, and belly. In addition they have a straight tail covered with long, bushy, black hair. Males, usually weighing about ten pounds (4.5 kilograms), are heavier than females. Dhole look very much like many members of the genus *Canis* (such as wolves, coyotes, and domestic dogs) except the skull is shorter and the snout is wider. Another difference is that female dhole have 12 to 16 teats rather than the ten teats found on the wolf and domestic dog.

Bloodthirsty?

Dhole are actively hated by hunters because they can drive away their sport, while farmers believe dhole kill their livestock. The dhole therefore is badly mistreated everywhere within its range. The persecution is so severe that the dhole has become rare outside well-protected areas such as wildlife reserves. The

The dhole resembles a dog or a fox and, like those animals, it is a member of the Canidae family. As carnivores, these animals present a threat to domestic livestock and compete with human hunters for prey. As a result, the dhole has been badly treated throughout its range.

feeding at the carcass—each individual eating for a while, then lying down nearby while another pack member takes a turn.

If the captured animal is small relative to the size of the pack, each dhole attempts to get its share by quickly gulping down as much as possible. No matter what size the kill, fighting among pack members over food is almost unheard of. In fact juveniles, when they first start participating in hunts, are often given the first meal at a kill.

A social carnivore

Dhole are capable of many of the types of vocal communication associated with dogs and wolves—with the exception of the bark. Unlike wolves, dhole vocalize little during the hunt, often yapping or whimpering only during the final stages. They have been known to vocalize sometimes when hunting in heavy cover, presumably in order to keep track of the positions of fellow pack members.

A dhole pack is an extended family unit consisting of a pair and their offspring and typically numbering from 5 to 15 individuals. Packs of up to 40 have been reported, but groups this large are thought actually to be a clan composed of several related packs. The pack protects its territory and often has several den sites within its territorial boundary. Dhole regulate pack numbers by restricting breeding to a single dominant

dhole is not alone in receiving this kind of treatment; elsewhere in the world both the wolf and the African wild dog are similarly hunted. Many villagers, however, do not mind having dhole packs around because the dhole rarely attacks humans. Villagers are also sometimes able to obtain meat by following the pack and driving the dholes off the kill.

Dhole are daytime hunters and seem to rely heavily on their keen sense of smell in tracking prey. When large prey is brought down by a pack of dhole, some pack members either quickly swallow chunks of its flesh or run off with larger pieces in order to eat it before it is snatched away. After this initial feeding frenzy, pack members often take turns

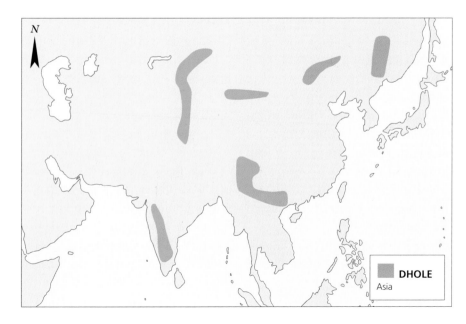

female. When conditions are very good, more than one female in the pack may bear young, although this is rare. Females usually give birth between November and March to between four and eight pups. Observations of both wild and captive packs indicate that the mother—and the young at a very early age—are provided with regurgitated meat by other pack members. Pups leave the den when they are about 70 to 80 days old and join in kills at seven months. Major predators like the dhole play an important part in the earth's ecosystems by controlling populations of their prey,

but local people who believe the dhole are competing with them for the same resources still persecute this animal, and its numbers continue to decline. Increasing human populations throughout areas of Asia occupied by the dhole will lead to an increase in kills stolen from dhole packs by local people. Humans have used poison to reduce the dhole population, and some governments still pay bounties on dhole. The number of studies of dhole are few and have been done in India. Counting local populations has been difficult because dhole are evasive when

humans are around, and they can cover large distances quickly. Because of this, there is no estimate of the total population for the species. It is thought that nine of the ten subspecies are threatened and are declining, while only one subspecies in India is common.

Stopping the decline

Protecting habitat in preserves and parks will help to halt the population slide. People in its range must cease their active persecution of dhole packs.

Terry Tompkins

See also Dogs.

Dibatag (Clark's Gazelle)

(Ammodorcas clarkei)

ESA: Endangered

IUCN: Vulnerable

Class: Mammalia
Order: Artiodactyla
Family: Bovidae
Subfamily: Antelopinae
Tribe: Antelopini
Weight: 55–77 lb. (25–35 kg)
Shoulder height: 31½–35½ in. (80–90 cm)
Diet: Leaves, twigs
Gestation period: 180–210 days
Longevity: 10–12 years
Habitat: Semidesert
Range: Ethiopia, Somalia

THE DIBATAG, or Clark's gazelle, is a tall member of the antelope family with extremely fine-boned legs and torso and a long, slender neck. It is similar to another antelope found in the southern

portion of its range, known as Waller's gazelle or the gerenuk. Both types are found in Somalia, but the gerenuk extends into Ethiopia, Djibouti, Kenya, and Tanzania in East Africa.

Only the males have horns. The dibatag has thin horns curving forward. Both the dibatag and gerenuk have a unique capability: their pelvis is so flexible that they can stand erect on their back legs and feed on leaves high off the ground. Except for the giraffe, this allows the dibatag to feed on food that other animals cannot reach. This limits competition for food.

Dibatag are usually found in small groups of females. Males are occasionally found with them, but usually they live separately until breeding season. They are very skittish and difficult to approach unless they are used to humans, and then they are quite docile. Dibatags have been kept very little in captivity, and there are no captive populations. Probably the zoo in Naples, Italy has the most experience in breeding

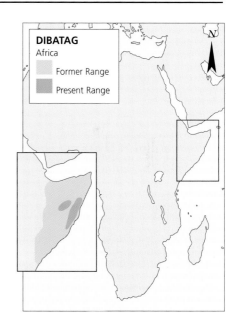

DIBATAG
Africa
Former Range
Present Range

dibatags. Many years ago there was a small breeding group, but that was one of the few groups ever brought into captivity.

Unusual runners

In the wild, dibatag have an unusual way of running. When excited, they hold both their head and long, slender tails erect. The tail moves forward while the neck moves the head backward. The dibatag is a beautiful and delicate

453

The dibatag is a tall member of the antelope family with extremely fine-boned legs and torso.

animal that is preyed upon by lions, leopards, cheetahs, hyenas, wild dogs, and smaller cats, although the decline has been caused mainly by poaching and the destruction of habitat for raising livestock. Goats, which have a high grazing level, compete with the dibatag for food. The Somalian population is declining because of poaching, habitat loss, and competition with domestic livestock. In Ethiopia the dibatag has been hunted by local people. While the dibatag is a protected species in Ethiopia, it does not occur in any protected areas. A reserve in the Ogaden area has been recommended.

Warren D. Thomas

Dibbler

(Parantechinus apicalis)

ESA: Endangered

IUCN: Endangered

Class: Mammalia
Order: Marsupialia
Family: Dasyuridae
Weight: 1½–3½ oz. (40–100 g)
Head-body length: 5½–5¾ in. (140–145 mm)
Diet: Insects, nectar
Gestation period: 44–53 days
Longevity: 2–3 years
Habitat: Dense heathland with thick leaf litter
Range: Extreme southwest part of Western Australia and islands off the coast

AFTER 80 years without a sighting, this small, ratlike creature was thought to be extinct. Fossil remains indicate that the dibbler once occurred in coastal areas of Western Australia from Shark Bay on the west coast to Bremer Bay on the south coast. However, it seemed the dibbler's range had already started to shrink prior to the arrival of Europeans and had virtually disappeared during the 20th century. Then in 1967, when hunters attempted to catch some honey possums (*Tarsipes rostratus*) at Cheyne Beach, two dibblers

The dibbler has an unusual white eye ring that makes it appear as if it is wearing eyeglasses.

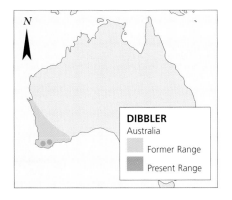

DIBBLER
Australia

Former Range

Present Range

were captured in live traps set on flowers. This discovery led to other searches. This involved live trapping as well as checking predator droppings for the distinctive hair of the dibbler. By 1984, only nine more individuals had been found; seven were live-trapped at Cheyne Beach, and two dead specimens were found that had been killed by domestic pets.

Dibblers are small brown-gray creatures with white flecks on the upper body and dull white to dingy yellow fur on the underparts. They look like their distant relatives the marsupial mice, but they have a distinctive white eye ring, a flat, tapering tail, and a coat of speckled fur.

Females come into estrus in March or April, and 44 to 53 days after mating give birth to a litter of up to eight young that are nursed for a few months in an abdominal pouch. They reach sexual maturity at 10 to 11 months of age in the first breeding season after birth.

Dibblers forage at night, and search for food at dusk and dawn. They are agile climbers when in search of insects and nectar in low shrubs, but also forage for insects and other invertebrates in ground littered with leaves. The nest is an enlarged chamber at the end of a tunnel burrowed in the litter.

An uncertain future

The outlook brightened for the dibbler in 1984. After the discovery of a dead individual in Fitzgerald River National Park, extensive live-trapping yielded 17 dibblers. In 1985 more individuals were found on Boullanger and Whitlock Islands off the coast of Western Australia. Cheyne Beach is now part of a flora and fauna reserve, but this has not assured the dibbler of protection. Another threat has been the death of Banksia shrubs. They bear flowers used by the dibbler as an insect and nectar source. Protection of the mainland and offshore populations may allow researchers time to determine and protect the dibbler's habitat needs, since habitat protection is so essential to preserving this species.

Terry Tompkins

Dikume

(Konia dikume)

IUCN: Critically endangered

Class: Actinopterygii
Order: Perciformes
Family: Cichlidae
Length: 5 in. (13 cm)
Reproduction: Egg layer
Habitat: Deep open water
Range: Lake Barombi-Mbo, Cameroon

THE WEST African crater lake called Barombi-Mbo in the country of Cameroon is the only stronghold of the cichlid species commonly called the dikume. Barombi-Mbo is a small (but deep) and relatively infertile fresh-water lake only about 1½ miles in diameter (2.4 kilometers), yet it is the primary source of food for the village of Barombi on its northern shore. Anglers guard their right to fish the lake and the dikume and other threatened cichlids are sought by people as food.

Because the dikume is found only in Lake Barombi-Mbo, the species is vulnerable to overfishing and any number of natural or human-made catastrophes. However, the desire on the part of the Barombi villagers to maintain exclusive fishing rights on the lake may work to the advantage of the dikume and other cichlids. The villagers have been able to maintain a workable balance for decades between the amount of fish they catch and the natural supply available, and Cameroon authorities hope that this can be continued.

Cichlid traits

All cichlids present a fairly flattened and rounder appearance (like a plate on edge) than other streamlined and torpedolike fishes. Most have broad, hardened mouth parts that are used to scrape algae from surfaces or to crush hard food items. In addition to teeth on the jaws, the mouth contains hundreds of teeth on a platelike bone at the base of the mouth and throat to hold food; these teeth within the throat are called pharyngeal teeth. Cichlids have a long gut to efficiently absorb the nutrients of the food they swallow. The length of the gut is often more than two-and-one-half times the length of the fish. A distinctive characteristic of the dikume is the long, spiny dorsal fin on the back that can extend from just behind the head all the

DIKUME
Africa

are quite large for better vision in deep water. The body, gills, cheeks, and eye areas of the dikume are heavily scaled. The coloration is silvery with a faint stripe down each side and a large dark blotch on the gill covers. The dikume is less colorful than other cichlids because colors are less important in deep-water, low-light environments.

While all cichlids are egg layers, the way in which they reproduce varies. Some engage in mouthbrooding. After eggs are laid by a female and fertilized by a male, one of the parents picks up the eggs and guards them in a chamber in the mouth cavity. They are incubated until they hatch after one to two weeks, when the offspring still rely on the parent for protection. Because of its preference for deep

water, the breeding and parental habits are difficult to observe.

This species is a bottom and water column feeder, with a preference for mosquito-like insects called *Chaoborus*. Most often, immature *Chaoborus* can be found in bottom sediments, and this is where the dikume also eats. When the immature larvae are ready to emerge from the lake, many are caught by the dikume as they make their way to the surface.

Along with measures to prevent pollution and to prevent the introduction of harmful non-native fishes like the large and aggressive Nile perch (*Lates niloticus*), conservationists look to continue the ban on fishing. They aim to educate the people of Barombi as to the delicate balance of the ecosystem that they exploit.

William E. Manci

way to the tail section of the body. The segment near the tail is longer than the segment near the head and the profile of the head is pointed, with a flat and angular forehead. The mouth is upturned, but the dikume has a slight overbite, and the upper teeth protrude forward. The eyes

DOGS

Class: Mammalia

Order: Carnivora

Family: Canidae

Dogs (canids) belong to the same family as coyotes, foxes, jackals, and wolves. They occur naturally on most continents.

Dogs have trim, muscular bodies, thin limbs, bushy tails, and large ears.

Canids often travel over wide ranges in pairs or packs, and they share their prey.

Wolves live in cold climates, while some dogs live in desert habitats and may eat vegetation instead of rodents and birds. The domestic dog (*Canis familiaris*) was probably reared in Europe and accompanied people as they colonized parts of the world.

African Wild Dog

(Lycaon pictus)

ESA: Endangered

IUCN: Endangered

Weight: 37½–79½ lb. (17–36 kg)
Shoulder height: 23¾–30½ in. (610–780 mm)
Diet: Carnivorous
Gestation period: 79–80 days
Litter size: 6–16
Longevity: 11 years
Habitat: Grassland, savannah, plains, and open woodland
Range: Southern Africa, eastern Africa; remnant populations in west and central Africa; areas south of the Sahara

ON THE AFRICAN plain, a commotion among some grazing gazelle causes the herd to break into a full gallop. Soon a lone Thompson's gazelle (*Gazella thomsoni*) is separated from the herd, running rapidly, followed closely by a group of animals with white-tipped tails and mottled fur coloring. The African wild dog is on the hunt.

Although little is known of how plentiful these carnivores were during the mid- to late-19th century, anecdotal reports suggest they were once more numerous than they are today. In the 1800s packs of several hundred individuals were routinely spotted. It is known that vast herds of grazers—especially of springbok (*Antidorcas marsupialis*)—roamed the same range. The springbok was hunted extensively. Their population at present numbers only around 500,000 individuals.

Apparently during the same period in which the antelope declined, the African wild dog also suffered a parallel decrease in numbers.

Just like a domestic dog?

The African wild dog is comparable in stature to a medium-sized German shepherd with the exception of its long, slender legs. Generally, males and females look alike and show little difference in size. There is, however, individual variation in the mottled, multicolored pattern of the short coat of fur. The one apparently unvarying color trait is the white tip of the tail, which may help the dogs recognize each other on the open plain.

The wild dog has relatively large rounded ears and, unlike the majority of the canine family, four toes, not five, on each foot.

Another characteristic of the wild dog is its strong, musky odor, which is believed to be used

The coat of the African wild dog is a mottled pattern of short fur showing a random arrangement of black, yellow, and white.

as a scent marker so that individuals can track the pack if they become separated.

Cooperative canids

This species, like only a few other members of its family (such as the wolf and the dhole), is highly social. Individuals exhibit several behaviors that help maintain the relative success of members of their pack and particularly of the young. Pack size in the latter part of the 20th century averaged about ten individuals but can number as many as 25 to 30. Pack members are related to varying degrees. A pack consists of several closely related adult males as well as one or more adult females that are usually related to each other, but not to the males. This situation is a result of males remaining with the pack they were born in while females—once they reach sexual maturity—are forced to leave their natal pack and gain acceptance into a new pack.

This, coupled with the birth of a higher percentage of males than females, results in a condition unusual for social mammals—groups containing more males than females.

Equally unusual is that generally only one female in a pack bears young each breeding season. Many scientists believe such groups, in which mature females help the dominant female (who is also their sister) raise her young, may be more successful at raising offspring to adulthood. This arrangement provides fewer mouths to feed than would exist with several females breeding.

Nomads

Births may occur at any time but are most common during the second half of the rainy season, usually from March to June. Packs are wide-ranging during most of the year, covering anywhere from 578 to 1,543 square miles (1,500 to 4,000 square kilometers). When a litter of pups is born, the pack is restricted by the need to return to the den site, and the home range can become as small as 62 square miles (160 square kilometers).

After a gestation period of nearly three months, females give birth to a litter which ranges in number from 6 to 16 but averages about ten. The young first emerge from the den around three weeks of age and begin to take solid food at about this time. During the three-month period when the pack is anchored to the den site, the young always have at least one pack member—usually, but not always, the mother—guarding them. Meanwhile, the rest of the pack hunts. The pups, and any other members that have remained behind on guard, are fed regurgitated food when the pack returns from the kill. The pups are usually completely weaned by 11 weeks of age and begin to follow the pack on

hunts. Over a period of time they become better able to keep up with the rest of the pack and the whole pack resumes its usual wide-ranging behavior.

Open hunters

The hunting technique of the African wild dog differs from that of most predators on the African plains, even from other social animals like the African lion (*Panthera leo*). While most predators are secretive, using a slow stalk or an ambush, the African wild dog approaches a group of potential prey quietly, not attempting to hide, until the prey stampedes. At this point the pack concentrates on an individual, one that may be old or sick and shows signs of slowness, and chases it. These dogs can sprint at speeds up to 41 miles per hour (66 kilometers per hour) until they tire. Such chases have been known to last as long as an hour and range as far as 3 to 3½ miles (5 to 6 kilometers) before the prey is captured or the pack gives up.

When the prey is caught, it is usually killed via disemboweling, if large, or dismembering, if small. The pack then eats voraciously until satisfied or until the prey is entirely consumed. Even though the initial feeding may seem like a free-for-all, observers have been surprised by the lack of fighting over the kill among pack members. In fact, when the young are first able to remain close enough to the pack to reach a fresh kill, they are allowed to eat before those who led the chase and made the kill.

The prey of the African wild dog vary greatly in size. The smaller wild dog of eastern Africa specializes in smaller forms like

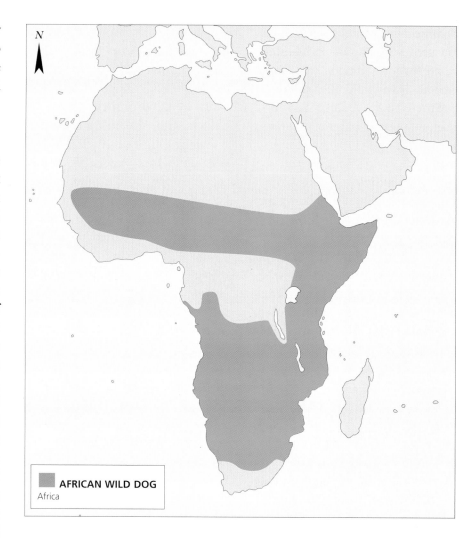

AFRICAN WILD DOG
Africa

the springbok and gazelle, while the larger central and south African wild dog (weighing about 60 pounds, or 27 kilograms) will take prey as large as zebra (*Equus* spp.) and gnu (*Connochaetes* spp.). Different packs seem to concentrate on particular species. This has led some to suggest that prey preference may be learned; experience in pack hunts may result in wild dogs knowing how best to chase and bring down a particular species.

The threat

Like many African predators, the wild dog has been adversely affected by people who have overhunted African game during the past century. In addition, this species has been targeted by

humans for eradication. Such malice toward the animal is partly inspired by the wild dogs' hunting technique. Their behavior appears disgusting to those who mistakenly judge animal behavior by human standards. Nor has the wild dog's overstated reputation as a killer of livestock helped it win the support of humans. In addition, wild dogs also suffer from canine diseases, which they catch from domesticated dogs kept by local residents. The cause of their decline has been a combination of persecution and habitat loss.

The numbers of wild dogs that existed in Africa during the latter part of the 19th century is uncertain. African wild dogs have disappeared from 25 of the 39 countries where they were once prevalent, and only six populations are believed to number more than about 100 animals.

The total population today is estimated at 3,000 to 5,500. Most of these are in southern and eastern Africa, while only remnant populations remain in west and central Africa. Still, some populations remain viable and a number of conservation efforts are ongoing, including using private land for wild dog conservation in South Africa and the development of a program in northeastern Namibia with involvement of local people.

Bush Dog
(Speothos venaticus)

IUCN: Vulnerable

Weight: 11–15½ lb. (5–7 kg)
Shoulder height: 10–11¾ in. (260–300 mm)
Diet: Carnivorous
Gestation period: 67 days
Longevity: 10 years, 4 months in captivity
Habitat: Forests and wet savannah
Range: Eastern Panama south to northern Argentina

DOGS IN GENERAL have evolved as grassland predators, able to run down prey using their long legs and endurance. The bush dog of South America is an obvious exception to this norm. Although it hunts in packs, its odd short-legged appearance and its tendency to hunt near—or even in—the water makes it quite different from other canids.

The bush dog's short legs give it a very unusual appearance. In addition, its feet are webbed, probably an adaptation that has helped it become a water hunter.

Widely distributed in wooded areas on both sides of the Andes, the species is rare. This rarity, combined with the bush dogs' habit of dwelling in rapidly diminishing forests and avoiding humans, has resulted in an uncertain future for the species. Population figures for the bush dog are unavailable.

The short legs make the bush dog look somewhat like a dachshund. It has short ears and a short, thickly-furred tail. It is a deep reddish brown on the head and shoulders and dark brown to black on the back and tail. The underparts of the animal are generally the same color as the back, although there is often a light patch of fur on the throat. The short legs with webbed feet compliment its habit of pursuing prey in the water.

Hunting in packs

Active primarily in the daytime, bush dogs usually rest in a den inside a hollow tree or in a burrow at night. Occasionally hunting alone, bush dogs more commonly hunt in a pack of around six to ten individuals.

Although they are known to pursue prey as large as deer, bush dogs seem to prey mainly on large rodents that are found near water such as agouti (*Agouti* sp.), paca (*Dasyprocta* sp.), and capybara (*Hydrochoerus hydrochaeris*). While we usually think of rodents as being small, agouti are about half as large as bush dogs, pacas are about the same size or slightly larger, and capybara are eight to nine times as large as bush dogs.

The bush dog is an accomplished diver and swimmer and can even swim underwater. These dogs have been observed to chase and kill prey in the water.

While there are numerous observations of bush dogs hunting in packs, it is still not clear whether any pack member (other than her mate) helps the female to rear her young.

Like other dogs that are social and live in packs, such as the gray wolf (*Canis lupus*), the dhole (*Cuon alpinus*), and the African hunting dog (*Lycaon pictus*), the young have rarely been observed fighting over food.

Reproduction is controlled by self-imposed restrictions. Mature females do not come into estrus when living with a dominant female. In other words, it appears that only one female per pack is allowed to reproduce. Females are able to conceive at ten months of age and, if dominant and thus able to reproduce, come into estrus twice yearly.

Litters are usually born during the rainy season and range in size from one to six, with four being the average. The ability to have two litters a year and the early age of first reproduction offset the small litter size.

These factors could be of value in the recovery and survival of the bush dog, provided that enough suitable habitat is saved for the species.

The bush dog is at risk because of a number of factors. First, it is naturally quite rare and probably always occurred in low numbers. Second, as a predatory species some people find its behavior brutal and have hunted it intensively. Most important however, the bush dog is suffering from the loss or alteration of its habitat. The rain forests of South America are being cleared at a rapid pace, and this is the habitat of the bush dog. Even where forests still stand, increased human settlement and its effect on rivers and streams may lead to intolerable pressures on this small dog.

IUCN–The World Conservation Union, considers this animal to be threatened and it is classified as vulnerable to extinction. The bush dog is banned from international commercial trade under the Convention on International Trade in Endangered Species of Wild Fauna and Flora (CITES).

One factor that weighs in the bush dog's favor is its ability to breed in captivity. In addition to helping scientists better understand their breeding behavior, the captive population may become an important group for restocking areas that have lost their native populations.

Field studies to help to learn more about the habitat requirements and life history of this interesting little dog are still of vital importance if it is to be saved from extinction.

Terry Tompkins

See also Dhole.

Hector's Dolphin

(Cephalorhynchus hectori)

IUCN: Vulnerable

Class: Mammalia
Order: Cetacea
Suborder: Odontoceti
Family: Delphinidae
Weight: 90–120 lb. (40–55 kg)
Length: 45–60 in. (115–145 cm)
Diet: Fish, squid, crustaceans
Gestation period: Unknown
Longevity: Unknown
Habitat: Coastal ocean waters
Range: New Zealand

THE FAMILY Delphinidae consists of about 27 species of oceangoing dolphins. These include the common dolphin, the bottlenose dolphin, and the killer whale, as well as many other, lesser-known species. While Hector's dolphin is the only member of this family to be listed as a threatened species, many other species are in trouble. Even the common species have suffered population declines, either from pollution, hunting, or accidental capture and drowning in nets set for tuna and other fish.

Hunting dolphins for food is decreasing in some areas, but hunting is on the rise in other parts of the world, such as Peru and Sri Lanka. Legislation such as the 1991 United Nations resolution banning large-scale pelagic drift nets, and stricter enforcement of existing laws, such as those governing tuna purse seine nets, offer some hope for the oceangoing dolphins. However, the threat of pollution, especially the discharge of toxic chemicals into the oceans, has not yet been adequately corrected. Pollution can lower a dolphin's resistance to viral infections that can kill it.

There is an unusual group of dolphins found only below the equator in the Southern Hemisphere. These southern dolphins have some of the most restricted ranges of any oceangoing cetacean. One species is found primarily around the shores of Argentina, another can be found off the coast of Chile, and a third is found along the southwestern coast of Africa. The fourth—Hector's dolphin, also called the New Zealand white-front dolphin—is only found around the coast of New Zealand, primarily around the northeast coast of South Island. Here this little dolphin is never found more than five miles (eight kilometers) from the coast. It stays close to shore in shallow, turbid water, frequently in areas where rivers empty into the sea.

Unusual markings

Hector's dolphin has a small, torpedo-shaped body. The head has a short beak, with no bulge on the forehead. The dorsal fin is short and rounded. The shape is accented by a pattern of black and white markings on the head and body. Each species of dolphins has a different pattern. The body is mostly black or dark gray above, with markings below. The chin area is white, as is much of the belly. A dark band crosses under the body at the black pectoral fins. There is also a black teardrop within the white area of the belly. A band of white comes

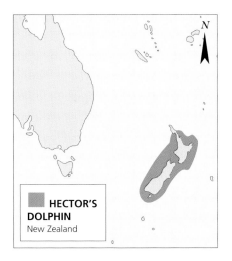

HECTOR'S DOLPHIN
New Zealand

up each side at the midline of the body and sweeps back toward the black tail. There is a white spot under each pectoral fin.

Hector's dolphins are usually found in pairs or groups of up to 20, but a group of several hundred has been recorded. They travel along the coastal waters of New Zealand, searching for fish and squid. Mating occurs in the winter, with births in November through February. It is thought that females give birth once every two years. The young are known to begin taking solid food at around six months of age.

Because these dolphins haunt the coastline, they are more prone to run afoul of fishermen, and more are thought to die from the effects of chemical pollution.

Only around 3,000 to 5,000 of these small dolphins can still be found within their tiny range.

Fortunately, New Zealand has begun to take some action, and studies are underway to determine the effects of commercial fishing on Hector's dolphin.

A sanctuary has now been established to protect this rare cetacean from any further decline toward extinction.

RIVER DOLPHINS

Class: Mammalia

Order: Cetacea

Suborder: Odontoceti

Family: Platanistidae, Iniidae

The families Platanistidae and Iniidae include five species of unusual dolphins. Four of these species are restricted to freshwater habitats and are commonly called river dolphins. They rarely, if ever, enter salt water. All four are listed as either endangered or threatened. The fifth is the franciscana or La Plata dolphin, and although it is a marine mammal, it is related to the other four river dolphins as well. It is found along the Atlantic coast of South America from Brazil to Argentina.

These dolphins lack the graceful shape and vibrant coloration of some of their ocean-going relatives. They tend to have subdued colors ranging from dark gray to light pink, with the underside frequently lighter in color. Their heads are marked by a high-domed forehead, or melon, that slopes down to a long, thin beak armed with more than 100 sharp teeth. The eyes are very small, and so it appears that echolocation (the emitting of sounds to judge direction and distance) is the primary sense used to navigate and find food. Behind the bulging forehead is a somewhat constricted neck area. The seven cervical, or neck, vertebrae of the backbone are not fused as they are in other species of dolphins and whales. This permits greater movement of the head. The dorsal, or back, fin is a simple bump or low ridge.

Dolphins have no gills like fish—they are mammals and surface to breathe air just like humans.

Because their range is more limited than that of oceangoing dolphins, river dolphins face more problems. Dams cause changes in a river dolphin's habitat, ones that oceangoing dolphins can avoid.

There is disagreement over the taxonomic status of these dolphins. Despite their similarities, many scientists now feel that these four may have each evolved separately from different oceangoing ancestors. Some scientists even place each genus into a separate family. It is unlikely that these arguments will be decided soon, and given the low numbers and extreme pressures these dolphins are under, it is possible that some species may vanish before an answer is agreed upon.

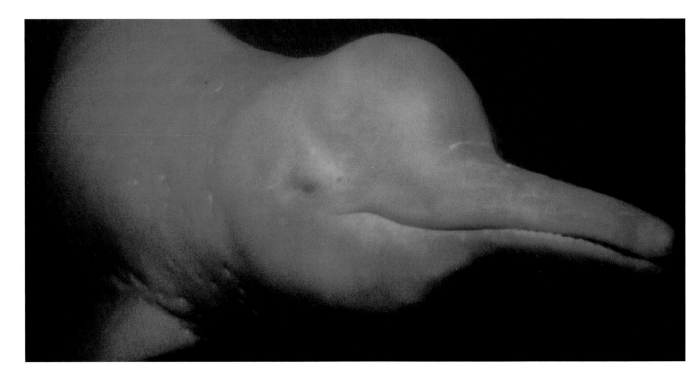

Amazon River Dolphin (Boto)

(Inia geoffrensis)

IUCN: Vulnerable

Weight: 175–285 lb. (80–160 kg)

Length: 80–100 in. (200–255 cm)

Diet: Fish, other aquatic animals

Gestation period: 300–330 days

Longevity: Over 20 years

Habitat: Major rivers and their tributaries

Range: Amazon and Orinoco river systems

OF ALL THE river dolphins, the boto, or Amazon river dolphin, is the most taxonomically controversial. Found throughout the Amazon and Orinoco river basins, this dolphin has three distinct populations. One is found throughout the lower reaches of the Amazon River, another is found in the Orinoco River and its tributaries, and the third is separated from the second by a 250-mile (400-kilometer) stretch of rapids in the Madeira River. This geographic separation has resulted in some very slight physical differences among these groups—just enough to cause scientific debate about whether the three groups should be categorized as distinct species. Unfortunately, all three groups have low populations and are extremely vulnerable to hunting by commercial fishers and habitat disruption from dams.

Like the other river dolphins, the boto has a long beak and a dome-like head. A constriction at the back of the head gives it a distinct neck. The eyes are small, yet functional. The dorsal fin is long and low and projects back toward the tail as a ridge. The pectoral fins and tail are large and wide.

The boto has small bristle-like hairs along the snout. These hairs probably serve as touch sensors and help it move about in the

The boto's color is distinctive and seems to vary with age. A young dolphin appears dark gray or blue-gray on the sides and back, with the belly region a silver-gray. As the dolphin becomes older it also becomes lighter, and older animals often display a light pink coloration.

dark, muddy waters of its river home. The boto also has two different kinds of teeth. Like the other river dolphins, the front of the beak contains many sharp, conical teeth. However, the back of the boto's jaws contains a series of flatter teeth that resemble molars (the Chinese river dolphin has the same two types of teeth). These teeth probably enable the dolphin to feed more easily on the various kinds of armored catfish that live in the rivers and on other animals with shells, such as crabs.

Flooded forests

This river dolphin may be found in pairs or groups numbering up to 20 animals but is also frequently sighted alone. It may also be found in the same area as

AMAZON
RIVER DOLPHIN
South America

another dolphin found in South American rivers, the tucuxi (*Sotalia flaviatilis*). The boto seems to remain within a specific home range set up along a stretch of river, using echolocation to hunt for food. In captivity it has been noted for spending time swimming and even searching for food upside down. While this dolphin does not appear to migrate, it does perform an unusual seasonal movement.

During the rainy season, the rivers and streams of the Amazon and Orinoco basin burst their banks and flood the surrounding forest. When this occurs, a number of species of fish move into the flooded forests to feed on the sudden bonanza of food, which includes drowned insects and even fallen fruit. This pattern of flooding and feeding has been going on for so long that some forest trees actually seem to rely on fish to help disperse their seeds. During the rainy season,

the boto also moves into the flooded forest. There it uses its sonar, wide flippers, and flexible neck to hunt the fish among the tangled roots and buttressed trunks of this strange and temporary habitat.

Scattered population

It is unclear exactly how many of these river dolphins still exist in South America. This is partly because there are many thousands of miles of rivers within its range—which includes Brazil, Ecuador, Bolivia, Peru, Colombia, and Venezuela. The fact that its range encompasses six different countries is a major problem. Each of these countries has different laws, enforcement records, development needs, and customs regarding wildlife in general and river dolphins in particular. At this time the boto is fully protected by law only in Brazil and Bolivia, but even there enforcement is difficult at best, especially in the more remote areas. While many local fishers respect and even fear the boto (many free them from their nets when they become entangled), some commercial fishers see this dolphin as a competitor and frequently shoot it on sight. There is even some trading traffic in dolphin body parts.

Like other river dolphins, the boto is also threatened by the development of dams and other water projects that increase siltation, lower water levels, and alter the cycle of flooding that the fish, dolphins, and even trees have come to rely upon. If this dolphin is to survive, special care must be taken to avoid disrupting the fragile and complicated ecosystem that is supported by the

seasonal cycles of these mighty rivers. Additionally, more must be learned about this rare river dolphin to determine its true status as well as its needs. Without a better understanding of its biology and behavior, future efforts to save it may be misguided and will undoubtedly fail.

Finally, a collective conservation effort must be made among the various countries whose borders include the Amazon river dolphin's enormous range. Without the cooperation of all six countries to maintain and preserve this dolphin's habitat, this dolphin may become increasingly endangered in the future.

Chinese River Dolphin
(Lipotes vexillifer)

ESA: Endangered

IUCN: Critically endangered

Weight: 160–265 lb. (73–120 kg)
Length: 69–100 in. (175–253 cm)
Diet: Fish
Gestation period: Unknown
Longevity: Unknown
Habitat: Major rivers and their lakes and tributaries
Range: Yangtze River system

THE CHINESE river dolphin, also known as the baiji, is one of the last large mammals known to Western science. The Chinese have known of this dolphin's existence in the Chang Jiang, or Yangtze River, for over 2,000 years, with the earliest written description dating from around

If it can survive the ravages of monsoons, declining prey populations, and irrigation projects, a Ganges River dolphin can live to 20 years of age.

Legendary dolphin

The Chinese river dolphin has been the subject of many local tales, one of which may have led to its continued survival within its densely populated range. It was told that the dolphin appeared in Tung Ting Lake after a beautiful princess threw herself into the lake and drowned—she was turned into a little dolphin. As a result of this legend, the fishers of the lake did not hunt the dolphin.

Although it is now protected by law in China, this river dolphin is still in danger of extinction. Recent estimates put the total population at only around 200 individuals. A number are caught in nets and accidentally hooked by fishers, which is the number one cause of death. They are also killed when they run into boat propellers, a more frequent occurrence as river traffic increases. It is thought that the noise from the boats' motors disrupts the dolphin's ability to navigate using echolocation.

However, like its distant dolphin relatives in the Indus, Ganges, and Amazon Rivers, the principal threat to the Chinese river dolphin lies in human disturbance of its habitat. Living in an area that contains over 380 million people, or eight percent of the world's population, this river dolphin is under constant threat from dams and other water projects. A gigantic hydroelectric dam is planned on the Chang Jiang River. The explosives used to build these structures can kill dolphins that are in the area. The finished projects are liable to block the migration of fish that the dolphin relies on for food and

200 B.C.E. However, it was originally described in Western scientific literature in the early 1900s from a specimen from Tung Ting Lake in China.

This dolphin was once thought to occur only in Tung Ting Lake, 600 miles (965 kilometers) up the Chang Jiang River. Because of the geographic and political isolation of China, little else was known of this rare dolphin by Western scientists until expeditions were mounted in the late 1970s. Surveys in late 1993 and early 1994 resulted in sightings of only nine animals. This river dolphin is now known to occur throughout the lower reaches and tributaries of the Chang Jiang River system in the Hunan Province of China. It can be found up to 1,180 miles (1,900 kilometers) from the coast.

In shape and size this river dolphin resembles others of the Platanistidae family; however, it differs in certain subtle traits. Like other river dolphins, it has a high-domed forehead, but its long beak curves slightly upward. The dorsal fin is short and triangular and continues toward the tail as a low ridge; the pectoral fins are short and wide. Its color is usually a blue-gray, fading to white on the underside. The eyes are small but functional, and the blowhole is oriented crosswise to the body and is elliptical in shape.

The Chinese river dolphin seems gregarious and is often seen in pairs or groups of between 3 and 12 individuals. It is also seen swimming with another cetacean that sometimes shares its river home, the finless porpoise (*Neophocaena phocaenoides*). They are easily told apart, however, as the finless porpoise is much smaller and darker and lacks a beak and dorsal fin.

separate the few remaining dolphins from each other. With the number of dolphins as low as it is already, splitting the dolphin population into smaller groups may result in keeping the few remaining dolphins of breeding age from being able to reach each other and mate.

Help from a relative

Although the situation for the few remaining dolphins looks dim, there is some hope. Conservation efforts include the development of at least one natural reserve. In addition, Chinese scientists have begun to develop a plan for a semicaptive breeding program for this dolphin. They are basing their plan on the methods used in successful captive-breeding programs for the oceanic bottlenose dolphin (*Tursiops truncatus*) in the United States. Unlike the program for the bottlenose dolphin, which used large tanks in aquariums, the Chinese scientists plan to use short outreaches of the Chang Jiang River itself as pens to hold the few remaining river dolphins of breeding age. It is hoped that these captive individuals will be as successful at breeding as their oceangoing relative, and that a viable population will be built up and become self-sustaining in their protected outreaches. However, captive breeding is not enough; this dolphin's river home must become less deadly.

River traffic, fishing, and dam and riverside construction must be reduced and regulated within areas where dolphins now live so that future reintroductions can ensure the survival of the wild populations of this critically endangered dolphin.

Ganges River Dolphin
(Platanista gangetica)

IUCN: Endangered

Weight: 175–185 lb. (80–84 kg)
Length: 80–100 in. (200–250 cm)
Diet: Fish and invertebrates
Gestation period: 300–330 days
Longevity: Over 20 years
Habitat: Major rivers and their tributaries
Range: Ganges, Brahmaputra, and Meghna river systems

THE GANGES river dolphin can be found in the major river systems that drain the southern Himalayan Mountain range. These are the Ganges, Brahmaputra, and Meghna Rivers and their tributaries, which flow through India, Bangladesh, and Nepal. This dolphin lives from the tidal zone of these rivers to the foothills of the Himalayas themselves. The species was once found in the Karnaphuli River in Bangladesh as well, but apparently no longer exists in that river. Its numbers are decreasing throughout the rest of its range.

This dolphin is also known as the "susu." It is so named for the sound it makes when surfacing to breathe, an act it performs on average every 30 to 120 seconds. It rarely leaps or otherwise exposes much of its body above water. Like all river dolphins, the Ganges river dolphin appears to have a simple social structure. It is usually found singly or in pairs, rarely in large groups.

This dolphin's color is dark gray or gray-brown above, with a similar but lighter coloration below. They have a long, thin snout that curves upward and is armed with as many as 130 sharp teeth. Their bulbous forehead is exaggerated by a noticeably constricted neck. The skull is asymmetrical, as it is in all members of the suborder Odontocetes (which includes toothed whales), but there is a bony outgrowth on the forehead, called a maxillary crest, that is unique to this genus. The unusual blowhole is a long slit on the top of the head, slightly to the left of center. The slit runs in the same direction as the body; most other cetaceans have a blowhole that is perpendicular, or that cuts across, the body. The dorsal fin appears as a long, low ridge along the back to the tail. The pectoral fins are large, wide, and squared-off at the ends, resembling large fans. The females are frequently larger than the males.

Perhaps the most striking physical attributes of these dolphins are the eyes, which are so small that they barely appear on the skin's surface. Their eyes have no lenses, and the optic nerves are reduced almost to the thickness of hairs. As a result, these dolphins are nearly blind. Most experts agree that the Ganges river dolphin cannot distinguish shapes, although their eyes probably function well enough to determine light and dark, or day and night, and to distinguish deep water from the surface.

Monsoon adaptations

The Ganges River is 1,560 miles long (2,510 kilometers) and is the major source of irrigation for India and Bangladesh. It lies within the monsoon belt of cen-

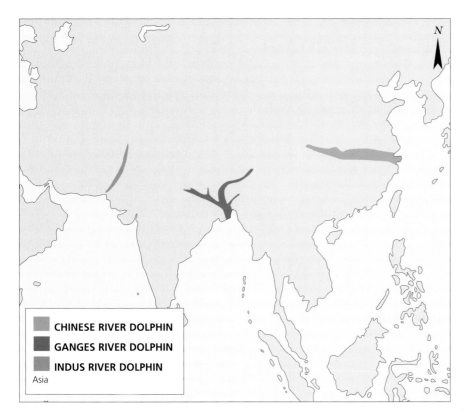

CHINESE RIVER DOLPHIN
GANGES RIVER DOLPHIN
INDUS RIVER DOLPHIN
Asia

tral Asia. For part of each year, extremely heavy rains fall and the land becomes inundated. The remaining water from the monsoon drains into these two river systems, and with the rain water comes a great deal of soil runoff. The result is that, for much of the year, the Ganges River runs fast and dark, and the waters become cloudy and dark brown or red from tons of clay and silt. Visibility in the water is reduced to almost nothing.

In conditions like these, it is no wonder that the Ganges river dolphin has such poor eyesight. For most of the year their eyes would be useless in the dark and murky river water. Yet the rapid flood waters' strength carries away many logs, branches, and other dangerous debris that could injure the dolphins. These animals have to find their way around, feed, and avoid the dangerous objects being carried downstream by the floods.

Like most other cetaceans, the Ganges river dolphins use echolocation. However, because of their poor eyesight and murky habitat, they must rely on echolocation more than any other cetacean species. Experts suspect that the strange maxillary crest on their skull may help concentrate their outgoing signals.

Another unusual trait of these dolphins is that they frequently swim on their side. It is thought that this helps keep them oriented, since their eyes can differentiate up (light) and down (dark), and their large pectoral fins would allow them to keep in contact with the river bottom. As they swim, they move their heads back and forth, probably to scan a wider area with their sonar.

Perhaps most interesting of all, these dolphins almost never stop swimming and using echolocation. Given the dark, swift, and dangerous water they must live in, this is not surprising. These

dolphins probably sleep during the brief breaks between sonar pulses. These breaks are rarely more than about seven seconds in duration, but it has been estimated that over a 24-hour period, these dolphins may sleep as much as other cetaceans.

Declining range

There are estimated to be only about 5,000 Ganges river dolphins left, and populations appear to be decreasing over much of their range in India, Bangladesh, and Nepal, where perhaps as few as 50 remain. Nonetheless, this species is doing better than its close relative, the Indus river dolphin (*Platanista minor*). Both species are under extreme pressure from the development of dams, irrigation, and flood control works that alter the river habitat. Lower water levels, siltation, a decrease in the populations of food fish, and splintering of the dolphin population into small groups are the major destructive effects of these water projects.

The Ganges river dolphin also faces pressure from pollution and hunting, for it lives in one of the most densely populated and poorest regions of the world. There is high demand for the dolphin's products, mainly their oil to use as fishbait, medicine, or liniment. While it may be the most numerically common of the river dolphins, it is also one of the most vulnerable. Local populations have become extinct in parts of its range, and this trend will continue unless efforts are made to forcefully preserve areas of river habitat. The Department of Zoology at Patna University in India has a program under way to study and conserve this dolphin. An IUCN action plan for the conservation of cetaceans includes six projects to help conserve this dolphin, including ways to restore habitat and evaluating the need for translocating populations isolated by dams or at risk from fishing.

Indus River Dolphin
(Platanista inor)

ESA: Endangered

IUCN: Endangered

Weight: 175–185 lb. (80–84 kg)
Length: 80–100 in. (200–250 cm)
Diet: Fish
Gestation period: 300–330 days
Longevity: Over 20 years
Habitat: Major rivers and their tributaries
Range: Indus River system

THE INDUS river dolphin (also referred to as *Platanista indi*) is found only in the Indus River system of Pakistan, primarily in the provinces of Sind and Punjab. Although this mighty river is 1,900 miles long (3,060 kilometers), most of the few remaining river dolphins are found in an 81-mile (130-kilometer) stretch of river between the barrages (artificial dams) of Sukkur and Guddu in Sind. This is partly because this area is the only stretch of river where the dolphin is protected, but it is also due to the enormous changes the Indus River has undergone in the past 100 years—changes that have had a negative impact on much of the wildlife of the river.

The Indus river dolphin differs very little from the Ganges river dolphin (*Platanista gangeticus*), causing some scientists to call it a subspecies. Like the Ganges river dolphin, the Indus river dolphin is a dull gray color with a lighter belly and a large, rounded forehead. The blowhole is situated lengthwise rather than crosswise as in other cetaceans. Like its close relative, the Indus river dolphin is almost blind. Its diminutive eyes contain no lenses. The main physical differences between the two species of dolphins are found in the features of the skull, especially the maxillary crest that is unique to this genus. The Indus dolphin's crest is smaller and more oval than that of the Ganges dolphin.

Target for hunters

While little is known about the natural history of this rare dolphin, it is thought to have a simple social structure, usually found singly or in pairs rather than in large groups. It is thought to spend much of its time swimming on its side, relying upon echolocation for hunting and navigating. This dolphin rarely exposes much of its body above the surface, performing a simple roll when coming up to breathe. This does not make it safe from hunters, as it breathes about once a minute. This makes it easy for a marksman to plot a dolphin's path and prepare for the shot when the dolphin surfaces next.

Although hunting has taken a toll on this dolphin's population, the major threat to it is the construction of irrigation barrages and dams for hydroelectric power. These works serve to separate the populations and do not allow for movement of dolphins or their fish prey along the rivers. Trapped in short stretches of shallow water, the dolphins can be easily caught by hunters, who shoot or net them from shore. There are probably only a few hundred Indus river dolphins remaining; most estimates place their numbers at around 500. Although they receive some protection in the province of Sind, the few dolphins that remain in the province of Punjab are unprotected, scattered, and physically separated from each other by water works.

One of the biggest problems concerning conservation work on this dolphin is the lack of data on its numbers, behavior, and general ecology. It is assumed to have similar habits to those of its close relative, the Ganges river dolphin. Studies must determine the dolphin's needs concerning space, food, and movement.

More information is needed to find out whether the protected population that exists between the barrages of Sukkur and Guddu is decreasing. The few dolphins that exist upriver should be tracked, a management plan drawn up, and laws passed and enforced to protect them. It may be necessary to begin a captive-breeding program, a system that is successful for bottlenose dolphins (*Tursiops truncatus*), and that is being tried for the Chinese river dolphin. Unless drastic action is taken toward protecting and managing the remaining populations, this dolphin will be the first cetacean to become extinct in modern times.

Peter Zahler

DOVES

Class: Aves
Order: Columbiformes
Family: Columbidae

Some bird species are so beautiful or intriguing that they become symbols in human culture. Doves, for example, invoke romantic images of gentleness and purity. They symbolize peace and goodwill. In contrast, pigeons do not conjure up pleasant images. Pigeons make messes. They roost around buildings and leave their droppings everywhere. Most people adore the dove and scorn the pigeon. However, nothing about their anatomy or behavior distinguishes one from the other. Biologically, doves and pigeons are the same kind of bird.

In many places, pigeons have found cities and towns that offer predator-free environments, where they can reproduce in great numbers. They form huge flocks that become intolerable to people. Many large cities spend enormous amounts of time and money to control rock doves (*Columba livia*), the bird commonly recognized as "the pigeon." These birds are poisoned and shot, and sometimes people are prohibited from feeding them.

There is also a popular recreational hunting industry for these birds. The money spent by hunters on guns, ammunition, food and lodging, guide services, and other things associated with hunting, influences local and regional economies. Hunters also pay revenue-producing license fees that are used to protect and enhance wildlife habitat. Many species that are not hunted also benefit occasionally from the money spent on hunted species.

Pigeons and doves are also valued for their homing nature and flying ability, which make them popular for racing.

Historically they were used as a rapid method of conveying messages over long distances. Also, their beauty is promoted by pigeon husbandry for competitive shows and the pet trade. Some foreign species are desired for zoo collections.

Several features make pigeons and doves unique. When they drink, they keep their heads down and their beaks immersed, sucking in the water and swallowing. Other birds have to dip their beaks, raise their heads, and tilt back in order to swallow. When pigeons and doves feed their hatchlings, they produce "pigeon's milk" from special cells lining their crops. It is not like the milk produced by cows or other mammals, but it is a thick liquid that nourishes the young until they can eat fruits and seeds. Young pigeons and doves reach their own beaks into the throats of their parents to scrape the "pigeon's milk" directly from the crop. No other birds produce such food for their young.

Ornithologists generally agree that the now extinct dodos and solitaires of the Mascarene Islands were related to pigeons and doves. However, since there are no surviving dodos or solitaires to confirm this theory, they are usually placed in their own family (Raphidae) and included in the pigeon order (Columbiformes).

The pigeons and doves form an easily recognized group of about 250 to 300 species. They range from about the size of a sparrow to that of a goose. Some are adorned with elegant crowns, some wear bright colors, and some are quite plain. A few pigeons and doves have very broad ranges and occur in high numbers. The extinct passenger pigeon (*Ectopistes migratorius*) of North America was the most abundant land-bird species in the world. Other pigeons and doves occupy very small areas and in very small populations.

Grenada Dove
(*Leptotila wellsi*)

ESA: Endangered

IUCN: Critically endangered

Length: 10 in. (26 cm)
Weight: Unknown
Clutch size: 2 eggs in captivity
Incubation: Unknown
Diet: Unknown, probably seeds
Habitat: Dry shrublands
Range: Southwestern Grenada in the West Indies

FIRST DESCRIBED in 1884, the Grenada dove was considered a distinct species for nearly a century. Then, in 1983, the American Ornithologist's Union reclassified the bird as a subspecies of the gray-fronted dove (*Leptotila rufaxilla*), but this has not been widely accepted.

The upperparts of the Grenada dove are a shiny olive-brown; the chin and throat are white. The upper breast and the sides of the neck are a pinkish tan, while the lower breast and belly are white. The sides are buff or tan with a cinnamon-colored underwing. The bare skin around the eyes is a pale blue, and the cheek and forehead are pinkish tan. The feet and toes are bright red, and the beak is black.

The gray-fronted dove inhabits wet or humid forests in South America. The Grenada dove inhabits dry shrublands. The gray-fronted dove shows large white tips on its tail feathers, but the Grenada dove shows only slender white borders on the tips. The gray-fronted dove has a grayish tan lower breast and belly, but the Grenada dove is very white. In field experiments, the Grenada dove does not respond to taped calls of the gray-fronted dove, but it does respond to taped calls of other Grenada doves. Based on this, most ornithologists still consider the Grenada dove a distinct species.

Grenada is the southernmost island in the Lesser Antilles of the West Indies. It lies 90 miles (144 kilometers) north of Venezuela and covers 138 square miles (344 square kilometers). A series of ridges and valleys break up the landscape. The Grenada dove probably never inhabited the entire island. It favors dry shrubland where small trees grow only 20 to 30 feet tall (6 to 9 meters). Today, suitable habitat for these doves has been drastically reduced. People build houses along the ridge tops and convert the lowlands between ridges to cropland, where they grow nutmeg, cocoa, sugarcane, bananas, and coconuts. Livestock grazing has severely damaged much of the island's native vegetation.

The Grenada dove survives only on the island's southwestern peninsula. An airport built in the early 1980s destroyed ten percent of the Grenada dove habitat remaining at that time. A quarry was opened nearby to provide fill material for airport construction. The quarry destroyed even more habitat, and no doves have been seen in the area since. The doves are concentrated in a small area of public land known as the Mount Hartman Estate. Dove habitat still survives on the hillsides, probably because the slopes are unsuitable for crops and are undesirable for building houses.

Preservation

Suggestions for protecting the Grenada dove focus on preserving the Mount Hartman Estate. At least one recommendation calls for designating it a National Critical Conservation Area. If carefully controlled, some grazing and woodcutting could continue on the estate without harming the Grenada dove. Trapping of other animals does not seem to be a factor in the bird's decline, but studies should be undertaken to monitor the population (believed to be about 100 birds in 1990).

The Indian mongoose (*Herpestes auropunctatus*) was released on the island many years ago and now occurs abundantly on the southwestern peninsula. Studies should be conducted to determine what effect, if any, the mongoose has on the dove. Finally, preservation actions should include enforcing the ban on further development of ridge tops. The Grenada dove can be bred in captivity, but it needs habitat to survive in the wild. So long as the bird breeds successfully, preservation efforts should be aimed at preserving space for it to live in.

Polynesian Ground Dove
(Gallicolumba erythroptera)

IUCN: Critically endangered

Length: 10 in. (25 cm)
Weight: Unknown
Clutch size: Unknown
Incubation: Unknown
Diet: Unknown
Habitat: Forests
Range: Tuamotu Archipelago in Polynesia

THE POLYNESIAN ground dove was just one tiny part of the Tahitian paradise that inspired the French artist Paul Gauguin. Tahiti is one of several islands in the Society Islands Archipelago. The Societies and four other archipelagos, including the

The Grenada dove lives on a tiny island in the Caribbean. Experts still debate its relationship to another dove in South America, *Leptotila rufaxilla*.

Tuamotu Archipelago, make up French Polynesia, an overseas territory of France. This territory includes about 130 islands that add up to 1,544 square miles (4,014 square kilometers) of land. Most of these are very small islands, or atolls, that support only scanty habitat for land animals. At 402 square miles (1,045 square kilometers), Tahiti is the largest island in the territory. Volcanic and mountainous, it supports more than half the territory's human population, an estimated 185,000 by the late 1980s. The larger islands depend on tourism and a modest harvest of coconuts, bananas, oranges, sugarcane, and vanilla. All the crops are grown in the coastal lowland areas.

On the male Polynesian ground dove, the middle back, rump, tail, belly, and sides are black. The wing is brownish, and the shoulder and upper back are a blackish brown with a purple sheen. The nape, the back of the head, and the cheek are slate gray, while the forecrown, forehead, chin, throat, and breast are white. Females of the species display more brown and less black than the males. The upper back, nape, back of the head, and cheek are medium gray; the forecrown, forehead, and chin are dingy. The lower throat and breast are a rusty orange brown. Both sexes have a black beak and dark feet and toes.

Virtually nothing is known about the Polynesian ground dove other than how it looks and that it is disappearing. Once common in the Society Islands, including Tahiti, it is now entirely gone from there. A few birds survive in the Tuamotu Archipelago, where they are limited to small atolls uninhabited by people.

No research has been conducted to learn the cause of this dove's decline. Probably the answer is connected to an expanding human population and its accompanying problems. Lost habitat, degraded quality of surviving habitat, imported exotic species, and excessive trapping or hunting are likely causes that should be investigated.

This Polynesian bird is another example of how rapidly a species can disappear before we have had a chance to learn anything about it.

Purple-winged Ground Dove
(Claravis godefrida)

IUCN: Critically endangered

Length: 7½ in. (19 cm)
Weight: Unknown
Clutch size: Unknown, but 2 eggs in related species
Incubation: Unknown, but 14 days for related species
Diet: Unknown, probably seeds
Habitat: Lowland forests
Range: Southeastern Brazil, Argentina, and Paraguay

BRAZIL IS THE HOME of the Amazon River and rain forest, a place of hungry piranha fish, jaguars, and anacondas. But among these carnivorous creatures lives a more docile one—the purple-winged ground dove.

Brazil covers an area larger than the 48 contiguous United States. Such a vast landscape supports many different kinds of plant and animal communities. Many of these plants and animals are unique to Brazil. Although rain forests received much public attention in the 1980s and 1990s, drier forests and shrublands in Brazil were actually more imperiled. The south and south-central regions of Brazil produce three quarters of the country's agricultural output, including coffee, cotton, cocoa, corn, rice, soybeans, and various fruits. Brazil is also a major producer of beef and pork. Birds such as the purple-winged ground dove cannot survive in landscapes cultivated for a single plant such as coffee. Unfortunately, Brazil's most

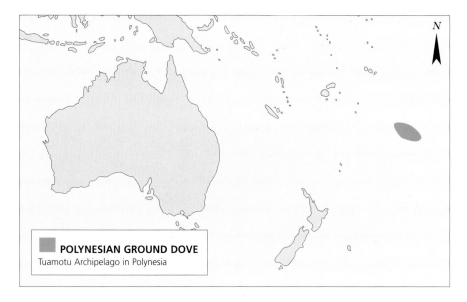

POLYNESIAN GROUND DOVE
Tuamotu Archipelago in Polynesia

The purple-winged ground dove is disappearing faster than it can be studied—much like the South American lowland forests in which it dwells.

important agricultural land lies within the range of the dove. The purple-winged ground dove has not been studied, so little is known about its natural history. What is known is that the species is disappearing from areas where it was once common. As a species becomes rarer, studying it becomes more difficult, yet specific information is essential so that people can control activities that cause the endangerment.

The male of the species has blue-gray upperparts, gently fading to pale neck and underparts. The face is almost white. The wings have three broad purple bands, and the outer tail feathers are white. The female's upperparts are a blending of tan and cinnamon browns; the throat and belly are dull white. The breast is pale brown, and the wings dis-

play the same purple bands as on the male. The tips of the outer tail feathers are buff on the female. Both sexes have pale beaks and a pink leg and foot.

Before plans to preserve the bird's habitat can be recommended, thorough field research

PURPLE-WINGED
GROUND DOVE
Southeastern Brazil
and Paraguay

must be done to verify its habitat needs. It may be willing to use secondary forest growth like the related blue ground dove (*Claravis pretiosa*). However, because it occurs in a much smaller area, it probably has more specific habitat needs that may hamper conservationists efforts to save it.

Socorro Dove
(Zenaida graysoni)

IUCN: Extinct in the wild

Length: 12–14 in. (30–35 cm)
Weight: Unknown
Clutch size: Probably 2 or 3 eggs
Incubation: Probably 14–15 days
Diet: Seeds
Habitat: Forest
Range: Socorro Island, 200 miles (320 km) south of Baja, Mexico

SINCE IT WAS first described in 1871, the Socorro dove has been treated as both a full species and a subspecies of the mourning dove (*Zenaida macroura*). Currently, most ornithologists accept it as a full species.

The Socorro dove looks like the mourning dove but is slightly larger and darker. It has gray-brown upperparts with a darker gray crown and a buff to pale rufous forehead. The underparts are paler, with more buff and a rufous hue. The inner tail feathers are longer than the outer feathers, which are tipped with white.

The first permanent human settlement on Socorro Island was a Mexican military base built in

471

SOCORRO DOVE
Pacific Ocean

GRENADA DOVE
Caribbean

1957. By the early 1980s about 125 people and some horses, burros, cats, chickens, and pigeons were living on Socorro. Sheep have grazed the island since 1869, and they have altered the vegetation on all the slopes below 1,968 feet (600 meters). Cats are also a danger.

The dove was last seen in 1958 and it may now be extinct, but about 200 birds survive in captivity. A new initiative means that while birds are reared in captivity, New Zealand wildlife experts will help Mexico to eradicate the cats and sheep. Only after the cats and sheep are gone will young Socorro doves be released into special aviaries built over surviving woodlands on Socorro. Here they will be trained to eat wild foods before they are set free.

Kevin Cook

DUCKS

Class: Aves

Order: Anseriformes

Family: Anatidae

Subfamily: Anatinae

The birds in the order Anseriformes are known as waterfowl. In many cultures waterfowl and their eggs are eaten. Waterfowl feathers are used as insulation for clothing and blankets. Feathers were once collected from wild waterfowl, but today feathers are taken from domestic birds. Exceptions in U.S. law allow Arctic peoples (such as the Inuit and Eskimo) to collect down from wild eider ducks. Many people collect waterfowl to keep and breed them, and there is economic value in waterfowl hunting. Each year U.S. hunters spend millions of dollars on recreational hunting. In addition to this, hunters buy licenses and pay excise taxes as a requirement to hunt legally.

This money helps finance wildlife management and even recovery projects for endangered species.

During the late 1800s in the United States an entire trade developed around hunting wildlife for market. As railroads and refrigeration became available, transportation and storage problems were resolved. This in turn led to even more hunting. Improved firearms and hunting techniques made this occupation efficient and lethal. Species disappeared from areas where they had lived for hundreds of thousands of years. In some cases they even became extinct.

By 1900 many forms of U.S wildlife were in jeopardy.

Individual states and the federal government passed laws to restrict or eliminate hunting of certain species. These laws typically were enacted after the protected species had already disappeared. During the 1930s, North America was struck by the worst drought in historic times. Waterfowl, already harmed by habitat loss, industrial pollution, and excessive hunting, suffered even further. It was clear that some kind of regulation was necessary to preserve both the wildlife hunting trade and the species that spawned it.

The United States adopted a system of restraint, and wildlife laws stipulate when legal species may be hunted, how they may be hunted, and how many may be taken. Since this system of regulation and restraint came into being, no waterfowl species have become extinct in the United States.

Hawaiian Duck

(Anas wyvilliana)

ESA: Endangered

IUCN: Vulnerable

Length: Males, 19–20 in. (48–51 cm); females, 16–17 in. (41–43 cm)

Weight: Males, 21½–26½ oz. (610–751 g); females, 18–23 oz. (510–652 g)

Clutch size: 2–10 eggs

Incubation: 28 days in captivity, 28–30 days in the wild

Diet: Plants such as green algae, rice, and other grass seeds; earthworms, snails, larval and adult dragonflies, and most probably other insects

Habitat: Wetlands

Range: Kauai, Hawaii, and Oahu in the Hawaiian Islands

THE MALLARD (*Anas platyrhynchos*) occurs nearly everywhere in the Northern Hemisphere, even on a string of islands in the Pacific Ocean. This great ocean isolated these island mallards from other mallards, and in time these ducks became unique to Hawaii, and thus became known as Hawaiian ducks.

The Hawaiian duck is highly patterned in tan, buff, and brown. Males are typically darker than females, showing a rich chestnut on the breast, a lighter chestnut on the side, and occasionally, usually on immature males, deep green specks on the head. The wing has a dark patch that varies from blackish green to deep purple, bordered by black, with white bands. The foot and toe of this species are usually orange, but dark gray and scarlet are known. The bill is usually olive green on males, and either dark gray or yellow orange with some dark spots on females.

Traditionally, ornithologists have regarded the Hawaiian duck as a subspecies of the mallard. In recent years the bird has been increasingly considered a distinct species. Wary birds, Hawaiian ducks are usually seen alone or in pairs. They fly well but stay within a general territory all year and do not travel among the

The Hawaiian duck is richly patterned, like other mallards—a species of duck that appears nearly everywhere in the Northern Hemisphere. The Hawaiian duck is usually considered a subspecies because of the unique characteristics that separate it from other mallards.

islands. Females build their nests on dry ground near water and in good cover. They lay from two to ten eggs, which need about 30 days of incubating to hatch. (Some observers believe the smaller clutch sizes indicate nests in which females have not finished laying). After the ducklings

HAWAIIAN DUCK
Hawaiian Islands

hatch, the female takes them to safety on the water to avoid predators. Black rats (*Rattus rattus*) and mongooses (*Herpestes auropunctatus*) are exotic mammals that raid nests for eggs and also kill young birds. Feral house cats (*Felis sylvestris*) are less likely to damage eggs, but they do kill ducklings.

The Hawaiian ducks also struggle with habitat loss. Once common on all the larger islands except Lanai and Kahoolawe, the duck disappeared after its wetland habitats were drained for agricultural, residential, and commercial development.

They used freshwater marshes, streams, and swamps from sea level up to about 8,200 feet (2,500 meters). The ducks even accepted taro fields which, when flooded, provided suitable artificial wetland habitat.

But many taro fields have now been converted to sugarcane, so even this artificial habitat is now less available.

Hunting pressure

This bird has also suffered from excessive hunting. During the late 1800s and early 1900s ducks were a favorite quarry. The population dropped drastically and so quickly that hunting was prohibited in 1925. The damage was already done, however. By 1949 the duck survived only on Kauai, Oahu, and Niihau. Protective action began in 1952, but the birds disappeared from Oahu in 1960 and shortly afterward from Niihau.

With protection, the Kauai population of Hawaiian ducks slowly recovered. By 1970 some 2,000 birds lived in undeveloped areas of the island. This was a healthy increase over the 1949 estimate of 500 ducks. From this stock, Hawaiian ducks were taken for recovery programs on other islands. The species has been returned to Oahu and Hawaii.

The U.S. Fish and Wildlife Service Recovery Plan calls for three self-sustaining populations. One population of 2,000 or more birds will remain on Kauai. Other populations of 500 birds are to be established on both Oahu and Hawaii.

Several wildlife refuges have been designated on the islands, and wildlife managers understand the vital need to maintain habitat quality.

Although the Hawaiian duck has not been removed from endangered status, its chances for survival look very good.

Laysan Duck
(Anas laysanensis)

ESA: Endangered	
IUCN: Vulnerable	

Length: 16 in. (41 cm)
Weight: 14–19½oz. (397–556 g)
Clutch size: Usually 3 eggs
Incubation: Unknown, probably 28–30 days
Diet: Brine flies (*Neoscatella sexnotata*) and moths (*Agrotis dislocata*)
Habitat: A single, salty pond and surrounding dry land vegetation
Range: Laysan Island in the Hawaiian Islands

THE LAYSAN DUCK is patterned in tan, brown, and chestnut, having an overall dark appearance. The wing displays a bright purple patch with a greenish sheen bordered with a white strip. Immature birds have a dark brown head with a green sheen and a white eye ring; the white becomes an irregular patch, mottling much of the head as the bird ages. The foot and toe are bright orange on males, duller on females. The male bill is a dull blue or bluish green, while the female bill is a dull yellow with black spots.

The Laysan duck is an ultimately doomed bird. Even if people correct all the harm that has been inflicted upon it, the Laysan duck will not survive for long. That is because it has become uniquely adapted to a naturally dying habitat.

Laysan Island lies 915 miles (1,463 kilometers) northwest of

LAYSAN DUCK
Laysan Island in the Hawaiian Islands

Oahu in the Hawaiian Island chain. Occupying only 913 acres (365 hectares) of land surrounded by the Pacific Ocean, Laysan today is just a shadow of its former size. A volcano formed it, and now the ocean, wind, and rain are washing it away. Geologists believe huge slabs of the Earth's crust, known as plates, float on an inner mantle of molten rock, or magma. In certain places, holes penetrate to the mantle and create hot spots. The plates move very slowly in a constant direction over these hot spots. Volcanos form from the magma that escapes through these holes and which then cools to become solid rock. For hundreds or thousands of years, the volcanos grow by repeated eruptions until the volcanic cone emerges above the sea as an island. Eventually, as the plate continues to move, the volcanic island drifts beyond the hot spot and the volcano becomes inactive. Without renewals of fresh lava, the island begins to erode under the natural processes of wind, rain, and waves, and eventually disappears altogether.

A delicate habitat

Laysan is such an island, and natural erosion has worn the once towering volcanic cone to a level just below the ocean surface. Corals and other reef-building organisms have grown abundantly enough around the shrunken mountain that a mound has formed from their ancient carcasses and rises above the waves. On this speck of land, the Laysan duck still survives.

A salty lake dominates the center of Laysan. Brine flies (*Neoscatella sexnotata*) breed in the lake, and the ducks feed on both the larvae in the water and on the winged adults. They also eat the caterpillars of a moth (*Agrotis dislocata*). The caterpillars come out of hiding in the late evening to feed on the foliage of *Nama sandwicensis*, a water leaf unique to the Hawaiian Islands, and on *Boerhavia diffusa* and *Tribulus cistoides*, vines common on Pacific islands. The ducks rest in the shade of these plants during the heat of the day and then begin feeding on the caterpillars at dusk and continue feeding through the night.

Europeans and Americans did not visit Laysan until after 1820. The duck was not collected until 1891, and its first scientific description was published in 1892. Called the "Laysan teal" for many years, the duck has caused endless speculation ever since its discovery.

Ornithologists are less sure about the Laysan duck's origin than about the history of human influence on the island.

A series of problems

Guano mining began on Laysan in 1891. Guano is the accumulated mass of bird droppings, and is rich in phosphorous and nitrogen compounds that are useful in making both gunpowder and fer-

The Laysan duck lives on a precarious bit of volcanic rock at the end of the Hawaiian Island chain. The island is a National Wildlife Refuge, but this will not be enough to save the species.

tilizer. On Laysan, terns and albatrosses were abundant for a long enough period to produce usable quantities of guano. The guano miners, unfortunately, took sport in shooting the ducks. They also brought European rabbits (*Oryctolagus cuniculus*) to the island. The rabbits fed on the few plants that could tolerate the high temperatures, sand, and guano of Laysan.

The United States annexed the Hawaiian Islands in 1898. The guano mining ended in 1904, and in February 1909 President Theodore Roosevelt signed an executive order that included Laysan in the Hawaiian Islands Bird Reservation. Japanese feather hunters either disregarded or did not know of the protection extended to the birds on Laysan. They landed there in 1909 and 1910 to collect feathers and killed many Laysan albatrosses and black-footed albatrosses (*Diomedea immutabilis* and *Diomedea nigripes*). Even after the miners and the feather hunters left, the influence of humans persisted on Laysan because the rabbits remained.

Rabbits eradicated

Without natural predators, the rabbit population grew large very quickly. By 1923 they had eaten the foliage of the island down to bare sand. Plants stabilized the sand and provided essential cover for several birds unique to the island, including the Laysan duck. When the vegetation disappeared, wind blew sand into the lake, partially filling it. A team was sent to Laysan with the specific assignment of eradicating the rabbits. These non-native mammals would have eventually starved themselves into extinction anyway, after denuding the island of plant life.

Once the rabbits were eliminated, the vegetation grew back. The Laysan duck population grew from a low of seven birds in 1912, to 33 in 1950, and 287 by 1976. At least 500 ducks were found in 1989, and many more live in zoos where they are carefully bred. Laysan ducks lay only three eggs per clutch, which means their rate

Many species of ducks throughout the islands of Hawaii and the South Pacific suffer from the same environmental stress. Because they are adapted to a unique environment, any change introduced by people harms the birds' ability to survive.

of population growth is quite slow. However, banding studies indicate that they have a longer lifespan than most other ducks, at least eight to 12 years, and probably even a little longer.

Laysan, now part of the Northwest Hawaiian Islands National Wildlife Refuge, was made a research natural area in 1967. The duck population is estimated at 500. Previous efforts to introduce the duck to other islands have not been successful, but other attempts may be made. Surveys and behavioral studies of this duck are under way. Only scientists are allowed on the island, and they must be granted permits before landing. The duck population is monitored, and the island is guarded against rats, mongooses, and other exotic species that could undo a half century of recovery.

Doomed island

All of these measures can be undertaken by people to help the Laysan duck survive, but people cannot prevent the ocean from one day consuming Laysan Island. When that happens, the Laysan duck will be doomed as a wild species, although it may survive in captivity indefinitely.

Mariana Mallard

(Anas oustaleti)

ESA: Endangered

Class: Aves
Order: Anseriformes
Family: Anatidae
Length: 21 in. (53.3 cm)
Weight: Probably 20–24 oz. (567–681 g)
Clutch size: Probably 2–10 eggs
Incubation: Probably 28–30 days
Diet: Probably seeds of aquatic plants and invertebrates
Habitat: Wetlands
Range: Mariana Islands in the western Pacific Ocean

THE MARIANA mallard may never have existed. Or it might be a species teetering on the brink of extinction. Knowing what action to take to preserve the Mariana mallard requires understanding this bird. Interpreting the Mariana mallard depends on understanding ducks, and the mallard in particular.

Mallards (*Anas platyrhynchos*) live north of the equator on all continents and many islands. Various cultures began domesticating them 3,000 to 5,000 years before Europeans colonized North America. After several millennia of selective breeding, people have developed domestic strains such as the large Cayuga, Pekin, and Raouen ducks, the peculiar Chinese racer, and the tiny call duck. These strains of mallards are much like the different breeds of dogs. They are the common ducks of barnyards and ponds in city parks. This poten-

tial for variation may turn up in populations of wild birds. When variations occur predictably according to their geographic location, the populations that show those variations are called subspecies. The mallard also interbreeds with other duck species, and the offspring are called hybrids. The mallard is known to interbreed occasionally with more than a dozen other duck species. Knowing about this facet of mallard behavior helps explain the confusion about the Mariana mallard.

A mystery

The status of the Mariana mallard has puzzled ornithologists for years. Ornithologists have considered this bird as both a discrete species and as a subspecies of the mallard. The Mariana mallard was never abundant, but its small population showed two distinct forms. One form closely resembled the mallard, and the other form resembled the gray duck (*Anas superciliosa*). Most ornithologists interpreted the forms as evidence that the Mariana mallard was actually a hybrid between the gray duck and the mallard. However, neither the mallard nor the gray duck has been found in the Mariana Islands. If the parental species does not occur on the Marianas, then the Mariana mallard may represent the beginnings of a new species. The final outcome, however, may never be known, because the last wild Mariana mallards were seen in 1979.

History

The Mariana mallard historically occurred only on the islands of Guam, Tinian, and Saipan in the

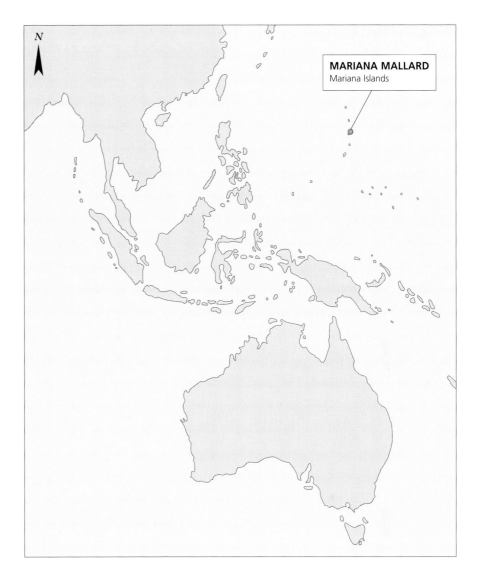

MARIANA MALLARD
Mariana Islands

western Pacific Ocean. At least 38 specimens were collected on Tinian and Saipan in the decade before World War II. Toward the end of the war, personnel of the United States Navy were stationed there. Records indicate that military personnel shot the ducks, if only occasionally. Duck hunting has persisted on the islands despite the presence of the highly endangered Mariana mallard. Wetland destruction on these three islands has further jeopardized the species. Almost no habitat remains on Guam, and the Mariana mallard has been seen on that island only once since 1946. Only Lake Susupe on Saipan and Hagoi

Marsh on Tinian still offer any suitable habitat for this species. In 1979 three Mariana mallards were trapped to begin captive breeding of the species. Two were kept, but they died in 1981 before they could reproduce. Mariana mallards have not been seen since the third bird, a male, was released after capture in 1979. It is possible that this species still exists, however.

As of 1990, some habitat endured at Lake Susupe on Saipan. It is dense enough that some Mariana mallards could survive there and escape detection. Perhaps this bird still survives and its story will someday become known.

White-headed Duck

(Oxyura leucocephala)

IUCN: Vulnerable

Length: 15 in. (38 cm)
Weight: Unknown
Clutch size: Probably 3–5 eggs; lays eggs in other ducks' nests
Incubation: Unknown
Diet: Aquatic plants and probably some invertebrates
Habitat: Open water
Range: Eurasia

THE WHITE-HEADED duck looks pudgy while floating on the water. It pulls its short, thick neck back so that its big head rides above its body, with its large beak resting on its round chest. With this stocky physique and its spiked tail pointing skyward, the white-headed duck lacks the sleek appearance so common to many other species of duck.

The male white-headed duck is reddish brown overall with a white cheek, chin, and forehead. The crown, the nape, and the throat are all black.

Females are more brown and less red overall, as well as less white on the head. The forehead, crown, and nape are dark brown. There is a dingy white line under the eye, with a dark brown line across a dingy white cheek. The bill is enlarged at the base; it is pale blue on males, and a dullish gray on the females.

Mallards live on all continents and islands north of the equator. The Mariana mallard is similar in appearance to the common mallard, shown here, and has been classified as both a separate species and as a subspecies.

Classification

White-headed ducks belong to a group known as the stiff-tailed ducks. Traditionally, ornithologists have recognized the group as a tribe (Oxyurini) in the subfamily of ducks (Anatinae). More recently, some ornithologists have elevated the group to subfamily status (Oxyurinae). Only eight or nine species are in the group, and the white-headed duck is the only member found naturally in Europe. The ruddy duck (*Oxyura jamaicensis*), native to North America, became established in England after some were intentionally released and others escaped captivity.

The white-headed duck originally lived in extreme southern Spain, portions of northern Algeria and Tunisia, and eastward to western China and Mongolia. The bird no longer occurs uniformly across this vast range but lives in isolated populations. In 1992 the world population was estimated to not exceed 210 birds, and only a very small number occur in protected areas.

In 1982 the population in the western Mediterranean Sea was estimated at about 2,000 birds. The greatest number of birds during the 1980s survived in Kazakh, primarily near the Aral Sea west to the Caspian Sea. These northern birds move south to spend their winters in Turkey, northern Iran, and Iraq. Southern birds remain in the same general area all year.

The white-headed ducks have been overhunted in Europe and have suffered from habitat loss.

Marshes and other wetlands have been drained for agricultural development and as a health measure against mosquitoes and other pests. White-headed ducks do not breed easily in captivity, but programs to encourage them have been in progress for years and have had some success. Captive breeding is a vital step to restoring bird species to the wild. Before such efforts produce significant results, duck hunting and draining of wetlands must stop.

White-winged Duck

(Cairina scutulata)

ESA: Endangered

IUCN: Endangered

Length: 24–30 in. (61–76 cm)
Weight: Unknown
Clutch size: Unknown
Incubation: Unknown
Diet: Unknown
Habitat: Swamps and wet forests with slow or standing water surrounded by trees
Range: Northeast India to Southeast Asia and Indonesia

THE WHITE-WINGED duck is dark overall, with blackish upperparts that have a blue or green sheen. The underparts are a deep chestnut brown. The head and neck are mostly white and marked with black streaks, spots, or both. The wing is black above with a bright patch of white and blue-gray. The underside of the flight feathers is black. The feet are yellow orange, as is the beak, which also has some black spotting.

Conflicting needs

To a person who makes a living cutting trees for wood, a hole in a tree wastes lumber and costs income. To the white-winged duck, a hole in a tree is a place to nest. The conflict between human interests and the ducks' needs is inevitable, and the duck is losing. Unfortunately, more has been written about the white-winged duck's slow but steady decline than has been written about how it lives.

Unlike most ducks, white-winged ducks, also known as white-winged wood ducks, are solitary birds of deep forests. They inhabit tropical climates where they have no need to escape winter by migrating, so they remain in the swamps and forest pools all year and never bunch together in flocks. Consequently, their population has never been as high or as dense as is typical among most waterfowl.

Within their forest habitat, white-winged ducks select tall trees where they find cavities for nesting. Their nests have sometimes been found as high as 82 feet (25 meters) above ground. Several American ducks nest in tree cavities, too. The wood duck *(Aix sponsa)* nests 20 to 40 feet (6 to 12 meters) above ground. After the ducklings hatch, the female whistles from the ground or water below the cavity. This lures the ducklings out of the cavity to join their mother. The light and fluffy ducklings survive the long fall without harm. White-winged ducklings probably behave in a similar manner, but how they exit the nest cavity has not been recorded. White-winged ducks cannot, or will not, nest without cavities in trees. Foresters, however, view trees with cavities as an aggravation. Dead and dying trees were believed to be the breeding site for insects that would spread damage to other healthy trees. Early foresters believed they could improve the health of a forest by removing those trees that were sick or already dead. The

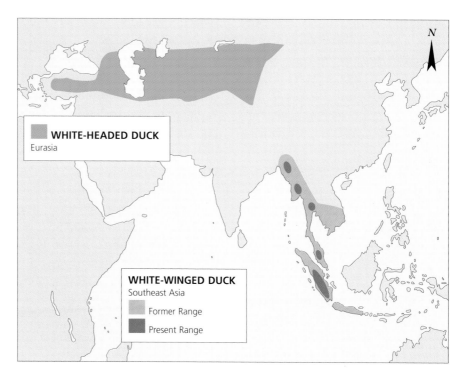

WHITE-HEADED DUCK
Eurasia

WHITE-WINGED DUCK
Southeast Asia
Former Range
Present Range

practice of cutting trees with cavities became standard procedure around the world. The practice did not eliminate or even reduce insect pests, but it did eliminate breeding populations of many animal groups that were dependent on cavities for nesting.

In the 1970s American forestry practices were challenged by wildlife experts, who insisted that forests, especially those on public land, should be regarded as more than just a lumber crop. As a result of this pressure, the American forestry profession has gained more awareness of its impact on animal species. However, using natural resources wisely is a concept that is slow in spreading to other cultures. Economically, some of these countries cannot afford to restrict the use of their resources. In the late 1980s people were still cutting trees with cavities where the white-winged duck lives.

Throughout the white-winged duck's range in Southeast Asia, tropical forests have been destroyed. They are cut for their marketable wood products and cleared to grow other crops—for-

White-winged ducks do not form strong pair bonds throughout the breeding season. The male courts as many females as he can, and the females build their own nests and defend territories around those nests. Males do not help to raise the ducklings.

est crops such as teak, rubber, coffee, mahogany, and fruits. The techniques that make efficient and profitable plantations eliminate habitat for birds like the white-winged duck. Consequently, the bird has disappeared from much of its natural range and survives only in scattered pockets of habitat. The wild population probably does not exceed 200 birds.

One small population of about 20 pairs inhabited the Pablakhali Wildlife Sanctuary in Bangladesh during the 1970s. The sanctuary is only 170 square miles (440 square kilometers) in size and lies entirely within the Kassalong Valley Reserve. The Bangladesh government closed the area to scientific investigations when it began a policy of resettlement. To resolve political turmoil among its people, the government opened the reserve and began leasing 6¼ acres

(2.5 hectares) of land to each family. By 1986 about 10,000 families had been relocated to the reserve. The settlers used dogs to hunt the ducks, and they set fish nets in which the swimming ducks become entangled. A small population cannot endure treatment like this for long.

White-winged ducks are now extinct on the Indonesian island of Java, but the largest known population persists on Sumatra. Very little is known about this group of white-wings except that it is in jeopardy. For many years the Indonesian government has tried to cope with the problem of severe human over-population on Java—1,500 people per square mile (2.6 square kilometers)—by a policy of transmigration. This policy calls for moving large groups of people from Java to other Indonesian islands. Sumatra is one island heavily affected by shifting the human population. Swamps have been drained and trees felled, all to accommodate the needs of an expanding human population. If provisions are not made to safeguard some habitat for the white-winged duck, it will disappear from Sumatra too.

An alternative

Plans to recover the duck include raising birds in captivity, then releasing them into suitable habitat. An international program of captive breeding has been successful, and activities are underway to release these birds into the wild. The problem is guaranteeing habitat for the birds. If reserves and sanctuaries are opened to settlement, they cannot also serve as a safe habitat.

Kevin Cook

Dugong
(*Dugong dugon*)

Class: Mammalia
Order: Sirenia
Family: Dugongidae
Weight: Average 900 lb. (400 kg)
Length: 10 ft. (300 cm)
Diet: Aquatic vegetation
Gestation period: 390–420 days
Longevity: Up to 70 years
Habitat: Coastal ocean waters
Range: Indian Ocean and southwestern Pacific

THE DUGONG BELONGS to a group of aquatic mammals, the sirenians. Although less well known than its cousin the manatee, the dugong has a much wider range. It is found throughout the southwestern Pacific and the Indian Ocean, from the eastern coast of Africa to Madagascar, India, Indonesia, and northern Australia.

Giant relative
The dugong is the sole remaining species in its family, the Dugongidae. Until recent times another member of the family, the Steller's sea cow, was known to humans. The Steller's sea cow was an enormous animal reaching almost 30 feet (9 meters) in length and weighing over 10 tons (9,080 kilograms). It was once commonly found around certain islands in the Bering Sea near Alaska, browsing amid the cold water seaweeds that grew along the rocky coasts. The sea cows were easily hunted and found to be extremely tasty, and within a few decades of their discovery they were hunted to extinction.

Although it too is facing extinction, the dugong is smaller, reaching up to 10 feet (3 meters), and is found only in warm tropical waters. Externally, it is recognizable by the shape of its tail. The dugong has a tail that appears as paired flukes, similar in appearance to a whale's or dolphin's tail. A manatee's tail, on the other hand, appears as a single broad fluke, more closely resembling a beaver's tail. The dugong relies on its tail for propulsion, using its rounded flippers primarily for steering. Like the manatee, the dugong has no dorsal or back fin.

The dugong is completely aquatic and never comes out of the water. It prefers shallow, sheltered bays and coastal areas, avoiding rocky shores with heavy wave action. It may wander up rivers occasionally, but it is not found in freshwater as frequently as the manatee. It grazes upon the thick sea grasses and other vegetation that grows in huge underwater meadows along the silty bottom. It is estimated that a dugong eats between 50 and 70 pounds (23 to 32 kilograms) of seaweed a day. The mouth is well designed for this type of grazing, pointing downward and containing thick, flexible lips and horny plates that grasp and grind the vegetation. The nostrils are placed high on the snout, allowing the dugong to breathe without exposing much of its body to the surface. A normal dive for a dugong lasts from one to three minutes, although it can stay underwater for much longer.

A lunar animal
There is no specific migration among dugongs, but certain migratory patterns occur within specific populations.

The more northern and southern populations will move to warmer waters during cold spells, and the heavy storms of the region's monsoon season will also cause local migrations.

The dugong appears to be active by day and at night. Its activity appears to be based more on the moon than the sun, for it follows the moon-influenced tides in toward the shore

The dugong (*Dugong dugon*) is totally aquatic, and never comes completely out of the water. It usually stays underwater for one to three minutes before it surfaces to breathe, but it can stay underwater far longer.

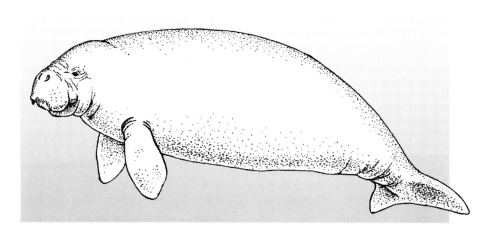

when feeding, regardless of whether the sun is up or not.

Although frequently found alone, the dugong is essentially a social animal. Groups of dugongs usually number between two and ten. The most common group is a mother and her calf, but there may also be some lasting bonds that form between mated pairs of dugongs, and larger assemblages could be family groups. Dugongs also occasionally gather in much larger herds, numbering into the hundreds, and in years past groups were counted that contained thousands of individuals.

Dugongs are extremely long-lived animals, surviving up to 70 years. A single offspring is the usual number born to a mating pair. Young dugongs may begin to graze when only three months of age, but will usually continue to nurse for another year, and will not reach sexual maturity until it is 10 or 15 years old. Females give birth only about every three to seven years.

Mortality

Despite its slow movements, a dugong is too large to be vulnerable to most predators. However, sharks and killer whales are known to take them in the wild. On occasion, dugongs have been known to drive sharks away by butting them, and killer whales rarely come into the shallow coastal waters preferred by the dugong. Storms may be a regular cause of mortality, for heavy seas are avoided by these animals, and strandings and deaths have been observed after large storms.

Humans are the most frequent predator of dugongs and their greatest threat. The dugong is highly prized for its tasty flesh,

Although it seems extraordinary, apparently sailors thought that the dugong (*Dugong dugon*) was a mermaid. The order it belongs to was given the name sirenia in honor of the "sirens" of Greek mythology.

thick leathery hide, teeth, and bones, and the oil is used for medicinal purposes. The bones have been used for carvings and jewelry. Dugongs are roughly estimated to number 100,000, but the actual number is not known. Their survival is in jeopardy because of three main factors: it ranges in a heavily populated part of the world where it is hunted for its meat; conservation laws are difficult to enforce at sea; and the dugong's rate of reproduction is slow. If not carefully monitored, any change in the dugong's situation could make it endangered.

Peter Zahler

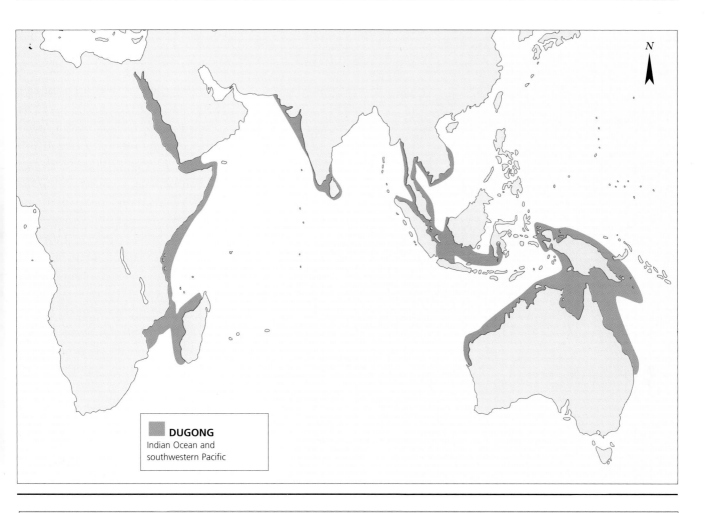

N

DUGONG
Indian Ocean and
southwestern Pacific

DUIKERS

Class: Mammalia

Order: Artiodactyla

Family: Bovidae

Subfamily: Cephalophinae

The duikers comprise a group of small antelope unique to Africa. They come in two types: the common duiker that inhabits savanna and open bush country and the forest-dwelling duikers. All 16 to 18 species of forest duikers belong to the genus *Cephalophus.*

The forest duikers are a diverse group, but they share many similarities. Their body configurations are all about the same, with the biggest differences being in color and size. The smallest duikers are the blue and Maxwell's duikers, weighing less than ten pounds (eight kilograms), while the largest are the yellow-backed, Jentink's and Abbott's duikers, weighing as much as 132 pounds (60 kilograms). They range in color from the grayish blue duiker to the striped zebra duiker. All duikers share the same basic shape: a stocky body with the front legs shorter than the rear legs and a back that is arched. Duikers have sloping shoulders that droop to a sharp muzzle, creating a streamlined look. Both sexes usually are armed with short, sharp, conical horns.

The term *duiker* is an Afrikaaner word meaning "diver." When surprised, duikers react instantly by fleeing in the opposite direction from whatever has disturbed them, rapidly disappearing into the bush. Their survival depends on their considerable swiftness. In spite of their brightly-colored coats, they blend very well into the forest.

As small and delicate as they may appear, duikers are in reality not so delicate. They are stocky animals, capable of sustaining substantial blows. Their most dangerous predators are humans. Today the duiker's environment has been disrupted by humans, and they are also hunted as one of the major sources of protein available to the people in western and central Africa.

They are almost always seen alone in the wild. Two together usually indicates a breeding pair that have come together temporarily or a mother that still has her young with her. A number of duikers have done reasonably well in captivity when properly managed. However, they are difficult animals to keep because they suffer from a range of common health problems. Their rapid rate of reproduction can make up for some of these deaths in captivity.

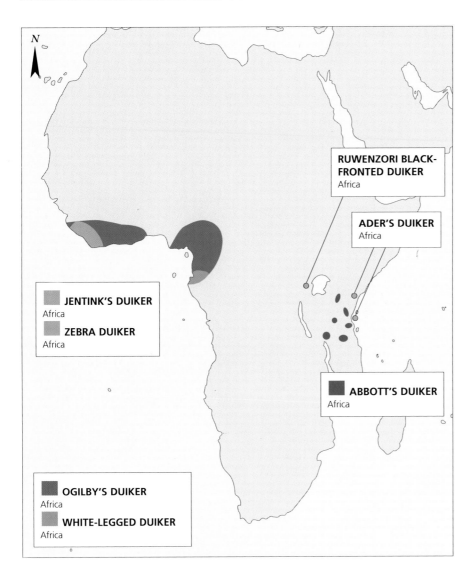

N

RUWENZORI BLACK-
FRONTED DUIKER
Africa

ADER'S DUIKER
Africa

JENTINK'S DUIKER
Africa

ZEBRA DUIKER
Africa

ABBOTT'S DUIKER
Africa

OGILBY'S DUIKER
Africa

WHITE-LEGGED DUIKER
Africa

Abbott's Duiker
(Cephalophus spadix)

IUCN: Vulnerable

Weight: 110–132 lb. (50–60 kg)
Shoulder height: 20–25 in. (50-65 cm)
Diet: Leaves, shoots, fruit
Gestation period: Unknown
Longevity: Unknown
Habitat: Thick uplands to high mountain forest
Range: Tanzania

ABBOTT'S DUIKER is one of the larger duikers, but it is not as large as the yellow-back or Jentink's duikers. It carries short horns three to four inches long (8 to 10 centimeters), and its coloration ranges from a dark chestnut brown to black. It has a reddish patch of long tufted hair on its forehead between the horns. It also has a small yellowish patch just above the tail and some reddish coloring on the belly and inside the legs. Its shoulder height is up to 25 inches (65 centimeters).

Shy creature of the night
Not a lot is known about this duiker because it is very shy and, like many of the other duikers, is primarily nocturnal. It has a given territory that it tends to fre-

quent, making it easy prey for dogs or for humans hunting them by laying snares.

The diet of Abbott's duiker consists of leaves and especially fruit. It is found in isolated montane forests in the east and south of Tanzania, including the slopes of Kilimanjaro.

It is estimated that there are less than 10,000 individual Abbott's duikers left in the wild, and most of those occur in areas that are not protected by law. In addition to this, the Abbott's duiker is rarely kept alive in captivity. Its relatively small range, the destruction of its habitat, and poaching have resulted in Abbott's duiker being a threatened species.

Ader's Duiker
(Cephalophus adersi)

IUCN: Endangered

Weight: 13–26.5 lb. (6–12 kg)
Shoulder height: 12–13 in. (30–32 cm)
Diet: Leaves, shoots, and fruit
Gestation period: 225–240 days
Longevity: 10–12 years in captivity
Habitat: Wet forest
Range: Zanzibar, coast of Kenya, and Tanzania

ADER'S DUIKER, or the dwarf red duiker, is often known as the Zanzibar duiker. It occurs both on the island of Zanzibar, where there are reportedly some 2,500 individuals, and in the Arabuko-Sokoke Forest on the mainland, where some 5,000 survive. The principal factors jeopardizing

Jentink's duikers have been successfully bred in captivity at Gladys Porter Zoo in Texas. This one is a resident of the Greater Los Angeles Zoo.

its future are habitat destruction for cultivation and poaching for their meat.

Ader's duiker is primarily diurnal. This duiker has a very unusual color pattern, being of a chestnut or tawny red color, with a broad white band on the rump and white speckling on the legs. Its fur is very soft to the touch and slightly oily, which helps repel rainwater in its humid habitat. They are also good swimmers. Ader's duiker is generally under 26 pounds (12 kilograms) and less than 31 inches (80 cm) tall. It lives on the leaves, shoots, and fruit found in the wet forests that this duiker inhabits.

Ader's duiker has been kept in captivity where it has lived for 10 to 12 years. It has not, however, become established in a breeding population. It would appear that this animal could become a healthy captive-bred species but there is currently no captive reservoir.

Jentink's Duiker
(Cephalophus jentinki)

ESA: Endangered

IUCN: Vulnerable

Weight: 121–154 lb. (55–70 kg)
Shoulder height: 29½–39 in. (75–100 cm)
Diet: Leaves, shoots, and fruit
Gestation period: 210–235 days
Longevity: 15–20 years in captivity
Habitat: Wet forest
Range: Sierra Leone, Liberia, and Ivory Coast

THE JENTINK'S duiker is one of the largest of the duikers. It is second in size only to the yellow-back, weighing up to 154 pounds (70 kilograms). It is a beautiful animal with a strange color pattern: the head and neck are a soft, velvety black with white markings around the lip, and the rear half of the body has a grizzled, salt-and-pepper appearance. A whitish stripe acts like a dramatic border between the front

and back of the body. The front and back legs are white below the shoulder. It is an unusually dark animal overall. It is found in the wet forests of Sierra Leone, Liberia, and the Ivory Coast in western Africa, where it feeds on leaves, shoots, and fruit.

Unusual history
Very little is known about these duikers in the wild and, in fact, they are considered to be the most endangered of all living antelope. Their history is quite unusual. They were first described by naturalists in 1892 in Liberia, when rubber plantations were first established in western Africa. Most of these duikers were simply killed or obtained from the locals for shipping to museums around the world. The remarkable thing was that every specimen collected at the time was a female.

Without evidence of the existence of a male, naturalists believed that the Jentink's duiker was simply a color variation of the yellow-back duiker.

Disappearing duiker
Eventually this duiker disappeared, and it was assumed for a while that the animal had become extinct. It was discovered again about eight or ten years later, again as a result of the development of rubber plantations. It seemed that people had stumbled onto another pocket of Jentink's duikers. A number were collected, and then they disappeared again as that population was exhausted.

Once again, it was thought that the species was extinct until the 1950s, when some females were caught alive. It was a continuing puzzle that only females were ever caught. Finally a male skull was discovered, ending confusion over whether they were actually a separate species.

Captive duikers

Two captive female Jentink's duikers were eventually sent to the Gladys Porter Zoo in Brownsville, Texas, where they were joined by the first live male ever to be caught. Another male-female pair had to be captured before a small population of ten Jentink's duikers was finally achieved. This, however, is from a very narrow gene pool and interbreeding can cause several other problems for the species.

Jentink's duikers that are kept in captivity are capable of living for between 15 to 20 years.

Jentink's duiker is a very endangered species because of the destruction of its habitat and the effects of constant poaching. Like all duikers, it is a valuable source of food in western Africa. Because of the extremely narrow range of the Jentink's duiker, poaching has a devastating effect.

The total population of Jentink's duiker is unknown, but it is estimated to be at several thousand and believed to be declining. Jentink's duiker is banned from international commercial trade under CITES (Convention on International Trade in Endangered Species of Wild Fauna and Flora).

Many more animals need to be captured to broaden the narrow gene pool as a reservoir against disaster in the wild.

With the ever-growing human population in western Africa causing a shrinking of their habitat, Jentink's duiker is in great danger of extinction.

Ogilby's Duiker
(Cephalophus ogilbyi)

IUCN: Lower risk

Weight: 31–44 lb. (14–20 kg)
Shoulder height: 22 in. (55 cm)
Diet: Leaves, shoots, and fruit
Gestation period: Unknown
Longevity: Unknown
Habitat: Wet forest
Range: West and central Africa

OGILBY'S DUIKER is a small duiker from the west coast of Africa, found from Sierra Leone east to Ghana, the Cameroons, and Gabon. One subspecies is found on the Bioko Islands. This duiker occurs in an area that is heavily populated. The duikers in that area, including Ogilby's duiker, are a major source of protein for the resident human population. Most of these duikers are caught by snares along forest paths.

Not much is known about the animal because it has never been kept in captivity to any great extent. It has a reddish orange coat with a white back stripe from the shoulder to the tail. It looks similar to other duikers such as the red-flanked duiker (*Cephalophus rufilatus*) and the bay duiker (*Cephalophus dorsalis*). These duikers live solitary lives, feeding on leaves, roots, twigs, fruits, and even small birds and mammals when they can catch them.

Their decline is due to encroachment of their habitat by humans as well as poaching. Although by the end of the 1990s the animal was thought to be at lower risk of extinction, there are only 25,000 left in the wild.

Ruwenzori Black-fronted Duiker
(Cephalophus nigrifrons rubidus)

IUCN: Endangered

Weight: 31–35 lb. (14–16 kg)
Shoulder height: 18–22 in. (45–55 cm)
Diet: Leaves, shoots, and fruit
Gestation period: 120 days
Longevity: 10–15 years in captivity in related subspecies
Habitat: Dense mountain forest
Range: Ruwenzori Mountains, Uganda

THE BLACK-FRONTED duiker, of which the Ruwenzori is one subspecies, gets its name from the black stripe that runs down the front of the face. The rest of the animal is a pale, fawn-tinted red, with lighter markings on the belly. Its weight can be up to 35 pounds (16 kilograms) and it can live up to 15 years in captivity. The Ruwenzori black-fronted duiker is usually found in mountain forest and swampy areas. Like all other duikers, Ruwenzori duikers spend time using their face glands to mark their territory. They follow the same paths through the forest from places where they shelter at night to daytime feeding areas.

Adaptive vocalization

An unusual trait of this duiker involves a vocalization. Most duikers make a stomping sound on the ground to raise an alarm. Because the Ruwenzori prefer more marshy ground, they have learned to make a clicking or thumping sound with their mouths that sounds very similar to the stomping sound made by their duiker cousins.

The duikers of the Ruwenzori mountains eat a wide variety of fruit and succulents, including wild impatiens and coffee plants. They have an aversion to people, so they do not pose a problem raiding people's gardens.

However, because of their habit of following the same trails in their territory, they are easily caught with snares. This leaves them very vulnerable to the risk of overhunting.

Because of the heavy disturbance of their environment, the Ruwenzori black-fronted duiker has been placed on the endangered list. The Ruwenzori have never been kept in captivity, so there is no captive population to back up the wild population. There are an estimated 2,500 of these duikers left in the wild.

White-legged Duiker

(Cephalophus ogilbyi crusalbum)

IUCN: Lower risk

Weight: 33–40 lb. (15–18 kg)
Shoulder height: 22 in. (55 cm)
Diet: Leaves, shoots, and fruit
Gestation period: Unknown
Longevity: Unknown
Habitat: Dense forest
Range: Western Gabon, possibly Congo

THE WHITE-LEGGED duiker is a subspecies of Ogilby's duiker, *Cephalophus ogilbyi*, and this particular form, called *crusalbum*, is found only in the dense forests of a small area of western Gabon and possibly Congo.

Little is known about this duiker, but it is assumed that it has similar characteristics to other *ogilbyi* duikers. It, too, is preyed upon heavily by the local population, and it is not difficult to catch because of its habitually-used territories and paths. Like Jentink's duiker, it has large, strong hindquarters.

Tiny range

Larger populations of duikers—such as the blue and Maxwell duikers—have huge groups spread over large areas and can tolerate some hunting pressure, but the white-legged duiker is in a precarious position because it has a tiny range surrounded by human habitation and has virtually nowhere to go. It has lower risk status, but unless protection is given, the hunting pressures will eventually overwhelm it, increasing the risk of extinction.

There are currently no white-legged duikers in captivity, and it is believed there are no more than 5,000 left in the wild.

The zebra duiker is one of the smaller members of the family Bovidae. Its distinctive striped markings make it popular as a captive animal in zoos.

Zebra (Banded) Duiker

(Cephalophus zebra)

IUCN: Vulnerable

Weight: 20–33 lb. (9–15 kg)
Shoulder height: 16–20 in. (40–50 cm)
Diet: Leaves, shoots, and fruit
Gestation period: 110–125 days
Longevity: 10–12 years in captivity
Habitat: Dense forest
Range: Western Africa

THE ZEBRA DUIKER is one of the smaller duikers. It is found exclusively in isolated pockets in western Sierra Leone, Liberia, and the southwestern Ivory Coast. It is most commonly found in east-central Liberia. The zebra duiker has a golden fawnish color with dark brown to almost black stripes that run horizontally across its back, which give it its other name: the banded duiker.

The elusive zebra duiker prefers primary forests with heavy vegetation, so it is rarely seen. It prefers lowland areas but may also be found in low montane and hill forests. The zebra duiker has short conical horns that sprout from a conical skull. These may be used in defending their territory from other duikers and may also be used to break open larger fruit. With its limited range, it is in a very vulnerable situation, primarily because of destruction and disturbance to its habitat. Unfortunately, it is also the victim of heavy poaching. The zebra duiker and all the other duikers in the west African area are killed and eaten for food.

In captivity

Zebra duikers have been popular in zoos as captive animals because of their attractive markings. With proper management they do well in captivity, but they are susceptible to skin infections. In general, zebra duikers have had only fair success in captivity. More study is needed to keep these animals healthy, and they seem to do better if no more than one pair is kept together. Their average life span in captivity is about eight to ten years. They will eat fruits and vegetables in captivity and will even eat dog food and other meat if it is offered to them.

Warren D. Thomas

EAGLES

Class: Aves

Order: Falconiformes

Family: Accipitridae

Historically, eagles have experienced a troubled existence with humans. European governments have paid bounties on birds of prey. People used to believe that birds of prey were bad, competing with humans for food such as rabbits, squirrels, partridges, and ducks. Only recently did people discover that birds of prey helped to control rabbit and rodent populations that, if unchecked, can destroy agricultural production.

Eagles were particularly vulnerable to slaughter. Being larger birds, they defend larger territories, so fewer of them live in a given area. The loss of a few, therefore, can be devastating. Its large size makes the eagle an easier target. Besides being shot, trapped, netted, and poisoned, eagle's nests were raided for eggs, their food supply was either depleted or was tainted with industrial pollutants and agricultural pesticides, their habitat was destroyed or modified and, in some cases, other species invaded their habitat, driving out the eagles.

As settlers opened up the west in the late 1800s, livestock production became a vital part of regional economies. All birds of prey were disliked, but eagles in particular were viewed as a menace to lambs and calves. Hunters now had modern firearms, and poison became a popular weapon as well. The most disastrous of these poisons came into wide use in the 1940s—sodium fluoroacetate, or 1080 ("ten-eighty" as it was called by bounty hunters). Extremely lethal even in trace amounts, 1080 did not break down in the body of a victim. Thus, a coyote could feed on a poisoned carcass and then wander off before dying. Its carcass then became poisoned bait for another scavenger. Other birds such as vultures, crows, ravens, and magpies then suffered poisoning and died, too. This slaughter was phenomenal in its scope and its effect.

The results of the bounty system in Europe was recorded in fairly accurate detail. Five European countries (Austria, Belgium, Denmark, Norway, and Spain) accounted for 517,620 birds of prey killed between 1951 and 1962. During the 20th century, humans deliberately killed as many as 20 million birds of prey on the European continent and adjoining areas of Asia and Africa alone.

Bald Eagle
(Haliaeetus leucocephalus)

Length: 31–37½ in. (79–95 cm)
Weight: 6½–16½ lb. (3–7½ kg)
Clutch size: 1–3 eggs, usually 2
Incubation: 35 days
Diet: Fish, birds, mammals, and carrion
Habitat: Forests near open water; also woodlands, prairies, and occasionally tundra
Range: North America

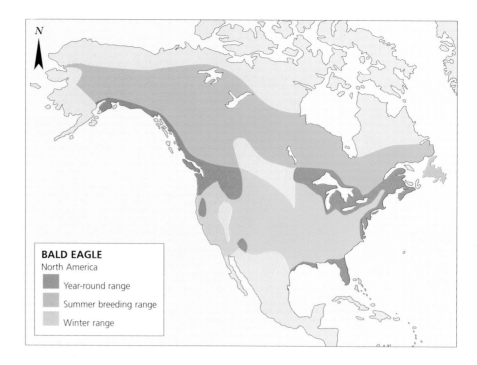

BALD EAGLE
North America

■ Year-round range
■ Summer breeding range
■ Winter range

PEOPLE HAVE revered and worshiped bald eagles, and they have also detested and persecuted them. In this respect the bald eagle, the national bird of the United States, has come to symbolize more than just a nation. It now symbolizes a social conscience about human behavior toward other creatures. Only during the last two decades of the 20th century have Americans realized how close they came to losing this species.

Revered but still hunted

Various Native American groups scattered about North America revered the bald eagle. Many Native Americans gave the bald eagle spiritual traits, and some believed the bird was able to fly to heaven. This reverence, however, did not protect the eagle but made it a target.

Native Americans frequently killed bald eagles in great numbers in order to collect the feathers for ceremonial purposes. The talons, wings, and feathers of bald eagles carried enormous prestige among some Native American groups. Despite the killings of this sacred bird, bald eagles managed to thrive.

European colonization of North America introduced many more complications into the eagle's environment. For example, European colonists brought with them their ancestral hatred for birds of prey. Eagles were seen as killers of fish, waterfowl, rabbits, squirrels, and other wild animals that could feed people. As colonists spread across North America, bald eagles disappeared from many of their native haunts as habitat was converted into cropland and towns. The Industrial Revolution brought a century and a half of chemical pollution of soil, air, and water. Pollution killed the eagles' food supply and, in some cases, the eagles as well.

Guns and poisons

Hunters traditionally used lead as shot in their guns. Decade after decade, people shot lead over marshes as they hunted waterfowl. The lead pellets accumulated until ducks and geese began eating them as grit for grinding the food in their gizzards. Poisoned by the lead, the ducks and geese became disabled and easy prey for hungry eagles. After eating several birds afflicted with lead poisoning, the eagles became poisoned in turn. Mining destroyed vast tracts of forest,

The incredible wingspan of the bald eagle makes it a spectacular sight to behold. This species was almost lost due to human carelessness.

and mine wastes polluted waterways, ruining food supplies for the eagles. Agriculture destroyed marshes, swamps, forests, and prairies, creating a double hazard. First, livestock growers, convinced that eagles killed their calves and lambs, regularly shot bald eagles. At first, the shooting was only from the ground. Later, with the development of technology, shooters took to the air in airplanes and helicopters. Dissatisfied with the results, ranchers began using poisoned bait to kill the eagles. The second problem created by agriculture was the poisons to improve crop yields.

Deadly poison

During World War II, the chemical compound dichlorodiphenyltrichloroethane, known as DDT, became widely used to kill lice on soldiers, prisoners of war, and refugees. After the war, experimentation proved DDT to be equally effective against insects that damaged food crops and trees valued for lumber and pulp—and especially potent against insects that carried human diseases. For 20 years DDT was used without regard for possible harmful side effects. After it is used, DDT does not break down in the environment quickly. Organisms that eat or absorb DDT store it in fat cells. If a predatory animal eats smaller animals that have absorbed DDT, eventually the predators accumulate enough DDT in their own bodies so that the chemical begins to interfere with normal life processes.

In birds, DDT disrupts calcium use in the body so females lay eggs with too little calcium in the shell. These thinner shells are

As the national bird of the United States, it would seem likely that the bald eagle would receive special protection from hunters, but this was not the case until the 1970s. By then, populations of the bird were already greatly reduced.

easily broken, and water is lost too quickly through small pores in the shell. The result is reproductive failure.

Attempts at recovery

Such pressures caused the bald eagle to vanish from much of its native range before the American public awakened to the seriousness of its plight. In 1978, the bald eagle was classified as an endangered species throughout the lower 48 U.S. states, except in Minnesota, Michigan, Wisconsin, Washington, and Oregon, where it was listed as a threatened species. In addition, the chemicals 1080, DDT, and other similar chemicals were banned except in tightly controlled circumstances. A large-scale public effort in education took the plight of bald eagles into classrooms and family homes, and extensive recovery plans got under way.

As part of recovery efforts, the U.S. Fish and Wildlife Service assembled the largest colony of breeding bald eagles in captivity at the Patuxent Wildlife Research Center near Laurel, Maryland, in a major effort to return healthy eagles to the wild. Patuxent's scientists enhanced the species' breeding potential by removing the bald eagle's first clutch of eggs and incubating them artificially. In all, 124 bald eagles were hatched at Patuxent. These captive-hatched bald eagles were an important source for restocking wild populations in certain areas and helped to reestablish a broader distribution.

Success story

In 1995 the bald eagle was reclassified as threatened under the Endangered Species Act and it has recently been announced that the bald eagle may be taken off this list altogether. A final decision is expected in July 2000. This is considered to be one of the greatest success stories of the Endangered Species Act.

From fewer than 450 nesting pairs in the early 1960s, there are now estimated to be around 5,748 adult bald eagle nesting pairs. Moreover, bald eagles have resettled in some portions of their historic range, in areas where they had been absent for decades.

In appearance, the bald eagle has dark, blackish brown plumage; the tail, undertail, and rump are white, with occasional black smudges in the tail feathers. The entire head and neck are white (giving the "bald" effect), and the feet and toes are golden yellow. The beak is yellow, massive, and hooked.

Slowly but surely the bald eagle has recovered, and restrictions have aided the eagle and other species recovering from centuries of abuse. If the bald eagle continues to improve in the wild, it will be a testimony to a new pride people have in safeguarding the environment for all living creatures.

Madagascar Fish-eagle
(Haliaeetus vociferoides)

ESA: Endangered

IUCN: Critically endangered

Length: 22.8–26 in. (58–66 cm)
Weight: Unknown
Clutch size: 2 eggs
Incubation: Unknown
Diet: Live fish and sometimes crabs
Habitat: Seashore, forested lakes, and rivers
Range: Western coast of Madagascar

MADAGASCAR DRIFTED free of the African continent millions of years ago. Isolated in the Indian Ocean, it became a place where plants and animals evolved in ways unlike the wildlife on the continent that lay only 250 miles (400 kilometers) to the west. Today, Madagascar covers 226,658 square miles (589,311 square kilometers), an area the size of Colorado and New Mexico combined. Almost ten million people now occupy the island, but in all that area, less than 100 Madagascar fish-eagles survive.

Fourteen species of birds of prey breed in Madagascar. Eight of them live nowhere else in the world, and the Madagascar fish-eagle is one of them. It belongs to the group known as the sea eagles in the genus *Haliaeetus*. This group of eight species includes the bald eagle (*Haliaeetus leucocephalus*) of North America. Although similar to the other sea eagles, the Madagascar fish-eagle differs in some important respects. It is generally brown overall, its breast is spotted with buff, and the flight feathers are uniformly brown, but small covering feathers are lightly spotted with paler brown. The tail is white, the crown and nape are light brown, the cheek is white, and the side of the neck, chin, and throat are whitish.

Adult Madagascar fish-eagles are not migratory like other sea eagles but remain in their nesting territories all year. Only the immature birds wander, and they avoid the adults' territories.

Fish-eagle diet
The fish-eagle prefers live food but sometimes eats carrion. It hunts from an exposed perch near water, where it can watch for prey. When it sees its prey, it takes to the air, swoops down near the water's surface, and plucks up the meal—getting only its toes and feet wet. A fish-eagle does soar, but alternates regular wing flapping with gliding.

Madagascar fish-eagles usually lay two eggs. However, the first eaglet to hatch usually kills the second eaglet when it hatches. This behavior is called "cainism," after the Biblical character Cain, who killed his younger brother Abel. In an

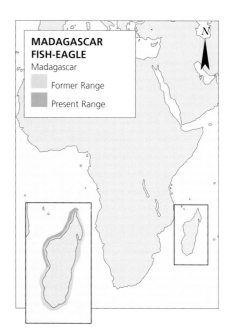

endangered species such as the Madagascar fish-eagle, cainism is not a healthy behavior. One offspring per pair, per year, in birds requiring at least four to five years before they can mate again, means slow population growth. With a captive-breeding program, one egg could be removed from each nest of two eggs without harming the wild population. The eggs could be hatched and the offspring could be used to bolster the wild population.

Only 40 breeding pairs and another 16 unpaired adults and immature birds were counted during surveys conducted from 1978 to 1986. They occur almost exclusively within 375 miles (600 kilometers) of coastline along the northern two-thirds of Madagascar's west coast. This strip includes three distinct habitat types: rocky coast, coastal mangrove forest, and inland lakes and rivers. Most fish-eagles live in the last habitat category. Ranging up to 55 miles (88 kilometers) inland, they inhabit forests along rivers and around lakes.

The Madagascar fish-eagle undoubtedly once occupied more

of Madagascar and occurred in higher numbers. It has suffered from human enterprise. Local fishers do not regard the fish-eagle as a competitor for fish. They do not eat the bird or use the feathers for personal decoration or ceremonial purposes. However, they readily kill fish-eagles when they find them.

Madagascar's problem

Madagascar became an independent nation in 1960, with a young government influenced by France. This caused problems of severe economic hardship during the next three decades, including food shortages. Madagascar then turned to its natural resources. Forests were cut for lumber products, then replaced with cultivated plantations of coffee, vanilla, cloves, and sugarcane. Swamps were drained to grow rice. Mining caused erosion of the land. The Madagascar fish-eagle lost forest habitat around lakes and rivers. Erosion muddied the waters, fish declined and became harder to see and catch. With fewer places to nest, fewer places to perch for hunting, and fewer prey fish to be caught, the eagle population dwindled.

As of 1990, Madagascar had 2 national parks, 11 integral nature reserves, and 22 special reserves. Only a single pair of fish-eagles was found to inhabit Montagne d'Ambre National Park and Ankarafantsika Integral Natural Reserve. Additional lands for protection have been proposed; a national park within a UNESCO World Heritage Site and a reserve on rocky islets along the northwestern coast. Without this action, the Madagascar fish-eagle will probably not survive.

New Guinea Harpy Eagle

(Harpyopsis novaeguineae)

IUCN: Vulnerable

Length: 30–35 in. (76–88.9 cm)
Weight: Unknown
Clutch size: Unknown
Incubation: Unknown
Diet: Primarily mammals
Habitat: Primarily coastal and montane forests
Range: New Guinea

THE NEW GUINEA harpy eagle soars back and forth, around and around, crossing the steep forested slopes of New Guinea. Compared to its overall size, the bird's wings look short and rounded at the ends, but its tail is long and narrow. The configuration of wings and tail gives it quick speed and great maneuverability among the branches of a dense forest. The New Guinea harpy eagle is on the prowl and it is seeking a special prey.

Quietly, it slips into the forest canopy and alights upon a horizontal branch, turning its head in search of prey. A movement attracts its attention. Soon a ground wallaby—a small, kangaroo-like marsupial—emerges from a clump of greenery. Before it can cross the opening on the forest floor, the eagle drops from its perch and seizes the wallaby. Its long, curved talons immediately grasp the animal's back. Crushing strength in the eagle's toes squeeze the air from the wal-

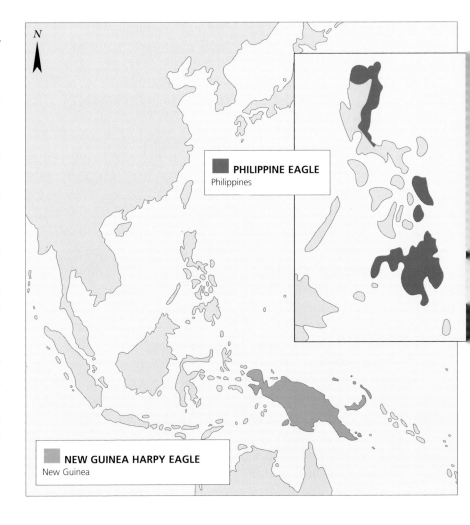

PHILIPPINE EAGLE
Philippines

NEW GUINEA HARPY EAGLE
New Guinea

laby's lungs and prevent it from taking another breath. With hardly a sound to mark the event, the eagle disappears back into the forest canopy where it will devour its meal.

Such is the life of the New Guinea harpy eagle. Little has been written about this eagle because so little research has been done on it. Most of the information about this medium-sized eagle comes from local people who inhabit the same forests. Many of them prize the eagle's wing feathers as ornamentation for their own bodies.

The New Guinea harpy eagle shares an English name with the more famous harpy eagle (*Harpia harpyja*) of South America, and it occupies similar habitats halfway around the world. But the New Guinea harpy is a smaller eagle with a much smaller crest. If they are related, it is by a common ancestor. The bird's upperparts range from dark brown to more of a gray-brown, with faint barring visible at close range. The wing and tail are dark above, light below, and barred. The underparts are mostly whitish, with pale brown or gray brown across the breast and down the sides. The unfeathered feet are yellow and long for an eagle. The large but thin beak is brownish black at the base and bluish white at the tip. Like all birds of prey, this eagle has bony prominences over each eye to shade their eyes from direct sunlight, like the bill on a baseball cap.

For all its regal bearing, the New Guinea harpy eagle faces an uncertain future. The forests of New Guinea are being cut for the world market in tropical woods.

Some of the forests are also being cut for agricultural development and for the mining of valuable ores. Some habitat can be lost, and the species will still survive. No one knows for sure how much habitat loss or alteration the eagle can endure. Further, no one has carefully surveyed New Guinea to determine how many harpy eagles live there.

More research needed
As of 1990 the New Guinea harpy eagle was considered to be vulnerable. If forest destruction continues, that status will undoubtedly slip to endangered. Before anything can be done to protect the eagle, basic research must be done on its behalf.

Only by making a study of its feeding habits, reproductive cycle, population size, and several other factors, will ornithologists be able to make recommendations for the eagle's preservation.

Philippine Eagle
(Pithecophaga jefferyi)

ESA: Endangered

IUCN: Critically endangered

Length: 30–34 in. (76–86 cm)
Weight: Males 11 lb. (5 kg); females 15.4 lb. (7 kg)
Clutch size: 1 egg
Incubation: 60 days
Diet: Large mammals and birds
Habitat: Dense rain forest
Range: Leyte, Luzon, Mindanao, and Samar islands in the Philippines

THE FOREST hushes as rain sends birds and mammals, insects and lizards, frogs and snakes scurrying for cover. When the shower ends, a group of crab-eating macaques cautiously emerges to resume their search for food. The forest chatter slowly revives in the drone of insects and birdsong. Suddenly, a rufous hornbill squawks excitedly. The macaques, alert to the call, look up, but before they can react, a blur of brown and white feathers shoots from the branches overhead. In a flash the bird snatches a nearly grown macaque from the branch on which it sits. With needle-sharp talons squeezing its back and chest as if in a vise, the monkey cannot even draw breath to scream. It probably never hears its fellow macaques screaming their outrage as the bird, bearing its prey, disappears among the trees to feed.

Local people knew of the great forest eagle for centuries. Ornithologists did not learn of the bird until an account of it was published in 1896. It was dubbed the "monkey-eating eagle" based on its appetite. Sometime during the 1960s people began calling it the Philippine eagle. This is the bird's official name today. Whereas the original name described the bird's feeding behavior, the present name honors its homeland.

Destruction of habitat
Although never abundant, the Philippine eagle historically occupied portions of several large islands and a couple of the smaller Philippine islands. A growing human population and modernization combined to destroy vital eagle habitat. Each

The Philippine eagle was never abundant, but once occupied a greater range than it does today. With the growing human population, removal of forests, and agricultural activities, this eagle has lost vital habitat.

pair of Philippine eagles needs five to ten square miles (12 to 25 square kilometers) of forested habitat. Some ornithologists have even estimated territories up to 40 square miles (100 square kilometers), but these have not been verified. Philippine eagles thrive best in primary forest. They also inhabit secondary forest after it has had a chance to mature to the point that it provides essential cover.

A camouflaged hunter
With short, rounded wings and a long, narrow tail, Philippine eagles are splendid flyers within the tangled world of forest canopies. They sit upright on horizontal branches. Their white undersides resemble the pale bark of some trees and possibly the large, shiny leaves of some plants. Their mottled brown wings and back probably help

them hide in dappled shadows. Thus concealed, they can sit and watch for their prey. Some animals, however, invariably discover them. Just as American crows (*Corvus brachyrhynchos*) often gang up on great horned owls (*Bubo virginianus*) in the United States, rufous hornbills (*Buceros hydrocorax*) often mob Philippine eagles. The mobbing spoils the predator's advantage of surprise and interferes with its ability to capture prey.

Deforestation
As people cut down forests to produce lumber and to open land for agriculture, the eagles lose the space they need. Mindanao supports more eagles than any other island. At 38,235 square miles (95,587 square kilometers), it is larger than Maine but smaller than Indiana. Forests once covered two-thirds of Mindanao or about 25,490 square miles (63,725 square kilometers). By the early 1970s cutting had reduced the forest area to 11,600 square miles (29,000 square kilometers)—scarcely the size of Vermont. Unfortunately, the first forests to be cut are lowland forests, which the Philippine eagle prefers. The cutting also leaves fragments of forests that may not be large enough for the eagle to use effectively and the forest-cutting operations usually leave roads behind. Farmers use the abandoned roads to gain access to the remaining forests.

Opening the forests creates another hazard for this eagle. Reduced cover makes it easier for people to find. People hunted the Philippine eagle for centuries using arrows, traps, and crude firearms. These methods did little

harm to the Philippine eagle. Dense rain forest helped to hide the eagle from hunters. Smaller forest tracts, however, and more roads and human settlements have enabled people to find more eagles. Modern firearms and traps have also made killing and capturing the Philippine eagle much easier.

Sadly, there is an incentive for hunters because stuffed and mounted "monkey-eating eagles" have long fetched good prices from those who collect novelties. Also farmers kill the eagles to protect their livestock.

Banned from trade
Modern zoos have higher ethical standards than some zoos have demonstrated in the past. They will not purchase birds captured illegally. This eagle is also banned from international commercial trade under the Convention on International Trade in Endangered Species of Wild Fauna and Flora (CITES). Philippine law also protects the eagle from being killed and captured for export.

The government, likewise, regulates forest cutting, but much cutting is done illegally because the Philippine government lacks the resources to enforce the law

A program of research, public education, and nest monitoring was initiated by the Philippine government in the 1960s, but its effectiveness is doubtful. This eagle now numbers no more than 200 in the wild. Conservation efforts include the enforcement of protective laws and reforestation. Captive-breeding efforts are also under way, with a single chick hatched in 1992 from an artificially incubated egg.

Spanish Imperial Eagle

(Aquila adalbertii)

ESA: Endangered

IUCN: Vulnerable

Length: 31–33 in. (79–84 cm)
Weight: 7–9 lb. (3.1–4 kg)
Clutch size: Usually 2 eggs, occasionally 3
Incubation: Probably 43 days, as in related species
Diet: Small- to medium-sized mammals and carrion
Habitat: Dry woodlands
Range: Spain, parts of Morocco

FOR THOUSANDS of years, the ancient peoples of Asia and the Middle East lived alongside a great golden brown bird with a massive beak and sharp talons. To the English-speaking world it became known as the imperial eagle (*Aquila heliaca*). It ranges across portions of Siberia, Mongolia, and China westward to Europe and the Middle East. Migrations take these birds as far south as Kenya in Africa and into Southeast Asia. A few of these eagles once occupied a portion of Iberia and Morocco. These eagles of northwestern Africa and southwestern Europe are considered by many ornithologists to be a distinct species called the Spanish imperial eagle.

Both imperial eagles closely resemble the more widespread golden eagle (*Aquila chrysaetos*). All have a rich brown plumage overall, with a golden nape. The imperial eagles differ from the golden in having a grayer base to the tail and whitish shoulder patches that the golden eagle lacks. The Spanish imperial eagle's shoulder patches are larger and whiter than those on other imperial eagles. The ranges of the two imperial eagles do not overlap, either. They are widely separated in Europe and Africa.

Historically, the Spanish imperial eagle inhabited central, western, and southwestern Spain; portions of extreme eastern Portugal; and some areas of Morocco across the Strait of Gibraltar. The Moroccan population has disappeared entirely, but immature birds from Spain apparently wander across the strait to North Africa. Ornithologists suspect that only a few birds, if any, survive in Portugal. It appears that virtually all the remaining Spanish imperial eagles live in Spain.

Habitat encroachment

As people converted the fertile plains to agricultural uses, the range of the Spanish imperial eagle gradually shrunk. It survived in those areas less suited to crops and grazing.

Aside from habitat encroachment, other destructive factors are affecting this eagle. There is

N

SPANISH IMPERIAL EAGLE
Europe

deliberate shooting and trapping. Rabbits, a food source for the eagles, are eradicated as agricultural pests. Eagles collide with and are electrocuted by power lines. People innocently, and sometimes deliberately, disturb their nests, which can destroy breeding success. New agricultural techniques and crops allow previously marginal land to be cultivated, taking with it more liveable habitat. Spanish imperial eagles nest in large trees but, unlike golden eagles, not on cliffs. The size and accessibility of their nest makes them an easy target for people who are merely curious as well as those who are intent on destroying eagles.

Estimates in the early 1980s put the total population at 70 to 100 pairs, plus an unknown number of nonbreeding immatures. Spanish imperial eagles live up to 22 years, but they take five years before they are ready to breed. They have some potential for slow population growth if protected, but experts disagree about any present population improvement. In 1965 a reserve was created called Doñana, which became a national park. Where once there were only a few pairs, 15 pairs of Spanish imperial eagles were nesting in Doñana by the 1980s, but skeptics believe that the effort to protect the eagles has only improved census-taking methods, meaning that more birds have been found than in previous years without necessarily indicating a growth in the population. However, if enough areas like Doñana can be protected, the Spanish imperial eagle will probably survive well into the future.

Kevin Cook

Steller's Sea-eagle
(Haliaeetus pelagicus)

IUCN: Vulnerable

Class: Aves
Order: Falconiformes
Suborder: Accipitres
Family: Accipitridae
Genus: Haliaeetus
Description: Length: 33½–37 in (85–94 cm)
Weight: 11–20 lb. (4.9–9 kg)
Clutch size: 2
Incubation: 38–45 days
Diet: Mainly fish, especially Pacific salmon, and a wide range of other vertebrates
Habitat: Rocky coasts near water containing fish
Range: Kamchatka Peninsula, on Sakhalin Island, and on the coasts of the Sea of Okhotsk

CLOSE TO THE COAST on the Kamchatka Peninsula, in Russia's far east, looking out over the Bering Sea, you may see a huge dark bird circling quite low over the water. As it drifts closer you notice that it has white shoulders, a wedge-shaped tail, and an obviously massive yellow bill. It is clearly a very large bird of prey, and it is obvious, as it suddenly plunges into the sea, that it is a sea-eagle. This is one of the world's most spectacular raptors but sadly one which numbers only a few thousand birds worldwide—Steller's sea-eagle.

Weighing up to 20 pounds (9 kilograms) and with a wingspan of up to 8 feet (2.5 meters), few birds of prey outsize Steller's sea-eagle. It hunts for its favored fish either by plunging into the sea from a branch close to the shore, circling before diving, or wading in the shallows with its long legs. It always nests close to waters containing fish, building a huge twig construction in the branches of a tree or on a rocky ledge.

Persecution by hunters

Despite the fact that fish make up the major part of its diet, Steller's sea-eagles also sometimes take quite large mammals. This has led to persecution by hunters. Another problem has been a high rate of mortality among chicks, which often fall to their deaths from the nest. Although two eggs are usually laid, typically only one young is reared. The nests, which can measure 8 feet by 14 feet (2.5 meters by 4.25 meters), sometimes collapse, with fatal results. Another threat is from forest destruction, which removes potential nest sites. In a species that takes four or five years to reach sexual maturity, and then only produce one fledged young per season, recovery from any population decline is a long process, and conservation measures are urgently required.

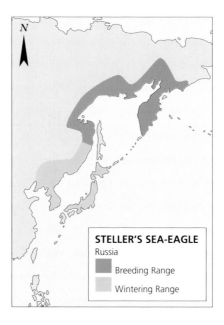

STELLER'S SEA-EAGLE
Russia
Breeding Range
Wintering Range

Steller's sea-eagle builds huge nests, sometimes measuring up to 14 feet (4.25 meters) wide.

The majority of the breeding population of Steller's sea-eagle is on the Kamchatka Peninsula. Birds move south in winter, though most of the breeders remain on the peninsula. Others breed on the island of Sakhalin, and on the northern and western coasts of the Sea of Okhotsk.

The Japanese island of Hokkaido provides important feeding, with about 2,200 birds fishing off its coasts in winter, and hundreds gather to feed on discarded fish and offal from the Japanese fishing industry.

Recommended conservation measures for the species, whose numbers are estimated to total only about 7,500 individuals, include paying hunters compensation for damaged skins and a more effective way of monitoring fluctuations in numbers. These measures may help this spectacular fisher to survive.

Tim Harris

EARWIGS

Class: Insecta

Order: Dermaptera

Earwigs have long, thin bodies and short wing covers that resemble those of the rove beetle, except for a pair of hooks that look like forceps. For this reason, earwigs are commonly called pincher bugs. Their hooks vary greatly in shape and length, depending upon the species, but are generally larger in the males. When an earwig defends itself, it bends its pinchers forward over its back like a scorpion; the hooks are actually above the earwig's head. These hooks are also used to seize other insects and invertebrates as well as to fold the hind wings under the hardened front wings.

The common name *earwig* has several possible origins. First, the extended wing of certain earwig species resembles a human ear. Second, the pincers of an earwig resemble instruments once used to pierce women's ears for earrings. Finally, there is the superstition that earwigs crept into the ears of sleeping persons. Because earwigs are nocturnal and readily crawl into crevices, a few people may have suffered this unpleasant experience.

Like all insects, Dermaptera have three main body regions: a head, thorax, and abdomen. The entire body is elongated and flattened, an adaptation that allows earwigs to live in cracks and crevices. Three pairs of legs and two pairs of wings attach to the thorax. The front pair of wings are short, leathery, and lack veins; the hind wings, if present, are membranous and

rounded, with radiating veins. When at rest, the hind wings are folded under the front wings. Some species of earwigs have lost one or both pairs of wings.

Most Dermaptera are dark brown to black in color, although some species have reddish markings. The vast majority of species are less than 1 inch (2.54 centimeters) in length, although a few approach 2 inches (5 centimeters) in size.

About 1,800 species of earwigs have been noted in all parts of the world except the polar regions. The greatest number of species occur in tropical and warm, temperate areas. Approximately 20 species are known from North America, including several species that have been introduced. In California there are more introduced species of earwigs than native species.

Habitat of bark

The scientific name for earwigs, Dermaptera, is derived from the Latin words *derma*, meaning "skin," and *ptera*, meaning "wings." It refers to the thickened or skinlike front pair of wings typical of this insect order.

Earwigs are commonly found living in crevices under the bark of dead trees and in fallen logs, under debris on the ground, under rocks, and in soil crevices. Earwigs rely greatly on their sense of touch, which is why their antennae are continually feeling out their surroundings. Because of their reduced and hardened wings, many species are poor

fliers; however, they compensate by being excellent runners. Birds are common predators of earwigs, and European naturalists have also seen bats feeding on earwigs. Other enemies include insectivorous mammals, lizards, other insects, spiders, and centipedes.

Dermaptera have chewing mouthparts and are generally believed to be omnivorous, although some species are pure carnivores or plant feeders. Their food consists of the tender parts of plants, fruit, decaying animal and plant matter, and other insects. A few species are highly

The only endangered earwig species is also the largest: the St. Helena earwig. This insect makes its home on the island of St. Helena in the South Atlantic and is restricted to a dry portion of the island with stony soils and little vegetation.

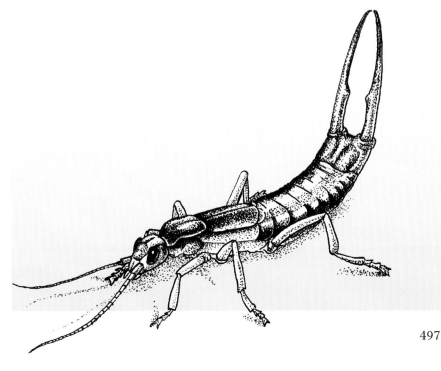

specialized ectoparasites, meaning they act as external parasites of mammals in tropical areas.

Family life

Unlike most insects, female earwigs care for their offspring. Eggs are laid most commonly at the bottom of a short burrow excavated by the female beneath debris on the ground. Female earwigs remain with their eggs and young nymphs, which resemble the adults except for their lack of wings. Maternal care is probably essential for successful reproduction since the eggs are very susceptible to molds and fungi due to the humid environments where they are laid. Females of several species are known to lick their eggs and nymphs, presumably to rid them of fungal spores that might other-wise kill their offspring during these life stages. The nymphs and their mother earwig often remain together for several months, at least until the mother dies. In some species, the brood nymphs even remain together for some time after they mature.

A threatened species

Only one earwig is considered an endangered species (listed as critically endangered by IUCN): the St. Helena earwig (*Labidura herculeana*). However, this is also the largest earwig species in the world, with specimens typically measuring 1½ to 2 inches in length (3.8 to 5 centimeters). This species is known only from the island of St. Helena in the South Atlantic, about eight degrees south of the Equator. There the earwig appears to be restricted to a portion of the island that is dry and barren with stony soils and little vegetation.

The St. Helena earwig lives under stones or in burrows made in the soil. This species is incapable of flying. The most famous resident known to have lived on St. Helena was the French emperor Napoleon, who was exiled to the island in 1815. This island became a dependency of England in 1834.

Although the earwig populations have been declining, reasons for their decline are presently unknown. Further study of the St. Helena earwig is needed to learn more about its habitat requirements, life cycle, and natural history, so that appropriate conservation measures can be taken.

Richard A. Arnold

Long-beaked Echidna

(Zaglossus bruijni)

IUCN: Endangered

Class: Mammalia
Order: Monotremata
Family: Tachyglossidae
Weight: 11–22 lb. (5–10 kg)
Head-body length: 17.6–30.2 in. (450–775 mm)
Diet: Earthworms
Longevity: 30 years in captivity
Habitat: Humid montane forests and meadows
Range: New Guinea

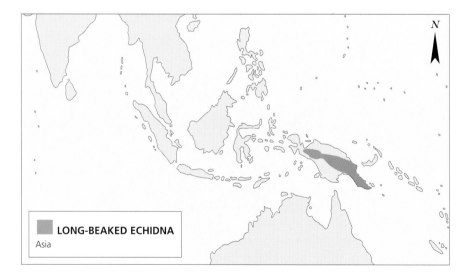

LONG-BEAKED ECHIDNA
Asia

THE LONG-BEAKED echidna is one of the three remaining members of a mammal group that possesses intermediate traits between reptiles and mammals. While it is possible that these strange mammalians may be able to help us understand the transition from reptiles to mammals, two of the three—including the long-beaked echidna—are classified as endangered today. The external egg and the simple mammary glands are the best-known "primitive" traits of this group. However, there are a number of other anatomical characteristics that are more closely associated with reptiles than with mammals. These are the skeleton, the structure of the eye, and the single opening that

The echidna is also called a spiny anteater.

serves the digestive, excretory, and reproductive systems.

Fossil evidence indicates that members of the genus *Zaglossus* were widespread in Australia during the Pleistocene epoch from ten thousand to about three million years ago. It is believed that climatic changes long ago dramatically reduced the wet conditions favorable to earthworms in Australia. Since earthworms are the major, if not the only, food of the echidna, these climate changes may have caused the echidna to disappear from that country.

No taste for ants

This species is also referred to as the spiny anteater. Echidnas are covered on the back and sides with short spines in between the hairs of their coat.

The anteater name arose due to the mistaken idea that this species was similar in its dietary habits to its close relative, the short-beaked anteater (*Tachyglossus aculeatus*).

The long-beaked echidna has a downward-curving snout that accounts for two-thirds of the length of its head. The eyes are small while the ear openings that lie partially hidden in the fur are quite large. (There is no external ear structure.) The spines range in color from white through gray to black; they are short and almost hidden in their brown-to-black fur. There are usually no spines on the underparts. The animal has strong legs with long claws on the middle three toes of each foot. These are probably used to dig for worms and to wedge the body into tight places for defense, although the long-beaked echidna has few predators besides people.

Little is known of the life history and day-to-day habits of the long-beaked echidna. Although the echidna is somewhat common at elevations of 3,300 to 13,000 feet (1,000 to 4,000 meters) in the humid central highlands of New Guinea, its density was estimated in 1974 to be only about four animals per square mile (1.5 per square kilometers). It is believed to be primarily nocturnal, finding its food within the litter on the forest floor by using its senses of smell and hearing.

Other than an indication that its breeding season may occur during the summer monsoons, little else is known of this species breeding habits. We do know that the long-beaked echidna, like the other two monotremes, the short-beaked echidna and the duck-billed platypus (*Ornithorhynchus anatinus*), produces its young by laying an egg that it incubates outside the body. It also has mammary glands that open into a temporary pouch where newly hatched young reside and nurse. It is not known how many young are produced.

New threats

While a change in climate may have driven the long-beaked echidna from Australia, it is the behavior of humans that threatens the species in New Guinea. Since the echidna is considered to be a delicacy and is eaten in ceremonial feasts, it is hunted by native people. As human populations have increased, hunting pressure has increased, and the echidna has vanished from the wide areas it once inhabited. Despite the hunting pressure, the total population was estimated to be 300,000 in the early 1970s.

However, increasing loss of habitat to agriculture is believed to be the overriding long-term threat to the echidna.

For this reason, the most important protective measure is the rapid establishment of national parks and reserves to protect the long-beaked echidna against further habitat loss.

Terry Tompkins

Chinese Egret

(Egretta eulophotes)

ESA: Endangered

IUCN: Endangered

Class: Aves
Order: Ciconiiformes
Family: Ardeidae
Subfamily: Ardeinae
Tribe: Ardeini
Length: 27 in. (69 cm)
Weight: Unknown
Clutch size: Probably 3–5 eggs
Incubation: Unknown
Diet: Probably aquatic animals
Habitat: Estuaries
Range: Korea and China to Philippines and Indonesia

PEOPLE WHO WORE them called them "hats." People in the clothing industry called the hat trade "millinery." Those who designed the hats called it fashion. Ornithologists called it outrageous. "It" was the social fad of wearing feathers in hats. During the three decades from 1880 to 1910, fashion-conscious women the world over clamored for hats styled not only with feathers, but with wings and even entire bird skins. For the fashionable, the cost of a hat was only money. For the birds that surrendered the feathers, the cost was near extinction. Some species taken to the brink by this trade have recovered. The Chinese egret has not.

Historically, the Chinese egret bred along the Chinese coast from Hainan in the South China Sea to as far north as the Korean Peninsula. Islands in the Yellow Sea were particularly important nesting areas. After the breeding season, Chinese egrets would wander. They have been found in Japan and as far northeast as the Aleutian Islands near Alaska. These far northern birds might have been immatures because the young wander more than the adults. Ordinarily, adult Chinese egrets migrate south to warmer areas after breeding. They are known to winter in extreme southeastern Sumatra, Borneo, Celebes, and the middle island

The Chinese egret was one of many birds that was killed for its feathers, which were used in the hat trade.

group of the Philippines, including Palawan, Cebu, Samar, Bohol, and Panay. They have also been seen in Thailand's southern peninsula, which suggests the species might also be found in coastal Cambodia and Vietnam.

The Chinese egret closely resembles the Pacific reef-egret

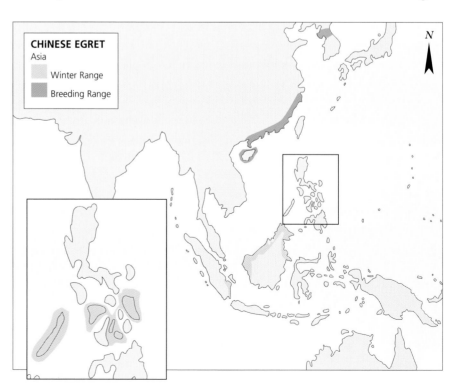

CHINESE EGRET
Asia

    Winter Range

    Breeding Range

(*Egretta sacra*) and the plumed egret (*Egretta intermedia*).

During the 1880s and 1890s plume hunters worked without any limitations. Early in the 1900s the United States passed laws that regulated interstate trade in feathers and bird skins. This legislation was an attempt to use the law to restrict wildlife exploitation. Some historians suggest that the law was not as instrumental in ending the slaughter of birds as was the scarcity of the birds themselves. Plume hunters ran out of birds to kill profitably. By then, the fashion trend had moved on to other styles that required fewer plumes. Some species particularly victimized by plume hunting eventually recovered, such as the snowy egret (*Egretta thula*) in the United States. The Chinese egret never recovered, for unknown reasons.

Its decline also is due to the enormous human population that has crowded the coasts of China, Southeast Asia, and the islands of Indonesia, Malaysia, and the Philippines. People have changed the character of the land, leaving few places for birds not able to adapt. The Chinese egret may prefer a special habitat or food that has disappeared from its range. This could explain the species' failure to recover to the same extent as some of its relatives. About 250 pairs breed on islands off North Korea's western coast.

Another 20 or so pairs breed on islands offshore from Shanghai in the Yellow Sea. A few egrets may breed on rocky islets near Hong Kong. In 1986 ornithologists working in the Philippines found 181 Chinese egrets—108 on Palawan and 73 on other islands.

The estuaries, coastal flats, and river mouths where egrets are seen must be protected from human development. Research must be done to determine the egret's natural history: what it eats, how it catches its prey, where it nests and why, where its migration routes are, and when it uses them. This information can help determine protective action.

Kevin Cook

Eastern Giant Eland
(*Tragelaphus derbianus gigas*)

IUCN: Lower risk

Western Giant Eland
(*Tragelaphus derbianus derbianus*)

ESA: Endangered

IUCN: Endangered

Class: Mammalia
Order: Artiodactyla
Family: Bovidae
Weight: 2,200 lb. (1,000 kg)
Height: 57–73 in. (145–185 cm)
Diet: Leaves and shoots
Longevity: 23–26 years
Habitat: Dry scrub bush
Range: West-central Africa

THE GIANT ELAND is so named because it is one of the largest African antelopes—certainly one of the most impressive and elegant. The most spectacular features of these animals are their spiral horns, which measure from 31 to 48 inches long (80 to 123 centimeters). The name "giant" is an apt description, since males can weigh more than one ton (900 kilograms).

Compared to the common eland, the giant eland has longer legs, with much brighter black and white flashings on the legs and on the pasterns (the portion of the foot between the hoof and the fetlock). The giant eland has a white chevron between the eyes that is characteristic of other elands and it is also typical of the spiral-horned antelope. When males become sexually mature they develop a large pendulous flap of skin, known as a dewlap, that hangs from their neck and turns almost black.

Diminishing range

Giant elands are found in southern Sudan and the Central African Republic, into northern Cameroon and southern Chad. They have also been known to live in Senegal and Mali.

However, the populations in Guinea are most probably extinct, and the total population across their entire range is rapidly diminishing.

Runs and hides

Giant elands are an animal of the scrub forest and brush. They prefer more dense vegetation than does the common eland. They probably browse (that is, feed off leaves and shoots of bushes and trees) more than the common eland, which tends more toward grazing. All elands are very wary and quick to flee when frightened in the wild; however, giant elands are even more wary than the common eland, so they are very difficult animals to approach.

Despite its large size, the giant eland is a wary animal and is quick to flee when frightened.

Gregarious females

The males prefer solitary living in the wild, or in some cases they congregate in small bachelor groups. The females, however, are very gregarious, and their calves stay with them until their second year, leaving just before the new calves are born. The females usually give birth to just one calf after a gestation period of between 255 and 270 days.

The giant eland's biggest problem in the wild is that of escaping human hunters. In addition, political struggles and civil wars in the part of the world it inhabits have ruined much of the giant eland's natural range. Troops have often lived off whatever meat they could kill in the forest; thus, an animal as big as a giant eland provided a very attractive source of food.

To make matters worse, large military units have been stationed in parts of these countries where there were once substan-tial populations, and the troops were told to live off the land. The western subspecies, *Tragelaphus derbianus derbianus*, has been reduced to barely 1,000 individuals because of encroachment by people and competition from domestic animals.

The stronghold of the western giant eland has been Senegal, where there are perhaps 700 to 800. However, Senegal is experiencing population growth and has suffered many years of severe drought. Therefore, the western giant eland is considered to be in danger of extinction.

Eastern giant eland

It was thought until fairly recent times that the eastern subspecies of giant eland (*Tragelaphus derbianus gigas*) still persisted in substantial numbers. This is incorrect—it is considered to be at lower risk of extinction but probably close to becoming an endangered species. Years of drought, constant competition from domestic animals, and heavy poaching are the culprits.

Dim prospects

The prospects for both the western and eastern forms of the giant eland's survival in the wild are not promising.

However, the situation of elands in captivity does show some hope. Several breeding pairs have been shipped around the world, with mixed success. A pair that came to North America after World War II never reproduced and was simply lost. A second group was shipped to Antwerp, Belgium, to a place called Plankendahl, where they bred reasonably well. Another pair went to Paris but did not survive, and a few animals were sent to Pretoria, South Africa.

Meanwhile the Plankendahl group all died of tuberculosis. But from the few that were sent to South Africa, a small group

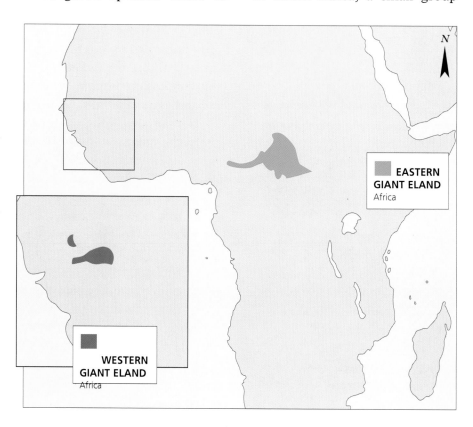

EASTERN GIANT ELAND
Africa

WESTERN GIANT ELAND
Africa

The giant eland is among the largest of the African antelopes. The distinctive horns, tan coloration, large, pendulous dewlap, and unusual striped markings, are all typical features of the species.

managed to persist, even though there was a high level of inbreeding among the animals. A small group was caught around 1984 in the Central African Republic and taken to two zoos in North America—Los Angeles and Cincinnati—where both populations have flourished. There are currently 22 in all.

However, the gene pool is narrow and needs to be enlarged. But captive breeding may yet be the answer to the problems of the giant eland.

Other conservation measures may be necessary to ensure its continued existence.

Warren D. Thomas

ELEPHANTS

Class: Mammalia

Order: Probosidea

Family: Elephantidae

Before they can read, small children can often recognize and identify a picture of an elephant. Children, however, are not alone in their enthusiasm for these large animals. As the stars of circuses the world over, elephants have long enjoyed an almost universal popularity.

By far the largest living land mammal, the elephant easily weighs twice as much as either the hippopotamus or the rhinoceros—the second and third largest mammals, respectively. Although the adult giraffe is taller, a mature elephant typically outweighs a giraffe by as much as 7,000 pounds (3,178 kilograms).

Elephants live in herds that are led by females and consist of female relatives and young bull elephants. At maturity, bulls are banished from the herds. Either they become solitary, or they associate with smaller groups of other mature males. These males periodically join up with the larger herds to mate but are soon driven off again.

An elephant is sometimes called a pachyderm and is grouped with the hippopotamus and rhinoceros—other animals with loose, thick skins. The wrinkled but not quite hairless skin of pachyderms requires the conditioning of water and mud. Like other pachyderms, an elephant delights in bathing in water—sometimes completely submerging itself and sometimes gathering mud, dust, and water in its trunk in order to spray itself lavishly. This is known as wallowing behavior.

The elephant often naps standing up but generally lies down to sleep, often in the middle of the day. When lying down, the animal breathes at only half its normal rate. It appears to sleep for about five hours out of every twenty-four and spends most of its waking hours foraging or wallowing.

To maintain its strength and body weight, an adult elephant may require more than 300 pounds (136 kilograms) of food a day. Consuming this much food requires so much chewing that an elephant's molars are soon worn down and are replaced by others.

Elephants develop six sets of teeth altogether, top and bottom, not including the tusks. The first four sets, considered milk teeth, are soon replaced by other, more durable teeth.

When a worn-down sixth set is not replaced, an elephant will probably die of starvation.

Noisy stomachs

Elephants are known for their noisy stomachs, but what was once thought of as a byproduct of a powerful digestive tract is now regarded as a means of communication. It is believed that a grazing elephant signals a sense of personal well-being with its growling stomach. Sudden silences are apparently thought to be a danger warning.

An elephant makes a trumpeting sound using its long muscular trunk to frighten or warn intruders and, if disturbed, may charge a stranger with little or no warning. The trunk, head, tusks, and weight of an elephant make formidable weapons. Normally not aggressive, an elephant is sometimes prone to tantrums. When enraged, an elephant becomes a fierce enemy. Bull elephants have been known to repeatedly charge into train locomotives and injure themselves before retreating.

Ritual combat

Bull elephants engage in combat, which is ritualized and designed to establish dominance and mating privileges. Ritual combat helps reduce the risk of serious injuries that could easily ensue from the elephant's sharp pointed tusks. Occasionally, however, these encounters develop into much more aggressive confrontations and can result in the death or maiming of one or both bull elephants.

A medieval myth that elephants feared mice was disproved in 1938 when Francis G. Benedict and Robert C. Lee put rats and mice in some elephants' hay and observed that the giant mammals were indifferent to the presence of the rodents.

African Elephant
(Loxodonta africana)

ESA: Threatened

IUCN: Endangered

Weight: Up to 13,230 lb. (to 6,000 kg)
Shoulder height: 10–13 ft. (3–4 m)
Diet: Grasses, foliage, branches, barks, shrubs, fruit
Gestation period: Approximately 660 days
Longevity: Up to 55 years
Habitat: Savannas, open ranges, tropical forests
Range: Most of Africa south of the Sahara

THE AFRICAN elephant is the world's largest land mammal, standing several inches higher and weighing about 1,000 pounds (454 kilograms) more than its Asian counterpart. Of the two elephants, the African has the larger ears and tusks, a flatter forehead, and a swayed back. The African elephant has two finger-like projections at the end of its trunk where the Asian has just one; the trunk is more wrinkled as well. The hind feet of the African elephant have three nails and the front feet four, but both front and rear feet of the Asian elephant have five nails. The African is, however, less long-lived than the Asian elephant.

The African elephant will use its flatter forehead to push over small trees in order to get at the tender foliage in the higher branches. It is also more inclined to use its larger hooked tusks in combat and is more difficult to train than the Asian elephant.

African elephants are inclined to roam widely in search of whatever food or fruit is in season—or in search of watering holes or places to wallow. Historically, elephant habitats covered vast areas, therefore damage to them could be minimized. Now, increasingly hemmed in by roads and other products of human civilization, elephants are increasingly confined to protected areas too small to contain them. Trees have been

The developing countries of Africa have so many problems to contend with that saving the elephant is not always a high priority.

denuded of foliage and bark, and water has become scarce. Yet the animals continue to reproduce. Given the difficulty of relocating these animals, those concerned with saving herds often must kill individual elephants in order to prevent the wholesale starvation of many elephants.

The presence of too many elephants in a region can be destructive to the populations of other herbivores, as well; these other animals must compete for the food the elephants are eating. This in turn has had an impact on carnivore populations whose continued survival depends on the relative abundance of other herbivores.

The African elephant's spectacular tusks have played a large role in the animal's population decline. Elephants are killed and mutilated for ivory that brings high prices in illegal trade.

Many scientists insist that there are two African subspecies, *Loxodonta africana africana* and *Loxodonta africana cyclotis*, or the bush elephant and the forest elephant. Forest elephants are said to be smaller, have straighter tusks, shorter ears, and slightly darker skins. Other experts dismiss these differences as superficial, attributing them to diet or habitat.

Whether or not they constitute a different subspecies, forest elephants are generally under less pressure from encroaching civilization and are harder to hunt and kill in the dense jungles. For this reason they are faring better than the animals living in the more vulnerable bush country.

The African elephants living in drier regions find water in times of drought, using their tusks to bore into mud to find it.

Trunks

Anatomically, the trunk is the elephant's nose and upper lip. Paired nostrils run its entire length. Entirely muscular, the trunk is extremely useful. An elephant can pick up and hand a coin to its keeper. The trunk is

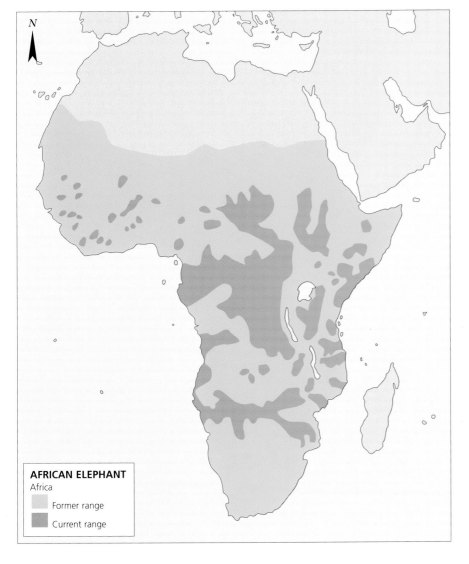

N

AFRICAN ELEPHANT
Africa

Former range

Current range

also an exploratory organ. When it senses danger, an elephant lifts its trunk to see what's in the wind. An elephant may use its trunk to swipe tidbits of food from another elephant's mouth, to smell the mouth of another animal, or to test an interesting smell on the ground.

The elephant's trunk can also hold up to about two pints (four liters) of water. It can soak up mud or dust, which it sprays over its body to help protect its skin and to keep cool. In combat, the trunk can be used to deliver an elephant jab.

Some experts believe that elephants will deliberately throw things at people or animals.

Although they are useful in contests of dominance, trunks are generally not used in serious combat, although elephants have been known to pick up an enemy with their trunks and fling it or beat it against trees or rocks. In combat, however, the elephant will gore an enemy with its tusks or trample the foe to death.

Tusks are upper incisors, not canine teeth. Birth tusks fall out after a year. The elephant's permanent tusks begin to protrude beyond the lips after about two or three years and continue to grow throughout the animal's life. Generally, the older the elephant, the heavier the tusks. Two tusks taken from a bull elephant shot near Mt. Kilimanjaro at the turn of the twentieth century were said to weigh 460 pounds (209 kilograms). But tusks of such size have not been recorded since.

This elephant possesses a fine pair of tusks. The tusks are actually the upper incisors and continue to grow throughout the animal's life.

This baby elephant has hairs on its body that are retained as coarse, short bristles on the trunk and chin.

Tusk pairs taken from adult females rarely weigh more than 45 pounds combined.

Composed principally of dentine, a tusk is no different from an ordinary tooth. About one quarter of the tusk is hidden in its socket, and the base of the tusk is hollow and contains pulp. But the dentine in the elephant's tusks has a peculiar diamond pattern that gives it a distinctive luster not found in other ivory that can be taken from the hippopotamus, the warthog, walrus, narwhal, or sperm whale. Elephant ivory's pleasing luster has made it popular, and it is carved and fashioned into jewelry, piano keys, combs, and other finery. Tusks are rarely symmetrical and often one tusk is used in preference to the other, making the animal right- or left-tusked. Often the tusks spiral and cross over one another. When this happens, it becomes difficult for the animal to feed itself, but the tusks still come in handy as a support for the great weight of the trunk.

Over time, most African governments have come to see the value of protecting their elephants, if only as tourist attractions, but political problems abound. Ivory, for which the elephant has been slaughtered for hundreds of years, is bound up with world politics. In 1990, international trade in ivory and other elephant products was banned under CITES. As a result, African countries and the international conservation community have become divided. While poaching is lower in some countries today, it has increased in others. Also, the status of African elephants varies widely, with far more numerous, stable, and well-managed populations in East and southern Africa.

High ivory prices, combined with limited economic opportunities and large numbers of unemployed workers, caused a wholesale slaughter of African elephants during the 1970s. In Kabalega Falls National Park in Uganda, scientists counted more than 14,000 elephants in 1973. That year the poaching intensified, and by 1974 the count had dropped to around 6,000 and

Despite their massive size, elephants can be surprisingly gentle animals, but an elephant's tusks can be used as formidable weapons.

finally to as low as 2,200 one year later. Poaching led to a similar population drop in Tsavo National Park in Kenya, where the problem was worsened by a decade-long drought. The current total population is estimated at 300,000 to 600,000, compared to 1.7 million in the 1970s. Although recognizing the need to preserve these mammals, developing African countries lack resources for their preservation.

In 1997 CITES member countries agreed to allow limited, one-time shipments of raw ivory from three southern African countries, namely, Botswana, Namibia, and Zimbabwe, to Japan only. The decision followed extensive and often divisive debate in CITES meetings and

was based upon recognition that elephant populations and ivory itself is well managed in the southern African countries. This trade could only take place after a series of conditions were first met. This trade began in April 1999 and continues to be the subject of much disagreement. While strictly controlled, it is still experimental and its impacts will need to be closely monitored.

Renardo Barden

Asian Elephant
(Elephas maximus)

ESA: Endangered

IUCN: Endangered

Weight: Up to 11,500 lb. (to 5,221 kg)
Shoulder height: 8–8½ ft. (2.4–2.6 m)
Diet: Bark, branches, roots, leaves, grass, bushes, fruit
Gestation period: 630–690 days
Longevity: Up to 70 years
Habitat: Dense forests
Range: India, Nepal, Sri Lanka, southern China, Southeast Asia, Malaysia, and Sumatra

THE SMALLER EARS of the Asian elephant are said by some to resemble the outline of India, while the ears of African elephants are likened to maps of Africa. Because elephants cool themselves off by flapping their ears, and because the Asian elephant lives in humid environments with more readily available shade, some scientists speculate that the Asian elephant's ears are smaller because its need for cooling is less. Apart from being the smaller of the two elephants, the Asian or Indian elephant exhibits quite a few differences. The Asian elephant has a domed rather than a flattened forehead, an arched back, 19 pairs of ribs (the African has 21), 33 caudal vertebrae (the African has 26), and a trunk that is considerably smoother than that of the African. The African elephant stands with its head below the level of its shoulders, while the Asian elephant carries its head higher than its shoulders. The African has the leaner look, whereas the Asian appears slightly more squat and rounded, with shorter legs. Tusks are smaller in the Asian animal. Only male Asian elephants have tusks. Female elephants have small "tushes"—tusks that seldom protrude beyond the lip. The male's tusks are considerably smaller than those found in either male or female African elephants.

A few Asian elephants never develop tusks. Lacking the weight of tusks, these elephants develop different muscles. In India, tuskless males are known as

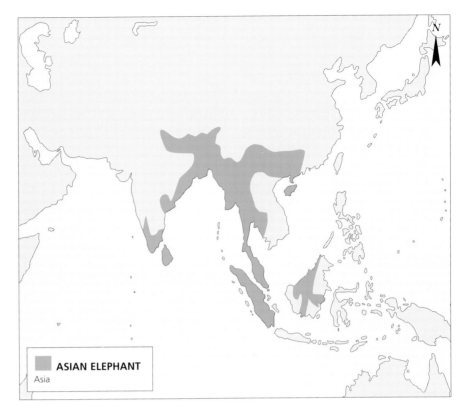

ASIAN ELEPHANT
Asia

Makhnas. The lack of tusks does not seem to place the Makhnas at a disadvantage in a ritualistic fight because tuskless animals have greater freedom of movement. Of course, in those rare violent encounters between bull elephants, a lack of tusks would be a decided disadvantage. In northeastern India the lack of tusks seems to occur in about 50 percent of the males. So common is this condition in some parts of India and Sri Lanka that some biologists believe that natural selection may now be favoring tusklessness. They surmise that, without ivory, the animals are less likely to be killed by hunters.

The Asian elephant is much closer to extinction than the African elephant. The reasons for this are many, beginning with the loss of habitat due to agricultural pressures and the clearing away of the heavy forests favored by this Asian mammal. The elephant is confined to increasingly smaller pockets of its range. When lack of forage forces it to wander in search of nourishment, an elephant will often raid a farming area where it is usually shot as a pest. Populations are highly fragmented. Today, there

The Asian elephant is in more danger of extinction than its African relative. As few as 38,000 animals may remain.

are only 38,000 to 51,000 Asian elephants, while there are estimated to be 300,000 to 600,000 African elephants. India has the largest Asian elephant population. In Sri Lanka, the population has declined by as much as 85 percent, predominantly because of habitat loss. There may be only 2,500 Asian elephants remaining there. The Sri Lankan Department of Wildlife Conservation is working with IUCN–The World Conservation Union, on several conservation measures, including identifying and protecting some of the high priority elephant populations.

Larger bull elephants are particularly inclined to stray from elephant sanctuaries. As a result, more males are destroyed as pests. Scientists believe this puts pressure on the gene pool; that is, with fewer mates, interbreeding occurs, and this can produce a smaller, less healthy population that may continue deteriorating.

Some Asian elephants are disappearing because they are more docile and easier to train than their African cousins. They have long been exploited as draft animals. Some are used in hunting while others are trained and exported to zoos and circuses. Thus, these elephants have been systematically removed from their natural habitats and sent into servitude or captivity. In Burma alone, nearly 4,000 elephants are used in the timber industry.

Finally, in both Africa and Asia, poaching for ivory has taken its toll. While Asian elephants are banned from international trade under CITES, protection and resources at national levels are often inadequate to deal with the problem. While Asian elephants are targeted by ivory poachers far less frequently than African elephants, poaching of male Asian elephants has negatively impacted the sex ratio in some areas, particularly in southern India.

However, a variety of measures has been undertaken, including adoption of national conservation plans and strict poaching penalties. In China, poachers—including two policemen—have been sentenced to death in recent years for poaching elephants.

Terry Tompkins

Golden-rumped Elephant Shrew
(Rhynchocyon chrysopygus)

IUCN: Endangered

Class: Mammalia
Order: Macroscelidea
Family: Macroscelididae
Weight: About 19 oz. (540 g)
Head-body length: 10.5–12 in. (27–31 cm)
Diet: Carnivorous
Gestation period: 42 days
Longevity: 4–5 years
Habitat: Moist coastal scrub and lowland semi-deciduous forest
Range: Coast of Kenya

THE GOLDEN-RUMPED elephant shrew is about the size of a domestic cat and is the largest representative of an old order of mammals. Experts differ about which group of mammals is the nearest relative of the elephant shrew. However, there is agreement on two points. First, the golden-rumped elephant shrew is similar in appearance to fossil forms that are 20 million years old. Second, evidence suggests that elephant shrews were formerly widespread, although today their distribution is restricted. This is especially true of the golden-rumped elephant shrew, which occurs in two separate populations on Kenya's coast.

It was given its common name because the nose extends well beyond the mouth and has the appearance of an elephant's trunk. Its mistaken connection with shrews arose because of an anatomical and a behavioral feature. Elephant shrews have small, relatively undifferentiated teeth, similar in appearance to those found in shrews. In addition, they have the habit of searching on the ground among leaf litter for invertebrate food, again, much like shrews. These creatures are not shrews, however, and in fact comprise an order all their own.

The nearly naked tail appears similar to a rat's, and the large hind limbs seem adapted for quick springing movements. The fur on the back is a deep reddish black except on the rump, where it is golden yellow. The fur on the face and underparts is slightly paler than that on the back.

Unlike most mammals, elephant shrews form monogamous pairs. These pairs use scent to mark and defend a common territory against other elephant shrews. Territories are usually about 4.3 acres (1.7 hectares) in size. Each member of a pair only drives off intruders of the same sex, suggesting that what is being defended is sexual resources, not food resources.

Even though pairs defend a common territory, they spend little time together and usually forage separately. They slowly search through ground leaf litter using their sensitive snouts and forepaws to locate prey such as beetles, termites, millipedes, ants, spiders, and other invertebrates. Elephant shrews have also been reported to occasionally eat small mammals, birds, and eggs.

Breeding

Breeding occurs throughout the year, and after a 42-day gestation period, the female gives birth to a single offspring. After a two-week confinement in the nest, the young one emerges and remains by its mother's side for about five days. The mother and offspring are seen together less and less often until the offspring goes off to establish its own home range.

The golden patch on the rump may have developed to dis-

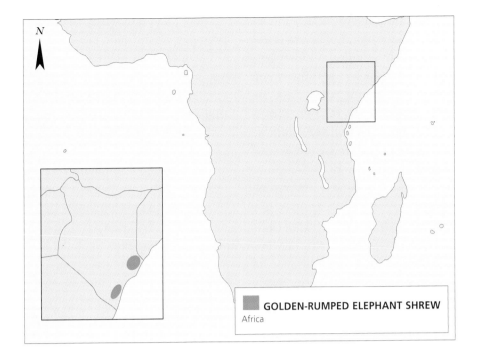

GOLDEN-RUMPED ELEPHANT SHREW
Africa

tract the attention of predators toward the rear of this species, increasing the likelihood of its escape. A golden rump, however, will not protect the elephant shrew from its major threats today—hunting and habitat destruction by humans. Much of the best habitat left within the species' range is highly sought

after for agricultural purposes. Although some areas within the range of the golden-rumped elephant shrew are protected in reserves, ongoing snare hunting and deforestation of what little suitable habitat remains outside these reserves are threatening the survival of this unusual animal.

Terry Tompkins

EUPHORBIAS

Tribe: Euphorbieae

Family: Euphorbiaceae

The Euphorbiaceae family contains some five thousand different species of plants that are divided into several tribes containing a total of three hundred genera. Euphorbias are a genus in the tribe Euphorbieae and examples of plants in this genus may be found all over the world.

These species vary enormously in size and shape, from tall trees to shrubs to very small plants only a few centimetres in height or diameter. Some are perennials and live for more than two years, while

others are annuals that live for only one year. Some Euphorbias are succulents and have adapted themselves to survive long periods of drought in their natural habitats by storing water in their stems, leaves, or roots, which then become thickened or swollen. In some cases, in order to prevent loss of moisture, the leaves are very tiny or even absent altogether.

In spite of all the differences between the many species of Euphorbia, there are some factors that are common to all of them. All plants contain a fluid, known usually as sap, that is generally quite clear. The fluid in euphorbias, however, is milky and often of a sticky or resinous texture. This is usually referred to

as latex. In some species the latex may be quite poisonous and after handling the plants, care must be taken to wash thoroughly any parts of the skin that may have been contaminated with the latex.

Another common factor in Euphorbias is that they all have a specialized type of inflorescence, called a cyathium, which may look like a single flower but, in fact, consists of several male flowers that have been reduced to a single stamen and that surround one, or occasionally more, female flowers that have been reduced to a single ovary. All of this is surrounded by bracts, which are sometimes large and colorful. The cyathium may also be surrounded by glands containing nectar.

A common example of a Euphorbia with large, colorful bracts is the Poinsettia (*Euphorbia pulcherrima*), which is popular at Christmas time. The bright red, pink or cream parts, which look like flower petals, are, in fact, colored bracts, and the true flowers are in the center of the bracts.

All euphorbias have tripartite seed capsules. The capsules are divided into three sections, each usually containing a single seed, but occasionally holding two or three. When the seeds are ripe, the capsules dehisce (pop open) and the seeds are scattered around, sometimes landing quite a long way from the parent plant. If conditions are right, they eventually germinate and form a new plant.

While many euphorbias are plentiful both in cultivation and in their natural habitats, some species are now endangered in their habitat and are protected by the Convention on International Trade in Endangered Species of Wild Fauna and Flora (CITES) regulations, which forbid their collection and sale.

Akoko
(Euphorbia haeleeleana)

ESA: Endangered

IUCN: Endangered

Height: Up to 4¼ ft. (14 m)
Leaves: Elliptic in shape 3–8 in. (7–20 cm) long, 1¼–3¼ in. (3.25–8.25 cm) wide, with stems (1.5–5.25 cm) long
Habitat: Sandy, infertile soil; among grasses and sedges
Range: Hawaiian Islands

EUPHORBIA HAELEELEANA was described by Derral Herbst in 1971 and is a species endemic to the Hawaiian Islands. The common name is Akoko, a name also used for other similar species.

It is a tree euphorbia with thick, succulent branches. The leaves are arranged alternately along the stems. The stems of the leaves are mostly smooth, but occasionally they may have pale-colored hairs. The parts of the leaves that join the stems may

EUPHORBIA ABDELKURI
Abd al-Kuri Island, Yemen

also be hairy, both on the top surface and underneath. The large cyathia are grayish brown and may also be hairy.

At first *Euphorbia haeleeleana* was found in only two locations, a single tree being discovered in Haeleele Valley and a larger population of about 150 trees being found in Mahanaloa Valley. The name haeleeleana was derived from the name of the former valley. These trees were found growing on the mountain slopes at a height of between 1,970 to 2,300 feet (600 to 700 meters) alongside other dry forest trees.

In 1985 further specimens of *Euphorbia haeleeleana* were found in the Wai'anae Mountains at a height of 1,700 feet (520 meters). in remnants of dry forest.

At the time when the trees were first discovered, seeds were collected and distributed to the Botanical Gardens of Honolulu, the Pacific Tropical Botanic Gardens, and the Lyon Arboretum.

Euphorbia haeleeleana has been gradually disappearing from its island habitat and is now on the endangered list issued by the Hawaiian Reforestation Foundation. It is hoped, in time, to reestablish the plant in its natural habitat.

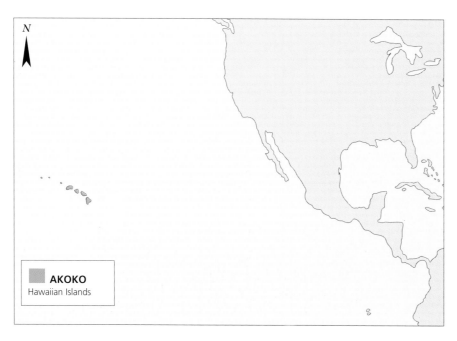

AKOKO
Hawaiian Islands

Euphorbia Abdelkuri

IUCN: Endangered

Growth: Erect branches up to 6½ ft. (2 m) long
Leaves: Spineless and leafless
Flowers: Small yellowish green clusters
Habitat: Mountain slopes
Range: Abd al-Kuri Island, Yemen

EUPHORBIA ABDELKURI takes its name from the island of Abd al-Kuri, which is the second largest of an archipelago, part of Yemen, which lies in the Arabian sea off the Horn of Africa. The largest of these islands is Socotra, which is the farthest from the continent of Africa. Two smaller islands, Samha and Darsa, lie between Socotra and Abd al-Kuri, the latter being the nearest to the coast

Older specimens of *Euphorbia abdelkuri* are a rather dull grayish green color, with a rough appearance.

of Africa. *Euphorbia abdelkuri* is endemic to the island of Abd al-Kuri and is not found on any of the other islands. It is a very rare plant and one that is much sought after by collectors of succulent plants.

The island of Abd al-Kuri is long and rocky and very barren. Its highest peak is at the western end of a long limestone ridge and this peak has an altitude of more than 2,300 feet (700 meters) above sea level. It is on the slopes of this mountain, called Jabal Saleh, at a height of about 1,650 feet (500 meters), that *Euphorbia abdelkuri* grows. It was first described by Balfour in 1903 in his book *The Natural History of Sokotra* and since then there have been several expeditions to the island, when botanists have made further studies of the plants.

Euphorbia abdelkuri is a shrub that branches densely from the base. The erect branches may be up to 6½ feet (2 meters) long and from 1½ to 3 inches (4 to 8 centimeters) in diameter. They are pinkish gray when young and at this stage have a particularly attractive rough, mottled appearance. This slowly disappears as the plant grows older and the stems gradually become smooth and a rather dull grayish green color. The plant is spineless and leafless and the small cyathia, which are yellowish green in color, are stemless and grow in clusters close to the body of the plant. The latex, instead of the more usual white, is yellowish in color and is extremely poisonous. Anyone handling the plant must do so with extreme caution.

In cultivation this euphorbia is not one of the easiest to grow. Care must be taken as far as watering is concerned. In habitat the climate is subject to monsoon winds. From May to October, which is the hot season, the winds blow from the southwest and are strong, but they do not bring a great deal of rain. Early in November, the northeast monsoon winds arrive and these are the ones that bring the rain to the islands and also cooler temperatures. Between the monsoon periods the islands have occasional tropical storms.

In 1967 the plant enthusiast Sir Michael Lefonu sponsored a botanical expedition to the islands, and plants of *Euphorbia abdelkuri* were collected and brought back for study and propagation. It is from these plants that most of the specimens in collections today originate. Propagation is best done from seed, but may be achieved by taking cuttings, although these take a considerable time to root. A more popular method of propagation is to graft part of the parent plant onto a suitable euphorbia stock, leaving the lower part of the stem to grow on. Offshoots may then be taken off and rooted.

Since 1967 more expeditions have visited the island of Socotra, and regular flights to the island mean that the plants are in danger of being collected by unscrupulous dealers. As are all the succulent Euphorbias, *Euphorbia abdelkuri* is protected by CITES. It is hoped that this will ensure that the island of Abd al-Kuri retains its indigenous flora and that careful propagation will ensure that it is always available through cultivation.

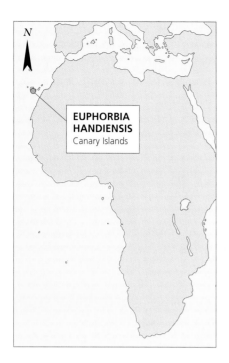

This *Euphorbia handiensis* displays a system of dense branching and prickly spines that resemble cacti.

Euphorbia Handiensis

IUCN: Endangered

Height: 3¼ ft. (1 m)
Leaves: Erect stems, sometimes with spines
Flowers: Small; yellow or pale yellowish green
Pollination: By greenbottles in habitat
Habitat: Basalt rocks
Range: Fuerteventura, Canary Islands

EUPHORBIA HANDIENSIS has been known in cultivation for many years, having been described by the botanist O. Burchard in 1912. It is endemic to the Island of Fuerteventura, the second largest of the Canary Islands, where it grows on the Jandia peninsula in the south of the island. In Spanish the letter *J* is pronounced as *H* and the name *Jandia* would sound like "Handia," from which

one can see how the name of the plant was derived. The peninsula consists of an old volcanic ridge with two main valleys running through it, the Gran Valle and the Valle de los Mosquitos. The valleys are wide and scattered with basalt rocks, among which the populations of *Euphorbia handiensis* grow. The Jandia peninsula is connected to the rest of the island by a region of sand dunes and is virtually uninhabited except for the southeast coast, where a large tourist area has developed over the years and is continually increasing in size.

Euphorbia handiensis is a small shrub that grows to about 3 feet (1 meter) in height. It branches densely from the base and these branches rebranch so that, with age, large specimens are produced. The stems are erect and are 2¼ to 3 inches (6 to 8 centimeters) in diameter, with eight to twelve angles. The furrows between the angles are quite deep. The spines are paired, or joined at the base where they join the plant stem, and they vary considerably in length. Some

plants may be virtually spineless, while others may have spines up to 2 inches (5 centimetres) long, and all variations between the two extremes may be found growing in the same area. People seeing the long-spined bushes could well think that they were cacti. The spine shields, which form where the spines grow out from the stem, are gray and they join together to make a hard, gray ridge down the angles of the stem. The color of the stems is bright green under good growing conditions, but if conditions are poor, the older parts of the stems tend to become gray and only the newest part at the top is green. The cyathia are small and grow on very short stalks, called peduncles. They are a bright yellow in habitat, but in cultivation in Europe, where the light is far less intense, the cyathia tend to be a pale yellowish green. Pollination is by greenbottles in habitat.

The climate on the Island of Fuerteventura is very hot and dry, the island being under the influence of the hot, dry winds that blow from the Sahara, only about 120 miles (75 kilometers) away. The island of Tenerife, the largest of the Canary Islands, is influenced by the trade winds, which, because of the high altitude of Mount Teide, bring rain to the area. Fuerteventura, on the other hand, is much lower and does not have the benefit of the influence of the trade winds. Its rainfall is extremely low and the rainfall for the whole year may fall in just one shower. When growing plants of *Euphorbia handiensis* in other parts of the world, it is important to remember this and to water the plants with care.

Plants of this species are available from some nurseries that specialize in succulent plants, but in habitat the number of specimens are declining. The main reason for this is the increasing tourist trade. As more and more hotels are built along the coast, more and more tourists arrive. Hiring cars and driving inland is a common pastime for many such visitors. Unfortunately, they tend to have no regard for the damage they do to plant life in their pursuit of pleasure. The road through the area where *Euphorbia handiensis* grows is a rough dirt track and so tourists drive over open ground and do not attempt to follow the road, causing damage to the plants in the process. Technically CITES regulations are in force to protect the plants, but little appears to be done to enforce the regulations and prevent the destruction. Goats roam the area where the plants grow, but they do not eat the plants or cause damage to them. The blame for the decline in the population of *Euphorbia handiensis* must be laid entirely on the damage caused by humans.

Euphorbia Obesa

IUCN: Endangered

Height: Up to 46 ft. (14 m)
Leaves: Arranged alternately on the stems
Flowers: Hairy; grayish brown
Habitat: Mountain slopes
Range: South Africa

EUPHORBIA OBESA was first discovered in 1897 by Peter MacOwan, who was at that time curator of Cape Town Botanic gardens in South Africa. He sent a specimen to the Royal Botanic Gardens at Kew, in England, under the name of *Euphorbia meloformis*, a somewhat similar species from the Eastern Cape of South Africa. The new plant was studied and found to be quite different from *Euphorbia meloformis* in many aspects and it was finally described as *Euphorbia obesa* by Hooker in 1903. The name was perhaps chosen because of the ball-like shape of young plants. Shortly after being described, the specimen at Kew died and it was not reintroduced until some twenty years later.

Euphorbia obesa is a dwarf stem succulent. Although ball-shaped when young, with age it elongates, and really old specimens may reach heights of up to about 12 inches (30 centimeters), with diameters of up to 3½ inches (9 centimeters). The plant usually has eight ribs, but specimens with seven, nine, and even ten ribs have been reported. The body is gray green with very attractive dull purple markings. This euphorbia is normally unisexual, with the small, grayish green cyathia normally being all male on some plants and all female on others. Therefore, cross-pollination between a male and female plant is required to produce seeds. Pollination is by insects.

Euphorbia obesa is probably the most popular species of euphorbia to be introduced to collectors of succulent plants, due to its unusual and attractive appearance. Very large quantities of plants have been collected from habitat. These have been grown in nurseries and in private collections, producing seed from which further specimens are grown. Seedlings of *Euphorbia obesa* are produced by the thousands by specialist nurseries and

EUPHORBIA OBESA
South Africa

there is no likelihood of the plant becoming extinct in cultivation. However, the situation in habitat is very different.

The home of this plant is in Kendrew, a small area of the Great Karroo in South Africa, in the Graaff-Reinet district.

The plants sometimes grow under small shrubs and sometimes among small boulders in fairly sandy soil. Their color blends in so well with their surroundings that it is often quite difficult to distinguish them.

Because over the years hundreds of plants have been collected from the wild and brought into cultivation, the number of plants in habitat is now dangerously low and the species is threatened with extinction in the wild.

Illegal collection

Although it is protected by law and anyone found collecting these plants is liable to prosecution, unscrupulous collectors have been known to offer payment to needy local people for collecting habitat specimens.

It would seem that although cultivated plants of *Euphorbia obesa* are readily available, there are some people who are only satisfied with plants taken from habitat. The local conservation authorities of the area have been successful in apprehending some of the plant thieves and now a special conservation area has been donated by a local farmer on whose land the plants grow.

Suitable fencing for it has been provided by funds raised by the Euphorbiaceae Study Group, an international group based in England. Regular checks are made on the area and it is to be hoped that this very endangered plant will once again become plentiful in its natural wild environment.

Telephus Spurge
(*Euphorbia telephioides*)

ESA: Threatened

IUCN: Endangered

Height: Up to 12 in. (30 cm)
Leaves: Succulent, riblike
Flowers: Small; grayish green
Habitat: Sandy soil under shrubs
Range: Florida to Apalachicola

EUPHORBIA TELEPHIOIDES is a perennial herb that is endemic to the coastal area of Florida from Panama City to Apalachicola. It is known from only 22 sites, all of which are within 4 miles (2.5 kilometers) of the Gulf of Mexico. The plants live among grasses, sedges, and other herbs in poorly drained, infertile, sandy soil. Some of the sites are actually seepage bogs, which are permanently wet, while other sites are savanna which are less damp but still poor as far as soil quality is concerned. *Euphorbia telephioides* has been known since 1860, when it was described by the botanist A. W. Chapman.

The species has a bushy appearance, with many smooth stems that may grow up to 12 inches (30 centimeters) in height. It has a stout storage root. The leaves are elliptical in shape, sometimes broader near the tip and narrower where the leaf joins the stem. The botanical term for this is *oblanceolate*. They are fairly large, from 1 to 2¼ inches (3 to 6 centimeters) long. They are attractive in color, with the midrib and margins usually being maroon colored.

The main threat to *Euphorbia telephioides* comes from the expansion of the tourist trade. Hotels and apartments are increasingly being built and this means that roads are required and that large parcels of land are being stripped of their normal vegetation. In addition, approval has been given for further development in the form of a golf resort, upgrading of general facilities, and an airport, all of which threaten the existence of local plants. The U.S. Forest Service's botanists are monitoring the situation and it is thought that in due course the state may set aside some land where the local plants may grow undisturbed and the future of *Euphorbia telephioides* and other species may be secured.

Daphne Pritchard

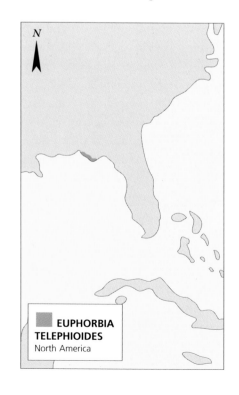

N

EUPHORBIA TELEPHIOIDES
North America

Lewis Eyebright

(Euphrasia campbelliae)

IUCN: Rare

Family: Scrophulariaceae
Stem: Erect, wiry, up to 4 in. (10 cm) tall
Leaves: Small, opposite, toothed, sometimes purplish underneath
Flowers: Dainty corolla up to 7 mm with two-lobed upper lip, larger three-lobed lower lip; predominantly white with some violet and a yellow spot on the lower lip
Habitat: Damp, heathy grassland near the sea
Range: Isle of Lewis in the Outer Hebrides, U.K.

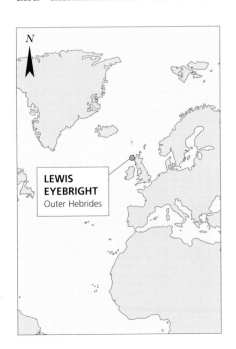

LEWIS EYEBRIGHT
Outer Hebrides

The bright white and yellow flowers of eyebright, which is still used today to treat certain eye conditions.

SPECIES OF EUPHRASIA are tiny, annual semiparasitic plants commonly known as eyebrights or, in Wales, Christ's eye. In the Middle Ages and later, extracts from them were used as a tonic for the eyes and to treat conjunctivitis and inflammation. In Britain there are about 20 species, all of which hybridize readily and are difficult to distinguish. Nine of the species are endemic to Britain. Germination occurs in spring and then the plants attach by suckerlike structures to the root system of a suitable host plant in their grassland and heathland habitats.

They absorb water and mineral nutrients but are able to manufacture their own sugars and starch in their leaves.

Seaside home

This species of eyebright is known only from the Isle of Lewis in the Outer Hebrides, where it grows mainly along the western coast of the island. It is found near the sea in damp, mossy, heathy grassland where grazing limits the growth of heather. *Euphrasia campbelliae* was first described as a species by a botanist H. W. Puglsley in 1940. It is thought to have originated by hybridization.

Other species of *Euphrasia* grow close by, but in slightly different habitats: *E. micrantha* in drier heath, *E. nemorosa* in drier grass-turf, and *E. scottica* in damper sites. Complex hybridization between these species may have given rise to *Euphrasia campbelliae*, which is listed as rare by IUCN-The World Conservation Union. It is not currently thought to be under threat of extinction, but due to its rarity, further assessment of the species is required.

There are no specific conservation measures in place for this rare species. Biodiversity Challenge, the plan for action compiled by voluntary conservation organizations in Britain, calls for maintenance of the populations of this annual endemic in its only world locations.

Sara Oldfield

Falanouc

(Eupleres goudotii)

Class: Mammalia
Order: Carnivora
Family: Viverridae
Weight: 4½–8¾ lb. (2–4 kg)
Length: 17½–25 in. (45–65 cm)
Tail length: 8½–9¾ in. (22–25 cm)
Shoulder height: 6 in.
Diet: Worms, ants, termites, and frogs
Gestation period: About 90 days
Longevity: 7–10 years
Habitat: Lowland forests and fields
Range: Madagascar

To MANY people the falanouc would probably look like it was made from spare parts. It is neither a fox nor a mongoose, a cat nor a weasel, a badger nor a civet—but it looks and acts a little like each one. In fact it is more like an insectivore.

As with other members of the Viverrid family, the falanouc is found only in the Old World, specifically in the lowland forests and fields along the eastern and western coasts of Madagascar.

The falanouc is one of about 70 species of viverrid. This family includes the civets, genets, fossas, linsangs, and other small Old World carnivores. Typically viverrids have long, slender heads and bodies; long, bushy tails; and short limbs. They are generally good diggers; they have five-toed feet and nonretractable claws.

Given its nocturnal habits and the comparative isolation of the falanouc's range, little is known about this creature, and much that is believed is subject to revision. The small falanouc has fur with a light reddish cast. There is also a larger falanouc (*Eupleres major*), most often found in

The falanouc is a member of an Old World family, Viverridae, consisting of small mammals with shy habits.

northwestern Madagascar, that has grayish fur. Both are nocturnal forest dwellers with similarly shy dispositions.

Even though their short, conical teeth resemble those of civets and mongooses, falanoucs are thought to feed primarily on worms, ants, and insects, a diet occasionally supplemented by a frog. Falanouc feet are unusually large, with long claws that are not quite retractable. When threatened, it "freezes," or it runs away.

Because the falanouc can store fat in its tail, some authorities suspect that the animal sometimes hibernates or at least experiences periods of reduced activity. Some observers claim that the falanouc is an essentially solitary animal, while others dispute this, insisting that the animal is as social as the fox. The falanouc has several vocalizations and other means of communication. It mates in the winter (in the Southern Hemisphere, around July and August). Experts doubt that falanoucs were ever very

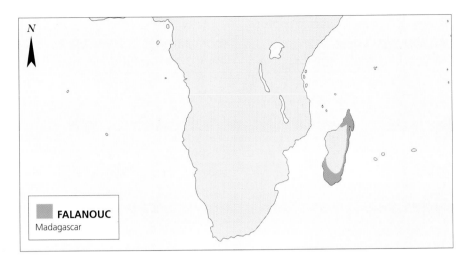

FALANOUC
Madagascar

fore have an immediate economic value to the people of Madagascar—an advantage not enjoyed by the falanouc. Not only do civets compete with the falanouc for food, but they may even prey upon their smaller cousins.

A still more direct pressure to falanouc populations is being applied by humans. The falanouc is looked on by many as a delicacy and is often trapped and eaten by people living in the region. Without further research or data about its current population, the status of the falanouc in the wild is in doubt, and, therefore, it will be hard to act on any recovery plan.

Renardo Barden

numerous. Now this animal is in decline. Habitat reduction is only part of the problem. Civets have been deliberately introduced into the falanouc's habitat, and they are natural competitors of the falanouc. In India and other places, civets are valued for the pungent fluid retained in small sacs near the genitals of both sexes. Their secretions are used to perfume the tobacco smoked by many people in certain Third World countries. Civets, there-

FALCONS

Class: Aves

Order: Falconiformes

Family: Falconidae

Falcons differ from hawks (family Accipitridae) in several conspicuous features, such as wing shape and flight behavior.

Other differences are not easily seen on wild birds but they can be noticed by examining captive birds at close range. For example, falcons have a bony plug in each nostril. The upper half of the beak has a single notch and a point on each side called a "tooth."

Falcons also have elongated outer flight feathers that give their wings a pointed appearance when they are fully spread.

Hawks have open nostrils without a plug, no tooth on the beak, and rounded wings.

While falcons are built for powerful flight, enjoying both quick and sustained speed, hawks are more suited for either quick pursuit or long, soaring flights. Falcons range in size from the sparrow-sized red-legged falconet (*Microhierax caerulescens*), weighing just 1½ ounces (43 grams), to the gyrfalcon (*Falco rusticolus*) at nearly 4½ pounds (2 kilograms).

Historically, the relationship between falcons and humans has been mixed. Some people admire the speed and power of falcon flight, while others are unfairly judgmental and disdain falcons because they eat other birds, such as songbirds.

While some human cultures protected falcons as birds of royalty, other cultures treated them as pests. They have been viewed as dangerous predators that compete for the same food as humans (falcons will prey on game birds such as ducks and pigeons), and as such have been systematically destroyed.

Falconry, an ancient sport that involves using trained falcons to hunt game birds, has reduced numbers in the wild.

Gray Falcon

(Falco hypoleucos)

IUCN: Vulnerable

Length: 13–17 in. (33–43 cm)
Weight: 12–22 oz. (335–624 g); females are heavier
Clutch size: 2–3 (rarely 4)
Incubation: Around 35 days
Diet: Birds, especially pigeons and parrots; small mammals; reptiles; large insects
Habitat: Arid and semi-arid savanna and wooded plains
Range: Breeds in interior of Australia; outside of breeding season, travels to coastal regions in northern Australia

THE DUSTY, dry plains of interior Australia have traditionally been inhospitable places for humans. Surface water is scarce and the heat of the summer sun is merci-

less. Across these vast savannas hunts the gray falcon, a bird which, like all the members of its family, shows an amazing mastery of the air in pursuit of its prey. The gray falcon will sometimes remain perched on a shaded acacia branch awaiting a movement from a lizard or small mammal. When the time is right, the falcon will glide silently from its hidden watch point to take its prey on the ground. It will soar for long periods at a great height, waiting for the opportunity to dive down onto a flying pigeon or other bird that has been oblivious of the falcon's presence.

Attractive bird

Like most falcons, the gray falcon has narrow wings and a longish tail. Its whitish underparts are marked with fine gray streaks, while its upperparts are a mix of several delicate shades of gray. Its pale gray tail shows darker gray barring and its flight feathers are almost black.

Because the recovery of the peregrine falcon has been so successful, it is no longer listed as endangered by the U.S. Fish and Wildlife Service.

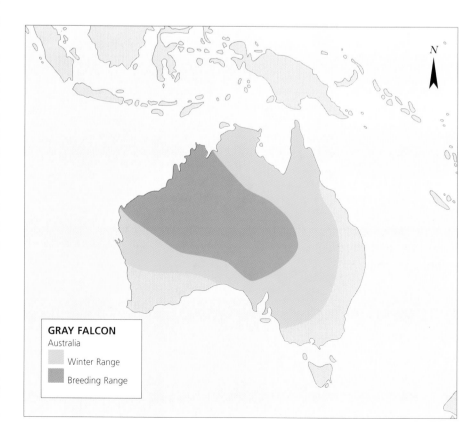

GRAY FALCON
Australia
Winter Range
Breeding Range

Altered habitat

Despite its hunting prowess, the gray falcon faces more threats than most other falcons. In recent years farmers have been successful in transforming large tracts of the acacia-dotted grasslands, which is the gray falcon's core habitat, into viable agricultural land. This trend has favored the larger peregrine falcon, which has a competitive advantage over the gray falcon. On the other hand, overgrazing by cattle has degraded some savanna country, reducing the number of nest sites and the amount of food available. In former years gray falcons were hit by the use of pesticides, which led to thinner eggshells. Like all falcons, illegal egg collecting and the taking of chicks for falconry have been continual problems. Consequently, this species is thought now to number only about 1,000 breeding pairs. In addition, its breeding range has contracted, so it is now found only within the 10-inch (250-millimeter) annual rainfall zone.

Two or three eggs are laid in a large stick nest taken over from another species, for example a crow, up to 80 feet (25 meters) above the ground. Research has shown a success rate of 1.9 fledged young per successful nest. Some dispersal of birds away from the breeding range takes place outside of the June-to-November breeding season. It is thought that the birds that migrate to winter in northern Australia are mainly juveniles.

To save the gray falcon from extinction, a number of measures need to be taken. It still retains a viable population, but the laws governing eggs and chicks need to be rigorously applied, numbers need to be monitored, and more needs to be understood about its breeding and feeding ecology if the decline is to be halted.

Northern Aplomado Falcon

(Falco femoralis septentrionalis)

ESA: Endangered

Length: 15–16½ in. (38–42 cm); females longer than males
Weight: 8–12 oz. (223–332 g); females larger than males
Clutch size: 2–3 eggs
Incubation: 28–31 days
Diet: Large insects, small reptiles, birds, small rodents
Habitat: Prairies and savannas
Range: Extreme southeastern Texas, and parts of Mexico

A GRAY BIRD bobs along just above the prairie grass. Its long, pointed, gray wings beat the air rhythmically. Its belly shines a golden rust color like a wheat field at sunrise. Startled by the passing shape, a horned lark pops into the air. Before the lark clears the grass to gain its full flight speed, a second gray bird hurtles from the sky and strikes it. The first bird swoops in to claim the carcass. A pair of northern aplomado falcons has taken another meal.

Never a common sight in the United States, the team hunting of the aplomado falcons disappeared altogether as the birds vanished from American grasslands. Recovery efforts initiated in the 1980s aim to restore the northern aplomado falcon to its remaining native habitat in the Southwest.

Bigger than an American kestrel (*Falco sparverius*) but smaller than a peregrine falcon (*Falco peregrinus*), the aplomado falcon measures just an inch or two smaller than an American crow (*Corvus brachyrhynchos*). As with all hawk and falcon species, the female is always a bit larger than the male. Aplomado falcons are uniformly gray above with a blackish tail that has a white tip and five white bands. The crown is dark gray but the forehead is buff. A white, buff white, or tawny white stripe originates behind each eye and extends backward to join on the nape. The chin, throat, and breast are white. Black patches on the side barely meet in midbreast and give the impression of an open vest. The belly is a pale tawny or a washed out cinnamon white. The yellow foot and toe are large and powerfully built, as is common for the birds of prey known as raptors. This species gets its name *aplomado* not from some geographic place but from a curious combination of Latin and Spanish. *Aplomado* may refer to the lead color of its back (in Latin, *plumbum*) or to its habit of dropping vertically on its prey just as one would drop a plumb line (in Spanish, *aplomar* or *plomado*).

A prairie bird

Northern aplomado falcons once hunted the coastal prairies of Texas. They also ranged over the dry mesquite (*Prosopis* sp.) savannas of western Texas and New Mexico. Early observers reported them in woodlands near desert grasslands. In Mexico they inhabited pine woodlands, hunting on the wing, either solo or in pairs, or watching for prey while perched on an exposed branch. Occasionally, a hungry falcon was seen to harass other birds and pirate their prey from them. Small- to medium-sized birds accounted for perhaps 90 percent of their diet; but they would take whatever was available. When breeding season arrived, the falcons searched out the abandoned nests of hawks and Chihuahuan ravens (*Corvus cryptoleucus*).

The northern aplomado falcon began disappearing in the late 1800s. By the 1940s they were nearly all north of the Mexican border. Only a few birds survived into the early 1950s in New Mexico. The causes of decline were habitat loss and degradation, leaving them nowhere to live.

Climatic changes probably altered rainfall patterns, which in turn affected their habitat. This creates pressure on a species to adapt or perish. Such changes occur over time, allowing the adaptation process to work. American cultural advances, however, changed the southwestern landscape faster than falcons could accommodate. The desire for agricultural land increased. Prairies lost their grass and became barren ground. Wheat and cotton fields extended from horizon to horizon. To force the land to yield an abun-

dance, people applied chemicals to kill damaging insects. The worst chemical was DDT.

It was not the most lethal pesticide, but DDT was so widely used in such great quantities that its influence was felt everywhere. It was found to accumulate in the body fat of animals and to kill animals who ate infected prey. Falcons are predators, so they were especially vulnerable. No research has clearly established DDT contamination as a cause of breeding problems in the northern aplomado falcon. However, breeding falcons in Veracruz had fragile, broken eggs during the 1960s and 1970s. The United States banned general DDT use in the 1970s, but Mexico and a number of Central American countries have not. The pesticide that kills more than just pests is still being used.

In a captive-breeding program in 1983, seven northern aplomado falcons produced 20 young birds in five years. Some young falcons were released in the mid-1980s on the King Ranch and Laguna Atascosa National Wildlife Refuge, both in Texas.

To ensure the continuity of the species, the U.S. Fish and Wildlife Service's recovery plan in 1989 called for 100 breeding pairs in the United States.

Peregrine Falcon
(Falco peregrinus)

Length: 16–20 in. (41–51 cm); females longer than males
Weight: Males, 19½–23½ oz. (550–660 g); females larger than males
Clutch size: 2–5 eggs
Incubation: 28–29 days
Diet: Other birds, small mammals, and insects
Habitat: Cliffs and rocky crags
Range: Every continent plus coastal and oceanic islands

THE PEREGRINE falcon is the world's most widely distributed land bird species, breeding on every continent except Antarctica. It is a great predator and possesses a matchless combination of speed, power, and maneuverability. This bird became greatly endangered and forced people to consider the acts that lead to extinction of a species. This was followed by action, which has now culminated in the falcon's successful recovery, and international attention has been focused on the plight of other species endangered by humankind.

A wanderer

Peregrine is an old word that comes from the verb *peregrinate*, meaning "to travel," especially far and abroad. This word is seldom used anymore, but the falcon keeps the name peregrine alive. It is appropriate to a species with global distribution. The species' wide range means that individuals in certain areas will show some predictable variability in

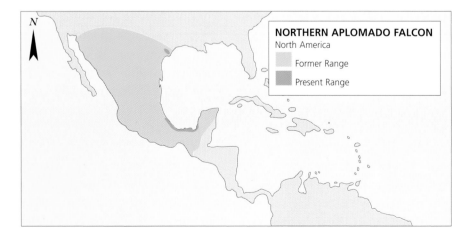

NORTHERN APLOMADO FALCON
North America
Former Range
Present Range

size or color or both. This diversity almost always leads to different interpretations of subspecies and their status.

In general there are 18 recognized subspecies of falcons, based on body differences and geography. All peregrines look much the same; they have dark upperparts ranging from pale, sandy gray to warm brown, medium gray, or dark gray. The underparts range from nearly pure white to somewhat buff, but always with distinct black or brown spots or short bars. Regardless of color, all peregrines have a hooded look created by the clean, sharp contrast of a dark cheek and light chin and throat.

In the past, not all subspecies of peregrine were equally endangered. Those in direct contact with industrial cultures suffered the most. Historically, people viewed predators either as dangerous or as competition for the same game birds. Eventually bounty systems arose in an attempt to wipe out an entire species. In areas where people found more pleasure in falcons, the birds were vulnerable to people who took eggs or nestlings to raise. Falconry is an ancient activity based on hunting game birds by using trained falcons to catch the prey. For centuries the only source of birds for this practice was wild nests.

Poisoned peregrines

Besides direct persecution, the peregrine has suffered indirectly in other ways. For instance, farmers have used strong, durable poisons for decades without considering the side effects. Because the peregrine falcon was the key species afflicted by mishandled

The peregrine falcon is found on every continent in the world, although not regularly in Antarctica. It is also seen on many coastal and some oceanic islands.

pesticides, people had to reconsider pesticide use. In researching the decline of peregrine populations, ornithologists discovered that birds living in areas thousands of miles from pesticide use were nevertheless carrying the pesticides. Most notable among these poisons was DDT. Originally used as a treatment for lice, DDT quickly came into use as an agricultural pesticide. It was sprayed in marshes and other wetlands to kill mosquitoes, on agricultural crops to kill insects, and on ornamental trees and shrubs to kill insects that blemished the foliage.

Eventually, DDT was found to accumulate in an animal's body fat. As one animal ate another, the DDT was passed along. Predators such as the peregrine falcon consumed enough poisoned prey to affect them badly. In the body, DDT interrupts calcium usage. When females lay their eggs, excessive

levels of DDT in their blood can prevent adequate calcium from being deposited in the eggshells. The thinner shells break easily and lose moisture quickly, killing the chick. Certain peregrine populations were more vulnerable to DDT than others. During the early days of the ecology movement (in the 1960s and 1970s), these inconsistent declines created debates over how to define an endangered species.

Before any deliberate action was taken on behalf of the peregrine, some populations vanished completely. Aggressive attempts to recover the peregrine led to new research and wildlife management techniques that have protected other species. Artificial brooding is perhaps the most important development. In this technique, eggs from wild peregrine nests are removed and incubated in artificial devices that compensate for water loss in the thinner shells. Artificial eggs replace the real ones in the nest so that the adult birds will continue to incubate and maintain the nesting territory. After the incubated eggs hatch, some chicks are returned to the nest for the parents to care for. Other chicks are placed on suitable nesting cliffs and fed in such a way that they do not associate people with food. After their normal fledging period, these young falcons become independent.

These techniques have boosted the wild peregrine population to near natural levels. In some areas, including the United States, the peregrine falcon is successfully recovered, and in August 1999 the Interior Department removed the bird from the endangered species list. However, many countries still use DDT and even harsher pesticides, and the peregrine falcon populations will still have to be monitored.

Kevin Cook

Taita Falcon

(Falco fasciinucha)

IUCN: Vulnerable

Length: 10–11 in. (25–28 cm)
Weight: 7½ oz. (212 g) for males; 11 oz. (306 g) for females
Clutch size: 2–4
Incubation: 31–33 days
Diet: Small birds, such as swallows and swifts, and insects
Habitat: High cliffs for breeding and roosting; hunts over semi-arid woodland and savanna
Range: Parts of Kenya, Uganda, Tanzania, Malawi, Zambia, Zimbabwe, Mozambique, and South Africa

IN THE HEAT of the midday sun, large numbers of swifts and swallows that nest in the rocky crags

of the Great Rift Valley in eastern Africa fly around thousands of feet above the lightly wooded valley bottom. Higher still, the dark silhouettes of vultures soar on stiff, motionless wings, looking for a dead animal to feast upon. Like a falling stone, a dark form materializes into a bird, its wings swept back as it plunges several hundred feet to capture one of the swallows. It carries its prey off to a nearby rocky ledge, flying with stiff, shallow wingbeats, somewhat reminiscent of a parrot. Its underparts, including most of the underside to its wings, are a rich rufous color.

This predator is a beautiful bird, the rufous of its breast marked with small dark chevrons, dark gray upperparts contrasting with small reddish patches on the head, a paler gray rump, and

The taita falcon (*Falco fasciinucha*) is a beautiful bird of prey. Its distinguishing features are a rich rufous-colored chest, small red patches on the head, and bright yellow legs.

bright yellow legs. This is a taita falcon, a bird with an extensive but very broken distribution in eastern and southern Africa.

Flying hunter

Birds of prey use a variety of strategies to catch their prey, and the taita falcon is one of a group of aerial predators that hunt their food entirely on the wing. It is a relatively small bird of prey, but nevertheless seems perfectly adapted to this way of life. It is only known from a small number of sites in one part of Africa, while others from its genus are widely distributed across the continent. The reasons for this

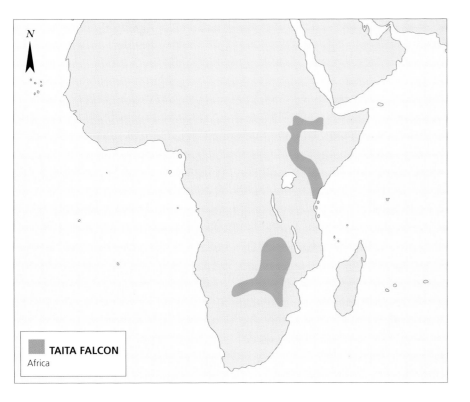

N

TAITA FALCON
Africa

It is possible that many taita falcon nests remain undiscovered because they are so inaccessible, and population estimates may be heavily understated. For example, although this falcon is thought to be widespread in very small numbers in Malawi, there are few definite records, while even in Zimbabwe only 50 breeding locations are known.

Pesticide problem

The taita falcon is a bird that feeds over wooded terrain, so deforestation may have reduced its numbers, and there is evidence from northern Zimbabwe that pesticide spraying has eradicated a section of the population by rendering it infertile. However, apart from controlling the use of damaging pesticides, it is difficult to construct a viable conservation policy for the species until more accurate estimates of its population exist.

Tim Harris

are thought to be because the taita falcon requires a highly specific habitat for nesting and roosting on high cliffs and gorges. Birds nest in a scrape or stick nest at the back of a shaded crevice in the cliff face up to 12,500 feet (3,800 meters) above sea level. Clearly this specialized nesting requirement limits its range, and there is also evidence that the species faces competition from its larger relative, the peregrine falcon, for these sites.

FERNS

Phylum: Pteridophyta

The fronds (leaves) of ferns have an astounding variety of shapes and sizes: some are undivided, others may be very finely dissected and lacy. They can range in length from just a few millimeters to about 23 feet (7 meters). The genus *Marsilea* has four-lobed fronds that look like lucky clover, while quillworts (the genus *Isoetes*) resemble tufts of grass or rush.

Ferns number some 12,000 different species and are found in all parts of the world. Most are found in tropical and temperate rain forests, although their full range of habitats is much wider, including sea cliffs, lakes, rivers, marshes, forests, moorland, rock crevices, screes, walls, and urban wasteland. They may be terrestrial, rock-dwelling, epiphytic (growing on other plants), or aquatic.

Ferns do not bear flowers or fruit but instead have a two-stage life cycle: the adult fern plant produces thousands of dustlike spores that under favorable conditions develop into small, mosslike prothallia (the gametophyte generation), in which male and female gametes, or sexual cells (equivalent to ovules and pollen in seed plants), unite to produce embryos that develop into new ferns (the sporophyte generation).

Many ferns are versatile, able to colonize disturbed habitats or even entirely human-made structures such as brick or stone walls. However, others are highly specialized and can survive only in particular natural habitats that are easily damaged by human activity. Such species may be seriously threatened with extinction. For example, the drainage of seasonal pools and shallow lakes destroys habitat needed by many species of quillworts, while the clearing of rain forests eliminates fern species that are unable to tolerate exposed, sunny conditions. Other species are vulnerable because they have small populations with limited distributions, like *Marsilea villosa*, which is restricted to Hawaii.

Alabama Streak-sorus Fern

(Thelypteris pilosa var. *alabamensis)*

ESA: Threatened

IUCN: Endangered

Class: Filicatae
Family: Thelypteridaceae
Subgenus: Stegnogramma
Fronds: Evergreen, 4–18 in. (10–46 cm) long and 1–2½ in. (3–6 cm) broad
Reproduction: Sori lacking protective indusia are produced along the veins
Habitat: Epipetric on sandstone cliffs
Range: Endemic to Winston County in northern Alabama

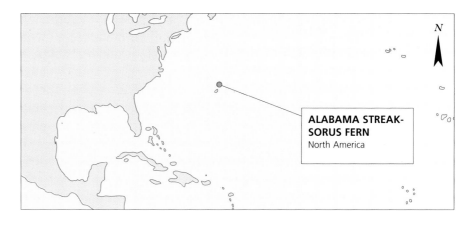

ALABAMA STREAK-SORUS FERN
North America

THE SUN SLOWLY RISES above a shallow river bordered by sandstone cliffs in what is now northern Alabama. There is something very strange about this place: tropical birds glide overhead; liverworts, tree ferns, and large palms line the sides of the sleepy river. Closer inspection reveals numerous tropical fern species covering the rocks, trees, and sandstone riverbanks. This scene is indeed odd, for it existed during the Eocene some 50 million years ago when much of the current southeastern United States exhibited a frost-free subtropical flora. This area was radically changed by the Pleistocene glaciation, which drove most of these tropical plants to extinction or pushed their distributions farther south into Mexico and South America.

Many of these sandstone cliffs, however, had eroded into what we now call rock houses. These semicircular cave-like recesses provided enough shelter from the cold glacier winds for a small number of species to survive. One of these species was the Alabama streak-sorus fern.

Taxonomy and distribution

Thelypteris pilosa belongs to the subgenus *Stegnogramma*, of which only this single species is known to occur in the New World. The species ranges from Honduras through northwestern Mexico and to the United States. This New World species has been separated into three varieties: two in Central America and Mexico, and one in Alabama. The Alabama streak-sorus fern, which is known as variety *alabamensis*, occurs only in a single county in the state of Alabama. All other members of the subgenus (about 15) occur in the Old World tropics. This unusual distribution has called into question the current taxonomic standing of the New World plants.

Recent scientific investigations have shown that the plants in Alabama and Mexico are very different from each other. Thus, it has been proposed that the Alabama streak-sorus fern is unusual enough to merit its elevation from varietal status to that of a species.

Species threats

If ever a happy story exists about an endangered plant, that of the Alabama streak-sorus fern is such a one. In 1918, Congress established the Alabama National Forest, which later became known as the Bankhead National Forest. Little did the lawmakers know that they were also protecting a yet unknown fern species. In 1949 the Alabama streak-sorus fern was discovered along the Black Warrior River within the national forest boundaries. Unfortunately, in 1969 a bridge was constructed that crossed the river and destroyed the only known population of this rare species. It was not until 1978 that the species was rediscovered 8 miles upstream. Since its rediscovery, the fern has been found to exist in 17 populations along the Black Warrior River. In another stroke of luck, in 1975 Congress established a national wilderness area where many of the current populations exist. With construction prohibited on the river, the Alabama streak-sorus fern will remain an intriguing species.

Eddie Watkins

Aleutian Shield Fern

(Polystichum aleuticum)

ESA: Endangered

IUCN: Endangered

Class: Pteropsida
Order: Filicales
Family: Dryopteridaceae
Height: Fronds to 7 in.
(18 cm) long
Fronds: Grass green in a
shuttlecock arrangement with
chestnut brown persistent
stalks (rachis) sparsely covered
in tan scales, which fall off
before the frond matures
Reproduction: Spores are
produced in the upper part of
the fronds in July and August
Habitat: Rock crevices from sea
level to about 1,300 ft. (400 m)
altitude
Range: Atka and Adak
Islands, Alaska

ALEUTIAN SHIELD FERN is probably one of the least well known
ferns in the world. Until recently
it was one of a select group of
plants that were known only from
the original collection and had
never been seen again. In many
cases this is because the plants'
habitat has been destroyed, due
in part to the logging of the
world's rain forests, but in some
cases it is just that these species
grow in very remote areas that
have been rarely visited by the
specialists who might identify
them. The latter was the case for
the Aleutian shield fern. It was
discovered in July 1932 on Atka
Island by a small party organized
by botanist Eric Hultén, who was

then in the process of gathering
information for the first complete
flora of Alaska and the Aleutian
Islands. The Aleutians form an
extensive arching archipelago
extending from the Alaska Peninsula to Kamchatka, thus dividing
the Bering Sea from the Pacific
Ocean. Atka and Adak Islands
are two of many small islands
that lie roughly halfway along this
archipelago. It is interesting to
speculate whether Hultén's assis-
tant, J. W. Eyerdam from Seattle,
realized the significance of the
small piece of fern, with its three
small fronds and battered old
stalks, when he dug it up and

popped it in his collecting bag.
But for those studying plant distributions and how they have
come about, the Aleutian shield
fern is of considerable interest. It
is unlike any of the other shield
fern species in North America.
So much so that when described,
the author worried whether it
should be included in the genus
Polystichum or the related genus
Dryopteris (wood ferns). However, it is very similar to some
dwarfed *Polystichum* species from

Little is known about the perennial
Aleutian shield fern, which inhabits
remote areas of the world. Because of
its rarity alone, it is worth conserving.

527

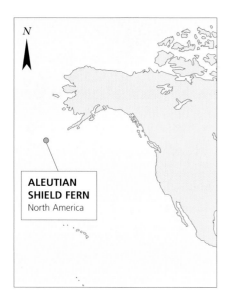

ALEUTIAN SHIELD FERN
North America

the mountains of southwestern China and the Himalayas, particularly *P. kruckebergii*, from which it differs only in its smaller, more rounded leaflets and scalier stalks. Like the islands it inhabits, it forms a link between Asia and America.

Description

Each frond consists of 15 to 25 pairs of sessile to shortly stalked, slightly overlapping leaflets or pinnae. These are 4 to 8 mm long, with toothed margins. The spore-producing structures (sporangia) cluster together in groups termed sori. Each of the upper leaflets of the plant has one sorus (rarely two) on its undersurface, this is protected by a flap of tissue, the indusium. The indusium is greenish and has a round to oval shape, with a ragged toothed margin and an off-center point of attachment. The spores are brown.

The species is so poorly known and the area of its occurrence so restricted that it must be considered of conservation concern. It is unlikely that it is in cultivation.

Fred Rumsey

Asplenium-leaved Diellia

(Diellia erecta)

ESA: Endangered

IUCN: Endangered

Height: 12 in. (30 cm)
Stems: Usually 3–9 stems up to 28 in. (70 cm) long, with up to 50 oppositely paired leaflets
Fronds: Brown to black central midrib, lanceolate
Reproduction: By spores
Habitat: Lowland forest
Range: Molokai, Maui, and Hawaii; historically also Kauai, Oahu, and Lanai

ASPLENIUM-LEAVED DIELLIA was first collected in 1840, but it was not formally described until 1854. Shortly after this another species of *Diellia*, *D. pumilla*, was described. It is now realized that

D. pumilla is merely an example of *D. erecta* with finely dissected fronds. *D. erecta* has been placed in two other genera since its discovery, and it is sometimes still recorded under these other names. These names are *Lindsaya erecta* and *Schizoloma erecta*. All of these fern genera are members of the spleenwort family.

The fronds, which emerge from a small darkly scaled rhizome buried underground, are lanceolate with brown to black central midribs, a common feature within the spleenworts. Along the midrib there are up to 50 small leaves (pinnae) oppositely arranged. These pinnae are up to 1½ inches (4 centimeters) long, and on their underside can be found the spore-bearing structures protected by their covers, the sori. The sori can be fused or separate and distinguish this species from the other members of the genus. Historically *Diellia erecta* was found in several sites

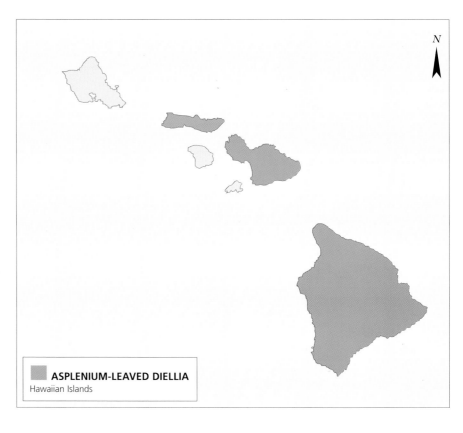

ASPLENIUM-LEAVED DIELLIA
Hawaiian Islands

on Hawaii, the Koolau mountains of Oahu, the Kokee area of Kauai, and several sites on Molokai, Lanai, and West Maui. The current distribution is somewhat less than this. Only three islands still support this species—Hawaii, Maui, and Molokai. Hawaii boasts two populations on state-controlled land; one population has 20 individuals whereas the other has only one plant. Maui has 38 plants at 7 sites, and 4 of these sites occur on private land. Molokai has 4 sites, but the number of individuals is unknown. All told there are 13 known populations across the state with a minimum of 63 individuals, although this figure in reality is probably higher.

All of the populations are found in lowland forest at an altitude of between 700 and 5,200 feet (210 and 1,580 meters). Like other endangered species on the Hawaiian Islands, the threats associated with continued survival are chiefly from habitat destruction caused by populations of cattle, pigs, and goats. Other hardships include competition with non-native species and a reduced future viability due to loss of genetic variation. On the positive side for the future of this species is the fact that the plant is spread over several islands. This may help the species survive if any natural disaster destroys whole populations on any one island.

Many species of *Diellia* have proven amenable to growth under artificial conditions, and it is hoped that future growth of this species will allow out- planting of cultivated samples into suitable habitats.

Gordon Rutter

Black-spored Quillwort

(Isoetes melanospora)

ESA: Endangered

Class: Lycopodiopsida
Order: Isoetales
Family: Isoetaceae
Height: Up to 4 in. (10 cm)
Leaves: Bright green arranged spirally around central rootstock
Reproduction: Spore cases (sporangia) containing thousands of microspores (male) or dozens of megaspores (female) are imbedded in the basal, inner side of fertile leaves (sporophylls); the minute (26–31 μm) microspores are covered in low tubercles, while the tiny (350–480 μm), dark gray to black megaspores are covered with low tubercles and mounds
Habitat: Vernal pools in open granite bedrock outcrops
Range: Western and central Georgia; northern South Carolina

THE DEMANDING environmental conditions of the granite bedrock outcrop habitat of the black-spored quillwort eliminates all but a few exceptionally durable vascular plant species. This small pteridophyte (fern ally) is an inconspicuous member of an exclusive association of plants and animals found in vernal pools that temporarily occupy broad, shallow depressions (weather pits) in the open rock face. These so-called flat rocks are ancient habitats, 6 million

years or more in the making. They endure punishing heat and drought in summer and killing frost in winter. For a short period in the rainy, temperate spring, though, the pools fill with water and explode with life. Black-spored quillwort is locally abundant in flat-rock pools, sometimes constituting virtually the only vascular plant life. After a few weeks of rapid growth and development, however, the increasing heat of summer dries up the pools, kills new plant growth, and returns the weather pits to their apparently lifeless condition for another year.

The black-spored quillwort is much like its nearby relative, the mat-forming quillwort (*Isoetes tegetiformans*), in many characteristics. Like its even rarer cousin, black-spored quillwort can form dense, lawn-like mats and have a distichous arrangement of leaves (in ranks, not spiraled), but in this species those are considered to be characteristics of immature populations. Typical mature black-spored quillwort plants grow individually and eventually demonstrate the spiral leaf pattern of all other North American species. Melanistic megaspores are typical of black-spored quill-

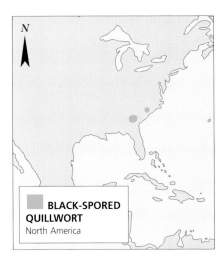

BLACK-SPORED QUILLWORT
North America

Black-spored quillwort is fighting for survival against quarrying activities and habitat destruction.

Diellia Falcata

ESA: Endangered

IUCN: Endangered

Height: Up to 3 ft. (1 m)
Stems: Brown, scaled at base, darker and smoother farther up the frond
Fronds: Up to 10 fronds each with up to 50 pinnae
Reproduction: By spores
Habitat: Lowland forest, less then 1,970 ft. (600 m) altitude
Range: Oahu, Hawaiian Islands

wort and are unknown in other North American species.

There were 11 populations of black-spored quillworts known in the southeastern Unites States, all in Georgia with the exception of one disjunct population in South Carolina. The latter is physically distinct from all other black-spored quillwort populations in several ways and may represent a separate taxon. Whatever their infraspecific relationships were, however, 5 of the 11 known black-spored quillwort populations have been destroyed in recent years. Most remaining populations have been variously impacted by rock quarrying, recreational abuse (especially all-terrain vehicle traffic), road building, and refuse dumping.

An Olympic solution

Most populations of black-spored quillwort occur in the heavily developed and expanding Atlanta area of central Georgia and are found in sites exposed to frequent public access. The population from which the species was originally described in the mid 19th century is situated by major recreational facilities in the heavily used Stone Mountain Memorial Park. Improved protection (fencing) was put in place in response to the enlargement of those facilities for the 1996 Olympic Games, however, and the population has actually increased in size in recent years. This simple response may be the key to the protection of other black-spored quillwort populations.

As with all other flat-rock plant and animal species, the quarrying of the granite bedrock outcrops continues to be the main cause of the destruction of their essential habitat. Only two to four black-spored quillwort populations are considered to be in a healthy state.

Like its close relative the mat-forming quillwort, the long-term prognosis for the black-spored quillwort is bleak indeed without an immediate conservation and protection program for all viable populations.

Daniel F. Brunton

A SYNONYM OF *Diellia falcata* is *Diellia erecta* var. *falcata*. Although some literature may refer to it by this name, it is now accepted that the name used here is the correct one. This is a distinct species, although it does have many similarities with *Diellia erecta*. This plant belongs to the fern family Aspleniaceae, the spleenworts. *Diellia falcata* grows in tufts with up to 10 fronds on each plant. From each frond there are up to 50 small leaves (pinnae) arranged oppositely. On the edges of the pinnae are the spore-producing sori, which are variable in number.

This is the most common of the six known species of *Diellia*. The exact population size is unknown, although a recovery plan is currently in development. The fern can be found in a number of lowland forest sites throughout the Hawaiian island of Oahu. It is believed that the historical distribution was much larger and that a steady decline has occurred in the numbers of this species. It was not until 1991 that this plant was listed as being endangered. The main threats are associated with activities of people in the area, competition with non-native species, and with the pressure associated with grazing from various animals. The majority of the animals posing a threat are introduced species such as goats. Some threat is related to land development. The majority of the land on which the *Diellia falcata* is known to occur is publicly owned national parks, but it is also known to occur on some military and private land. The work being carried out on this species is not as extensive as on other *Diellia* species, purely

Diellia falcata's fronds typically have up to fifty pinnae arranged oppositely.

because of the smaller threat. It should be remembered, however, that any species that is endemic to a small island is always at risk from natural disasters, particularly if the island is of an active volcanic nature.

The future of this plant

Research continues on the growth requirements of this species, and since it has proven possible to grow it under artificial conditions, it is hoped that future work will lead to a successful reintroduction plan. Many appropriate habitats for reintroduction exist, particularly in nature reserves. With successful cultivation and a wide choice of habitats, as well as a moderate natural population, the future for

DIELLIA FALCATA
Hawaiian Islands

this plant should be secured. With more individuals than any other *Diellia* species, there is less of a threat from loss of genetic diversity, which is the true measure of how successful a species will be in the future.

Diellia Laciniata

IUCN: Endangered

Height: Up to 24 in. (60 cm)
Stems: 2–5 present
Reproduction: By spores
Habitat: Mixed mesic forest, at elevations of approximately 1,970 ft. (600 m)
Range: Waimea canyon, western Kauai

DIELLIA LACINIATA
Hawaiian Islands

THERE IS no common name for *Diellia laciniata* although it is sometimes called Ida's fern. The taxonomy of this species is very confusing. Some authors regard it as a separate species, whereas others regard it as a subspecies or even merely a variant of *Diellia erecta*. To further add to the confusion, when *Diellia laciniata* was first recorded and published, it was classified as *Lindsaya falcata*. For the purpose of this account, *Diellia laciniata* is being treated as a separate species. If this is not the case, then it is true that due to the geographical isolation of the two *Diellia erecta* species, we are seeing incipient speciation. In other words with continued separation the two forms will eventually diverge sufficiently to produce two distinct species.

Diellia laciniata has fused sori. The sori are groupings of spore-producing cells on the underside of the leaves of a fern. The bases of the fronds of this species are covered in black cells. Breeding experiments done in the early 1950s at the University of California, Berkeley, showed that these characters are true breeding; that is to say, they appear generation after generation.

Threats

It is impossible to say with any certainty how many individuals of this species exist because of the taxonomic confusion. However, the numbers are exceedingly low. The threats suffered by *Diellia laciniata* are the same as those suffered by all the other endemic species of *Diellia* in Hawaii, namely competition with non-native species of plants for resources and space, grazing from alien species such as goats, a small amount of risk from human activity such as road and facility building, and finally the risks associated with natural disasters. This last risk is problematical in that all the wild individuals can be destroyed in only one single event. Since it is possible to grow *Diellia laciniata* in cultivation, there is a means of suitable recovery. However, before artificial reintroductions can be done, it is vital that more information be gathered about this species and its relation to other species. In particular the true relationship between *Diellia laciniata* and *Diellia erecta* needs to be divined; it is also important to figure out how *Diellia falcata* and *Diellia pallida*, which are very

similar to the other two species, fit in as well.

Measures to preserve the current known specimens should be encouraged (they are living on a relatively well protected nature reserve), but more work needs to be done before a full-scale recovery plan can be initiated.

If reintroduction is attempted before the full truth of the situation is known, there is a possibility that two distinct species will be put at risk.

Diellia Pallida

ESA: Endangered

IUCN: Endangered

Stems: 2 to 5 produced,
Fronds: Oblong lanceolate up to 24 in. (60 cm) long and 8 in. (20 cm) wide
Reproduction: By spores
Habitat: Dry rocky soils
Range: Koaie Stream valley and historically in Mahanaloa and Paaiki Valleys, western Kauai

THE CLOSEST LIVING relative to *Diellia pallida* is *D. falcata*. They can be distinguished by the fact that the base of *D. pallida* is only very sparsely scaly, whereas the latter species is densely scaly over the whole surface. On *Diellia pallida* the scales, when present, have very thin walls and are confined to the base of the stem. The midribs of the fronds are dark, a characteristic of this plant's family. The pinnae are simple and straight-margined (pinnae are the smallest subdivision of leaves on a fern frond). The sori (protective covers for the spores on the underside of leaves) are variable in shape. Sori are normally characteristic for particular species or genera. *D. pallida* was originally described in 1888 as a variety of *Lindsaya laciniata*. Various taxonomic changes and extra study resulted in the decision that *D. pallida* was a new species in a different genus.

This species is the lightest-colored member of the genus *Diellia*. The other species in this group bear black cells on the surface. These are absent on *D. pallida* even when it is grown under cultivation (this was first shown in the early 1950s). This species was first recognized in the Mahanaloa and Paaiki Valleys of western Kauai in the 1940s. Subsequently it proved impossible to find in these areas, and it was assumed it had become extinct in the wild. In 1987 a new location was discovered in the Koaie Stream valley on the eastern side of Waimea Canyon. This site was found at a height of 1,970 feet (600 meters), 5½ miles (9 kilometers) from the original locations. It should be stressed

that upon its discovery this site contained only a small number of mature plants on a steep slope at the base of a tree. In the adjacent area some immature plants were also found.

The main threat to the continuation of this plant is competition from alien species. Also problematical are feral goats. There is a limited amount of predation, but feral goats tend to erode the steep land on which the ferns live.

This rare fern has a very limited distribution. With only a few small examples known, it is very difficult to ascertain the true potential range, and since the species was first recorded in 1947, the historical range is of little help. The small numbers extant will potentially cause difficulties in the future because of a reduced genetic variation within the population.

It is possible to grow this species in cultivation, but if out-planting is attempted in unsuitable habitats, the work will be wasted. More information is needed to maximize the resources that are available and to give the greatest chance of success to reintroduction of this species.

Diellia Unisora

ESA: Endangered

IUCN: Endangered

Class: Filicopsida
Order: Filicales
Family: Aspleniaceae
Fronds: 3–12 in. (8–30 cm) tall, 1 in. (2.5 cm) wide
Habitat: Dry forest
Range: Oahu, Hawaiian Islands

THE GENUS *DIELLIA* is entirely endemic to the Hawaiian Islands. It contains six species, two of which are probably extinct, and only one of which is currently widespread. It is a genus with a recent origin, since it arose and radiated after the formation of the Hawaiian Islands, and this offers potential for research into the processes of speciation.

Appearance

Diellia unisora is a small perennial fern with an erect rhizome up to 1 inch (2.5 centimeters) tall and up to 10 millimeters in diameter. The rhizome is covered with the bases of old leaf stalks and a few black scales. The linear fronds are held on shiny black stocks and reach a height of 3 to 12 inches (8 to 30 centimeters) and a width of up to 1 inch (2.5 centimeters). The fronds have 20 to 35 pairs of pinnae, or leaflets, which gradually narrow toward the tip of the frond. The pinnae are strongly asymmetrical, with smooth margins. Spores are produced in a single sorus on the upper margin of the underside of each pinna.

D. unisora occurs on the island of Oahu, which was formed by

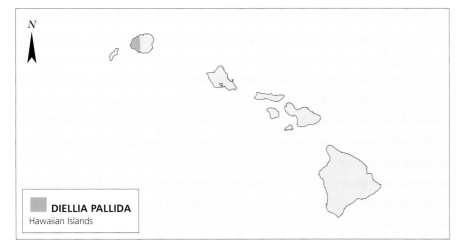

DIELLIA PALLIDA
Hawaiian Islands

N

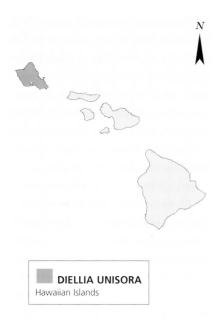

DIELLIA UNISORA
Hawaiian Islands

two large shield volcanoes that now form long, narrow mountain ridges. This plant grows on the western range of the Waianae Mountains, which lie in the rain shadow of the parallel Koolau Range. The Waianae Mountains receive 20 to 75 inches (50 to 190 centimeters) of annual rainfall, with only the summit area of Mt. Kaala receiving the higher values.

D. unisora typically grows in deep shade or open understory in dry forests at elevations of 1,740 to 2,490 feet (530 to 760 meters). It occurs on mossy slopes in rocky soil. Associated species include koa, *Metrosideros polymorpha*, strawberry guava, *Psidium cattleianum*, and a mixture of other alien and native vegetation.

Distribution

Historically this plant occurred on the slopes of the western side of the Waianae Mountains on Oahu. It is currently known to be extant at three localities in the southern region of the Waianae Mountains, in the South Ekahanui Gulch, the Palawai Gulch,

and the Paulii-Napepeiauolelo Ridge. These populations are contained in about 2 miles (3 kilometers) of land in part privately owned and in part owned by the Lualualei Naval Reservation. A total of 700 to 755 individuals exist.

Threats

The most serious threat faced by *Diellia unisora* comes from competing alien vegetation. *Schinus terebinthifolius*, an aggressive tree that was introduced as an ornamental in 1911, forms dense stands in the southern Waianae Mountains, displacing native vegetation. Likewise, *Psidium cattleianum*, the strawberry guava, can form dense growth, excluding other plants in the region where *D. unisora* exists. *Passiflora suberosa* is another immediate threat to some of the populations of *D. unisora*, because its vine habit can smother smaller plants.

Another threat comes from feral pigs, which have been present in the Waianae Mountains for 150 years. The activities of feral pigs, such as rooting and trampling the forest floor, can damage native vegetation, as well as encourage alien plant invasions. Feral pigs can also aid in dispersing non-native seeds, particularly those of berries. Finally, some populations are threatened by disturbances from military activities.

A recovery plan has been drafted for this species. It includes research into the life cycle and detailed surveys of the remaining populations of plants. Plans are also in existence to control fires and feral animals and to conduct weeding experiments.

Gordon Rutter

'Ihi'ihi ('Ihi'ihilauakea)

(Marsilea villosa)

ESA: Endangered

IUCN: Endangered

Class: Filicopsida
Order: Marsileales
Family: Marsileaceae
Height: 4–6 in. (10–15 cm)
Habitat: Cyclically flooding and drying mudflats
Range: Oahu and Niihau, Hawaiian Islands

MARSILEA VILLOSA is an aquatic fern that can also grow on land and survive periods of drought. It is a perennial with a creeping rhizome. This rhizome is villous (covered in reddish hairs), from which the plant takes its species name. Fronds rise from the rhizome on stalks or stipes that are from 4 to 6 inches (10 to 15 centimeters) long. The stalk is topped by a whorl of four terminal entire pinnae (leaflets), giving the frond a cloverlike appearance. When growing in water the fronds are hairless, the stalk is soft, and the leaflets float on the surface. The dry-land form produces short, stout stalks and the fronds are covered in hairs.

The reproductive structures of this fern are spore capsules known as sporangia. They are located in hard, bean-shaped structures called sporocarps, which rise from the rhizome on short stalks near the base of the fronds. The structures that hold the spores, called sori, are located inside the sporocarp on a gelatinous receptacle that absorbs water and bursts the sporocarp wall when mature. This receptacle can expand to many times the length of the sporocarp. Two rows of seven sori occur in each sporocarp. Each sori contains one megaspore and several microspores.

Life cycle

Marsilea is an unusual genus among the ferns because it is heterosporous (produces microspores and megaspores). In heterosporous ferns female and male gametophytes are produced from separate spores. Most other ferns produce only one type of spore; these develop into bisexual gametophytes. A gametophyte is an individual that has alternating generations bearing sex organs. *Marsilea* is also unusual because the gametophytes, which are the sexually reproductive stage of the life cycle equivalent to flowering plants, are completely contained within the spores. In most ferns the gametophyte stage of the life cycle is a small free-living photosynthetic plant body.

When the sporocarp of *Marsilea villosa* is mature and the receptacle has absorbed water and burst the sporocarp walls, megaspores and microspores are released and sink. The megaspore

The leaflets of 'Ihi'ihi (*Marsilea villosa*) are clover-like.

germinates inside the megasporangium and forms a single archegonium, which is the female reproductive structure. The microspores germinate and form antheridia (male organs) that produce free-swimming sperm cells.

Habitat and distribution

Marsilea villosa is adapted to grow in regions that alternately flood and dry out. An aquatic environment is necessary for reproduction, even though the sporocarps can remain dormant for decades; they seldom germinate in nature before at least two or three years.

Historically, *Marsilea villosa* occurred in at least 11 locations on Oahu, Molokai, and Niihau. Today it no longer exists on Molokai, and only five populations remain on Oahu and Niihau. It is possible that this species exists as sporocarps at other locations, and because of this trait exact surveys are difficult. The most dense remaining population is on a floodplain on Koko Head, near the city of Honolulu, where the plant forms a thick mat to the exclusion of other vegetation for ½ acre (0.2 hectares). This land is owned by the city and managed by the Nature Conservancy of Hawaii.

Threats

Marsilea villosa is threatened by changes in land management such as draining so that standing water never occurs. Animals and off-road vehicles can also do damage by tearing up clumps and allowing open space for alien plants to become established. *Marsilea villosa* cannot tolerate dense shade, so tree planting can interfere with its survival. Also, it cannot survive dry-season fires.

Christina Oliver

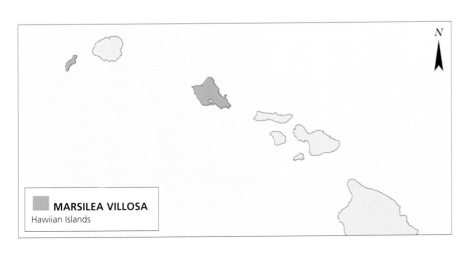

MARSILEA VILLOSA
Hawiian Islands

N

Louisiana Quillwort

(Isoetes louisianensis)

ESA: Endangered

IUCN: Endangered

Class: Lycopsida
Order: Isoetales
Family: Isoeteaceae
Leaves: Pale green, flaccid, thin, 10–16 in. (25–40 cm) long, arranged spirally around a central lobed rootstock
Reproduction: Spore cases (sporangia) containing thousands of minute microspores (male) or dozens of megaspores (female) are imbedded in the basal, inner side of fertile leaves (sporophylls)
Habitat: Emergent sandy clay banks and shoals along intermittent channels of sluggish streams in deciduous swamp forests
Range: Coastal plain of southeastern Louisiana and southern Mississippi

LOUISIANA QUILLWORT, an inconspicuous pteridophyte (fern ally) is found along cool, shallow creeks in quiet, deeply shaded, deciduous forest swamps. Such sites are often overtopped by giant oaks (*Quercus* spp.) and by bald cypress (*Taxodium distichum*), that quintessential symbol of swamps in the Deep South. The exotic nature of such habitat is underscored by the names of the often ancient deciduous trees that make up the dense Louisiana swamp forest canopy, including sweetbay mag-nolia (*Magnolia virginiana*), loblolly pine (*Pinus taeda*), blackgum (*Nyssa biflora*) and most particularly, laurel oak (*Quercus laurifolia*). Such sites echo the ringing calls of the brilliant prothonotary warbler, the brief, explosive song of the acadian flycatcher, and the occasional low hooting of the barred owl. This is a habitat where humans are clearly out of place.

Growing conditions

Louisiana quillworts grow in stands ranging in size from a dozen or so to thousands of individuals in very shallow water or, more frequently, on the wet, emergent sandy clay of lower banks, shoals, and intermittent side channels of woodland streams.

Mature plants are formed in late spring (April). While the peak of development normally occurs between April and early June, spore-bearing plants will continue to develop into early fall if sufficient water continues to flow in their shallow creek habitat. Most populations simply shrivel up in the intense midsummer heat, however, emerging anew in the cooler days of November and December.

The creeks inhabited by Louisiana quillwort are disaster prone. They are deeply flooded from time to time and are periodically heavily scoured by the floodwaters accompanying intense tropical storms moving northward across the Gulf of Mexico. Quillworts are sustained on their exposed creek bank locations through such times by being anchored into the densely intertwined tree rootlet mats that bind the creek bank together.

Poor competitor

Surprisingly, such impacts are actually to the quillwort's benefit. Louisiana quillwort, like most swamp quillworts in the southeastern United States, is a poor competitor. It would be quickly overwhelmed for growing space by other aquatic and even upland vascular plants were it not for the periodic renewal of its habitat. These disasters actually enhance the site by removing competing

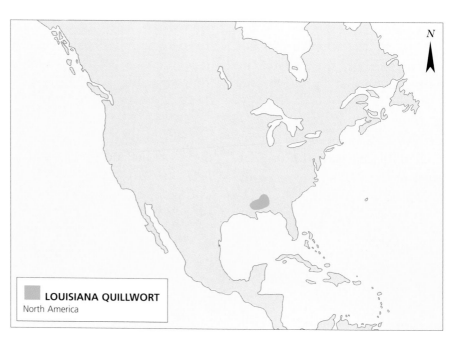

LOUISIANA QUILLWORT
North America

Louisiana quillwort (*Isoetes louisianensis*) is an inconspicuous plant that grows in shallow water. It can even survive floods by anchoring onto tree rootlet mats.

vascular plant growth, pushing back encroaching upland vegetation, creating new exposed sandbank habitat, distributing organic material throughout the quillwort stand, and even distributing plants along the stream.

Late discovery

Sequestered unobtrusively deep in its swamp habitat, Louisiana quillwort was not even discovered until the early 1970s. For years after this it was known only from a handful of sites, all on private lands, along Thigpen Creek in Louisiana.

Considerable concern was felt for its long-term viability as logging, water-quality degradation from agricultural runoff, wetland in-filling, and even beaver damming activity continued to reduce the necessary swamp forest wetland habitat of the species in this area.

Populations

The discovery of several additional populations in Desoto National Forest in adjacent Mississippi in 1996 substantially reduced the level of concern for the survival of the species. More encouraging yet, stream surveys by field botanist Steve Leonard and other workers within the Camp Shelby area of the national forest have since turned up dozens of new populations.

There are now 60 known Louisiana quillwort populations supporting about 16,000 plants in Camp Shelby and another 10,000 or more plants from elsewhere in the national forest. Populations of this species have now been found in ten counties in southern Mississippi alone.

The Atlantic coastal plain in the southeastern United States is rich in endemic plant species. Dozens of unique organisms have evolved over the last million years or so as vast areas of wetland and lowland habitat arose from the warm, subtropical seawater of the Gulf of Mexico. The Louisiana quillwort is one of the most geographically restricted of these. Its confined range in a common habitat suggests that it may also be a relatively new evolutionary experiment. Time will tell if it is a successful one, but the recent discovery of so many new populations within its range is grounds for considerable optimism. If after a 10-year monitoring program Louisiana quillwort can be shown to be flourishing in at least 10 separate watersheds, it will be considered for removal from the endangered species list in the United States.

Daniel F. Brunton

Mat-forming Quillwort

(Isoetes tegetiformans)

ESA: Endangered

IUCN: Endangered

Class: Lycopodiopsida
Order: Isoetales
Family: Isoetaceae
Height: To 2 in. (5 cm)
Leaves: Straight, bright green leaves arranged in ranks (distichously) along the rootstock
Reproduction: Spore cases (sporangia) containing thousands of microspores (male) or dozens of megaspores (female) are imbedded in the basal, inner side of fertile leaves (sporophylls); the dust-sized (26–33 μm) microspores are covered in spines while the tiny dark gray (275–375 μm) megaspores are covered with low, distinct tubercles
Habitat: Vernal pools in open granite bedrock outcrops
Range: Central Georgia

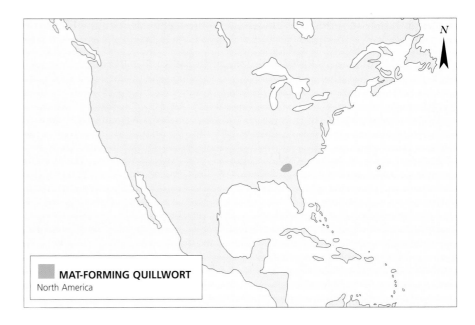

MAT-FORMING QUILLWORT
North America

THE MAT-FORMING QUILLWORT is an easily overlooked species, being a small, short-lived, and inconspicuous element of an inhospitable habitat. Indeed, it was only recognized as a distinct species in 1968. It grows for a brief period of time in broad, shallow pits eroded out of the face of open granite bedrock outcrops. These depressions are partially filled by a thin layer of sterile, acidic sand and gravel, the end result of thousands of years of bedrock weathering and the accumulation of wind-borne debris. Indeed, in his pioneering study of granite bedrock outcrop vegetation in the southeastern United States, Rogers McVaugh estimated that such mat-forming quillwort habitat was at least 6 million years old. For all those years, the flat rocks, as they are known, have endured unprotected exposure to the extremes of wind, sun, cold, and rain. The bedrock there virtually roasts under a brutally hot summer sun, with ground temperatures reaching more than 140 degrees Fahrenheit (60 degrees Centigrade). The bedrock is also splintered and cracked by frost in the subsequent cold spells of winter. Except in seepage areas where surface water collects after rainstorms, this is a bone-dry, desert habitat in which only scattered grasses, clumps of cacti (*Opuntia* spp.), and a tiny list of other remarkably durable herbs can endure.

Brief opportunity

Plant growth can occur only during the period of relatively cool temperatures that coincides with the late winter/early spring rainy season. The peak of development for mat-forming quillwort plants is usually in April. Some populations occur in pools devoid of associated plant life; others share their sites with Piedmont quillwort (*Isoetes piedmontana*) and/or with scattered individuals of a few other vascular plant species. Whatever the floristic makeup of the bedrock outcrop weather pits, their flooding each spring is followed by an explosion of growth as the dormant, previously invisible mat-forming quillwort plants burst forth. During this brief period the plants must extend rhizomes, mature spores, and produce new individuals. New leaves are initiated within two to four days. After a few weeks the pools dry up in the increasing heat of early summer, the plants wither, and the weather pit resumes its normal appearance as a slight, apparently lifeless dish of sand.

The mat-forming quillwort is a peculiar plant. It is the only North American quillwort to exclusively form dense, lawn-like mats and to have a distichous arrangement in the leaves in mature plants (in ranks, not spiraled around the rootstock). Indeed, the quillwort species most like this is the Southern quillwort (*Isoetes australis*) of southwestern Australia, another endemic of vernal pools on granite outcrops.

A number of other plants and animals have evolved to survive exclusively in the exceptionally demanding flat-rock habitat of the southeastern United States. These include other quillworts, the unique figwort Amphianthus (*Amphianthus pusilla*), the stonecrop *Diamorpha smallii*, and even invertebrates such as the fairy shrimp (*Branchinecta* spp.).

Their fragile, ephemeral wetland environment is often briefly shared by thousands of developing cricket frog (*Acris* sp.) tadpoles and salamander (*Ambystoma* sp.) larvae. However briefly, these vernal pools teem with life of all sorts.

Quarrying to extinction?

Only seven populations of the mat-forming quillwort have ever been found, despite a careful search of virtually every granite outcrop in western Alabama, Georgia, and the Carolinas in the early 1980s by flat-rock expert James R. Allison. Three of these populations have been destroyed. One of those was apparently deliberately obliterated. At least one other has been severely reduced in number and seems unlikely to survive much longer.

The main cause of the destruction of mat-forming quillwort populations has been rock quarrying. The largest granite outcroppings in Georgia are extensively mined for building materials. This has been identified as the direct cause of destruction for two populations,

has negatively impacted at least two others, severely threatens a third, and is the major potential threat to yet two other populations. The long-term survival of mat-forming quillwort is very much an open question. Only the scientifically important population at Heggies' Rock, Columbia County, Georgia, is secure. The latter is the population from which the species was described. The site has been purchased by the U.S. Nature Conservancy and is now protected from physical impact.

The discovery of previously undetected populations of mat-forming quillwort is unlikely. Potentially suitable habitat continues to be impacted by quarrying and other human activities. It is reasonable to assume, therefore, that the species' survival depends entirely on improved protection for the few known populations.

Daniel F. Brunton

Only improved protection will save mat-forming quillwort from threatening human activities.

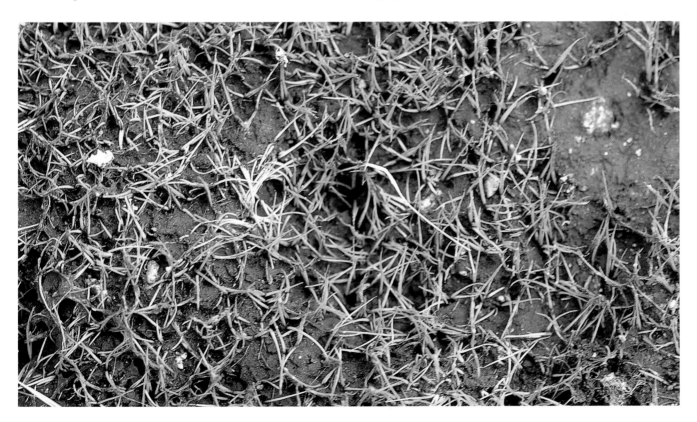

Papo's Maidenhair Fern

(Adiantum vivesii)

ESA: Endangered

IUCN: Endangered

Class: Pteropsida
Order: Filicales
Family: Adiantaceae
Height: Up to 28 in. (71 cm)
Fronds: Dull green with a lustrous purple-black stalk, spear-shaped, 8–11 in. (20–28 cm) long by 9–14 in. (23–36 cm) broad and twice divided into smaller leaflets. Each frond comprises three to four main divisions, or pinnae, the terminal one of which is largest. Each division has 10–13 pairs of narrow, blunt leaflets
Reproduction: By spores. Sori (clusters of spore-producing structures) are 1.5–3.5 mm long. The covering flap is gray brown and swollen with a ragged edge. Spores ripen in late summer
Habitat: Deeply shaded humus in limestone hollows
Range: Quebradillas, Puerto Rico

PAPO'S MAIDENHAIR FERN
Puerto Rico

THE RATHER ATTRACTIVE Papo's maidenhair fern is a recent discovery, found for the first time in 1985 but not formally described until 1989. It is only known from the one small area in Puerto Rico where it was first found. There it is locally plentiful in the Barrio San Antonio, where it forms small, dense colonies on deeply shaded humus in a sheltered hollow below limestone cliffs. It occurs at an altitude of about 820 feet (250 meters). The dull green leaves are closely spaced, produced at 5-millimeter intervals from the knobbly creeping rhizome, which is covered in patches by small, shiny yellow-brown scales.

One of 15 species of maidenhair ferns found on Puerto Rico,

The distinctive fronds of Papo's maidenhair fern (Adiantum vivesii) are spear shaped. The fronds are dull green and the stalks are purple.

Adiantum vivesii is named for Miguel "Papo" Vives, a local high-school chemistry teacher with a passion for ferns. He and a friend were present when George Proctor collected the first and perhaps still only specimen of this interesting and distinct species.

It is not known why the fern is so restricted in range, although more intensive searches may reveal additional populations of this species. No particular threats have been listed, but as with all species currently known from only one small area, one chance event could be responsible for the species' extinction. It is unlikely that this fern is in cultivation and unclear if any programs have been instigated or if there are plans to safeguard the plant. To protect the species, establishing plants in cultivation would be a high priority.

Fred Rumsey

Thelypteris Inabonensis

ESA: Endangered

IUCN: Endangered

Division: Pteridophyta
Class: Filicatae
Family: Thelypteridaceae
Fronds: Erect-arching, about 24 in. (60 cm) long and 4 in. (10 cm) wide
Reproduction: By spores. Sori covered by ciliate flaps or indusia
Habitat: Terrestrial in wet montane forests, high elevations 3,680–4,100 ft. (1,120–1,250 m)
Range: Puerto Rico

THELYPTERIS INABONENSIS is currently known from only two localities, one protected population in the municipality of Ponce and the other in the municipality of Quebradillas. The Ponce population is made up of 34 individuals, whereas that in Quebradillas is composed of only 12 individuals. These low numbers combined with such a small number of populations spells trouble for this rare fern.

Close relation

Dr. George Proctor, an eminent fern biologist, has spent his life studying ferns in Puerto Rico and has suggested that this species is closely related to a group of ferns from Costa Rica. This presents the intriguing possibility that the plants in Puerto Rico may have arrived from populations in Costa Rica or vice versa. These relationships, however, are unclear and a great deal more research is needed to develop accurate theories on the origins of this species.

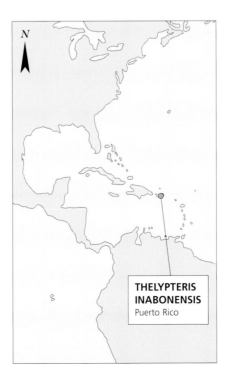

THELYPTERIS
INABONENSIS
Puerto Rico

Thelypteris Verecunda

Subgenus: Amauropelta

ESA: Endangered

IUCN: Endangered

Division: Pteridophyta
Class: Filicatae
Family: Thelypteridaceae
Fronds: Prostrate and spreading and of two different sizes. Sterile blades oblong: 1.5 in. (4 cm) long by ¾ in. (2 cm) broad; fertile blades narrowly spear-shaped: 6 in. (15 cm) long by ¾ in. (2 cm) broad. Sori have small indusia covered in simple hairs
Reproduction: As well as producing spores, this species exhibits an interesting form of asexual reproduction. Fertile elongate frond produce buds at the tips of the leaves that develop into and establish as new plants
Habitat: Moist shaded limestone rocks and cliffs, middle elevations around 660 ft. (200 m)
Range: Puerto Rico

THELYPTERIS VERECUNDA is exceptional in its rarity. The species is known from three localities in the municipalities of Quebradillas and San Sebastían. The population from San Sebastían and one of the two populations from Quebradillas have only a single plant each. The largest population from Quebradillas maintains only 20 plants. Currently, the taxonomic position of these plants is in a state of flux. It has been suggested by at least one author that this species may actually be a hybrid; however, these claims have yet to be tested scientifically.

Thelypteris Yaucoensis

ESA: Endangered

IUCN: Endangered

Class: Filicatae
Family: Thelypteridaceae
Fronds: 17–20 in.
(43–51 cm) long and
4–5½ in. (10–14 cm) broad. The sori are in the middle of the leaf with small ciliate indusia
Habitat: Steep, shady, rocky banks at high elevations of 2,780–3,940 ft. (850–1,200 m)
Range: Puerto Rico

THELYPTERIS YAUCOENSIS is perhaps one of Puerto Rico's least known ferns. Very little information is currently available on any aspect of its biology. The species is known only from three populations in the municipalities of Yauco and Ciales. The total number of plants from all populations is fewer than 65, and all occur on privately owned land, where protection laws are inadequate or not easily enforced.

Dwindling numbers

Given the small population sizes of all three *Thelypteris* ferns, removal of even a single individual could be harmful. Natural disasters such as Hurricane Hugo, which passed over the island of Puerto Rico in 1989, could have reduced the number of plants in the already critically small populations. At least one report suggests that populations of *T. inabonensis* were affected by this storm. Natural disturbances like Hugo pose a severe threat to the survival of these species.

Human threat

However, more immediate threats are those caused by humans. Frequently, collectors find ferns of such small size as *T. inabonensis* and *T. verecunda* ideal for their personal terrarium. Some collectors may actually search out endangered species to add to their prized collections and in doing so extirpate entire species from the wild. An additional concern is human alteration of the habitats where the species occur. This is especially critical for those populations that are found on privately owned property or on public property where enforcement of laws protecting the site is minimal. These rare ferns could potentially reveal a great deal about the evolution of plants restricted to small islands. Until the proper taxonomic relationships and biology of these rare ferns are better understood, they should be protected as endangered species.

Eddie Watkins

THELYPTERIS VERECUNDA
THELYPTERIS YAUCOENSIS
Puerto Rico

Black-footed Ferret

(Mustela nigripes)

IUCN: Extinct in the wild

Class: Mammalia
Order: Carnivora
Family: Mustelidae
Weight: 1¾–2½ lb. (760–1,080 g)
Head-body length: 14¾–19½ in. (38–50 cm)
Diet: Carnivorous
Gestation period: 42–45 days
Longevity: 12 years
Habitat: Short-grass prairie
Range: Formerly found in short grass prairie from southern Canada to southern United States

WHEN SETTLERS first crossed the plains and prairies of North America, they encountered vast expanses of land occupied by prairie dog towns. While settlers saw countless numbers of prairie dogs (*Cynomys* sp.) standing guard on their burrow mounds or scurrying about, what they rarely noticed were the other residents of these huge rodent colonies—the black-footed ferret. Since it is nocturnal and moves about primarily within the prairie dog burrows, only about 1,000 verified sightings of this ferret have been recorded since 1851.

Although estimates of their historic numbers are difficult to make, partly due to their secretive nature, some researchers have asserted that the black-footed ferret numbered around one-half million early in the twentieth century. By 1986 the number of black-footed ferrets had dramatically fallen, with only 20 known to exist.

Black-footed ferrets, like most members of the weasel family, have a long slender body that resembles a torpedo with short legs. Growing up to 19½ inches (50 centimeters) long, the black-footed ferret arches its back upright, both when moving about and when standing still. The background color of the fur is buff, changing to a slightly paler buff on the underside. The throat, muzzle, and a band across the forehead are white, while the top of the head and the midline of the back are brown. The most distinctive characteristic of this species is the black coloration of the mask, feet, and final one-fourth of the tail.

The ferret is solitary most of the year, with adults coming together only during the breeding season between March and April. Females give birth to a litter of from one to six kits, the average being slightly over three.

Young first appear above ground in July and by September they depart the den occupied by their mother. While female offspring remain in close proximity to their mother, males disperse a great distance in search of a territory and a mate.

Living with prairie dogs

The black-footed ferret is one of those unique species whose survival has become closely tied to a single source of prey. The black-footed ferret uses the burrows of the prairie dog for shelter and for a place to travel safely, unseen by predators, which include the coyote (*Canis latrans*) as well as some birds of prey. Although in captivity it accepts many types of small mammals as food, it appears to have relied almost exclusively on the prairie dog as a food source in the wild.

The ferret tends to remain within a particular prairie dog colony, rarely moving between colonies. The size of the colony is important to the ferret's existence. While the average size of a prairie dog town is 20 acres (8 hectares), the average size town occupied by a female ferret with

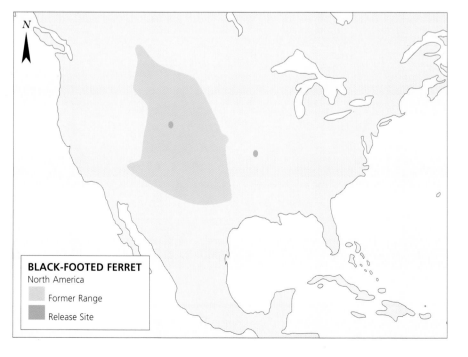

BLACK-FOOTED FERRET
North America

Former Range
Release Site

One of the most devastating problems the black-footed ferret faced was its reliance on a single source of prey—the prairie dog. As the size of the prairie dog colony diminished, this ferret's food source was seriously jeopardized. Plague and the virus canine distemper also reduced the ferret's population until it was extinct in the wild. Its status should improve due to the U.S. Fish and Wildlife captive-breeding program.

young was 89 acres (36 hectares). It is estimated that each individual ferret may require 124 acres (50 hectares) of prairie dog town.

A roller coaster existence

The saga of the black-footed ferret is a classic example of how deliberate manipulation of one species—the prairie dog—can have unintended consequences for other species. It is entirely due to the massive human effort to eliminate vast prairie dog towns (an effort estimated to be 90 percent successful) that the black-footed ferret has come to be extinct in the wild. The shooting and poisoning of prairie dogs was undertaken principally to prevent beef cattle from breaking their legs when stepping in prairie dog burrows as they grazed the open range.

During the late 1970s and early 1980s, the black-footed ferret was feared to be extinct. However, in late 1981 a population was discovered in Wyoming. An extensive survey of the area revealed the population to be substantial, estimated to be 129 in 1984. The excitement felt by conservationists soon faded, though, when this population was struck a double blow. First, a plague struck the prairie dog community, eliminating the ferrets' prey. Then, after black-footed ferret numbers dropped due to fewer prey, the ferrets themselves were devastated by contracting a virus called canine distemper.

Second chance

Despite all these problems, it now appears the species may receive one more chance. After the population dropped to just 20 individuals, 10 remaining individuals were captured from the wild in order to begin an intensive captive-breeding program. The black-footed ferret has performed well in captivity, and by 1991 the population had increased to 325.

Reintroduction of ferrets to the wild began during the fall of 1991 with the release of 49 individuals at a site in south-central Wyoming. By early spring of 1992, it was estimated that between six and ten of these individuals had survived. An additional 100 ferrets have since been released at the Wyoming site. The U.S. Fish and Wildlife Service hopes to firmly reestablish the black-footed ferret by creating 10 wild populations. More than 200 black-footed ferrets remain in captivity.

Human interference

The black-footed ferret is one of the more easily recognized endangered species whose decline can be directly blamed on human interference. Because its case has become so well known, its fate will be watched closely for two reasons: first, because it is crucial to see whether humans can muster the resources necessary to save a species whose numbers are so limited, and second, because it is a species that became extinct in the wild as a result of human actions.

The solution

Black-footed ferrets that have been reintroduced into the wild have been designated "non-essential experimental" populations under the Endangered Species Act. This allows a more flexible interpretation of the rules than is allowed for endangered species, and encourages cooperation in the recovery effort by landowners and other interested parties.

The aim is to establish 1,500 free-ranging ferrets in the wild by the year 2010.

Terry Tompkins

FINCHES

Class: Aves

Order: Passeriformes

Finches come in many shapes, sizes, and colors. The English name *finch* is a broad term given to many different birds that occur in several families. Two of the birds discussed here belong to the group known as the Hawaiian honeycreepers. They have proved to be a challenging group for

ornithologists to understand. New fossil material, new investigative techniques, and other evidence have led to different theories regarding their origin and relationships. All of the surviving members of the group are considered endangered or threatened.

The Saint Lucia black finch is from the family Emberizidae while the two honeycreepers belong to the family Drepanididae.

Saint Lucia Black Finch

(Melanospiza richardsoni)

IUCN: Lower risk

Length: 6 in. (15 cm)
Weight: Unknown
Clutch size: Unknown
Incubation: Unknown
Diet: Small fruits, seeds, insects, and snails
Habitat: Forests, plantations, and shrublands
Range: Mountains of Saint Lucia Island

IN THE DARKENED world beneath forest undergrowth, a black bird can easily disappear among the shadows. On Saint Lucia a small finch species does just that. Constantly pumping their tails downward, Saint Lucia black finches move easily among the dense plant life of forests and shrublands, searching the ground for food. Sometimes they use their beaks to flick aside plant debris. Other times they use a foot to scratch aside dead, fallen leaves or both feet to hop quickly

forward, then back. This shuffles the debris under which hide insects and snails, seeds and seedlings. They also use their feet to bend the stems of sedges (*Scleria latifolia*) so they can eat the seeds ripening on the ends.

Saint Lucia black finches are also at home above ground, moving about leaves and branches to pick insects and small fruits from the foliage and twigs—even chasing a flying insect now and then. When breeding, they build their nests in trees. Black finches are

SAINT LUCIA BLACK FINCH
Caribbean

well suited to the forested and shrubby island where they live. The island, however, may not be so well suited for them.

A volcano built Saint Lucia, which has an area of 238 square miles (595 square kilometers). Located in the Lesser Antilles, north of South America, Saint Lucia rises to 3,145 feet (959 meters) at Mount Gimie on the island's southern end. A pattern of valleys and ridges texture the island. Dry forests and shrublands once covered much of the lower slopes and coastal plains, and rain forests filled the higher elevations. Saint Lucia black finches originally inhabited all of the island's denser vegetation.

Habitat changes

As people settled Saint Lucia they cut the forests for lumber products and firewood. They also cleared forests and shrublands to provide space for grazing livestock. The northern coastal region has been heavily affected by grazing and has also developed into a resort hotel community that attracts tourists. The island's northwestern area has been largely converted to banana plantations. Such changes have harshly affected several birds, including the Saint Lucia parrot (*Amazona versicolor*), the Saint Lucia nighthawk (*Caprimulgus rufus otiosus*), and the Saint Lucia house wren (*Troglodytes aedon mesoleucus*). Apparently, the black finch adapts more easily to some habitat disturbance than do other birds, as it is found in different types of undergrowth: primary forest, the edges of banana plantations, under the trees on mahogany and blue mahoe (*Hibiscus tiliaceus*) plantations,

and on the borders around croplands, ravines, and coastal shrublands. More Saint Lucia black finches occur in primary forest than in other habitats, but they do not seem to require primary forest to survive.

The males plumage is entirely black, the foot and toe are pink, and the beak is dark; females have brown plumage overall with light streaks on the breast; the head is grayer.

Virtually nothing is known of the black finch's breeding habits. Few nests have ever been recorded or eggs counted. Some observers noted in the 1980s that young black finches were scarce. Reproduction may be unsuccessful because of predators such as Indian mongooses (*Herpestes auropunctatus*), black rats (*Rattus rattus*), and perhaps Virginia opossums (*Didelphis virginiana*). These mammals are exotic to Saint Lucia and are known to prey on eggs and nestlings of many bird species.

Unknown natural history

The origins of this black finch are also obscure. Some ornithologists think that the Saint Lucia black finch may have a common ancestry with the famous Darwin's finches of the Galápagos Islands. If this is true, it means that a general type of finch must have once inhabited northern South America. It is believed that individuals of this species wandered to both the Galápagos Islands and the Lesser Antilles. Over time, the island birds became more specialized and isolated from the mainland parent species. While the mainland species became extinct, the island birds continued to evolve until they became the species we know today. It is quite possible that the Saint Lucia black finch was the only distinct form to evolve in the Lesser Antilles; but if not, then the other Antillean species have already disappeared.

Not all ornithologists accept this explanation because the black finch and Darwin's finches have differences as well as similarities. The black finch has no close relatives still living; it is a unique species. Over the years this uniqueness has prompted ornithologists to classify the Saint Lucia black finch in four different genera. Each reclassification attempts to better explain their relationship to other species.

Despite all the uncertainty about origins and relationships, and despite the lack of information about this bird's natural history, the Saint Lucia black finch still survives. The Saint Lucia Forest Reserve has been established around La Sorciere, a 2,296-foot (700-meter) mountain in the north. The reserve holds some promise as a place where Saint Lucia's endangered birds might survive in protected undergrowth, free from exotic predators such as the Indian mongooses and black rats.

Laysan Finch
(Telespiza cantans)

ESA: Endangered

IUCN: Vulnerable

Length: 7½ in. (19 cm)
Weight: Unknown
Clutch size: 1–4 eggs, usually 3
Incubation: 14–16 days
Diet: Seeds, flower buds, leaves, roots, insects, bird eggs, carrion
Habitat: All vegetation types but prefers bunchgrass
Range: Laysan Island, Pearl and Hermes Reef, Hawaiian Islands

WHEN ONE endangered species preys upon another endangered species, the situation becomes difficult for those working to save

Because of the abundance of wildlife that lives on Laysan Island, including the Laysan finch, it has been designated as a refuge administered by the U.S. Fish and Wildlife Service.

them both. The Laysan finch almost became extinct in the early 1900s, as did the Laysan rail (*Porzanula palmeri*) and several other birds of that Pacific island. The finch managed to survive, but the rail perished. Ironically, the recovery of one endangered species may have helped push the other into extinction. The male Laysan finch is a yellowish bird overall. The yellow head is bright on the face, more golden on the crown. The yellow extends down the throat and onto the breast. The belly is white. The back fades from a gray collar to a yellowish green middle back, becoming more gray on the lower back and ending in a golden yellow rump. Both tail and wing are dark. The female is heavily streaked and appears both grayer and browner than the male. She has yellow only about the face, chin, and throat, all finely streaked. Both males and females have a very large, pale gray beak with a tiny hook at the tip.

Most visitors to Laysan island found these attractive small birds to be very tame. Some people reported catching them by hand. They were kept in cages in Honolulu as early as 1888 but were not described to ornithologists until 1890. They were not collected on Laysan by anyone who knew birds until 1891. Soon after their discovery, the Laysan finches were followed by guano miners. Guano, or the droppings of birds, is known as a rich source of phosphorous and nitrogen. It makes excellent fertilizer and was also used for many years for making gunpowder. The diets of seabirds probably explain why the coastal and island guano deposits are especially rich. By 1904, however, Laysan's guano supply was running out and could not profitably support a mining camp.

Mining directly affected the island, but miners also affected the birds. They shot them for food and for fun. One miner deliberately released European rabbits (*Oryctolagus cunicularis*) on Laysan. Without any natural pressures from predators or disease, the rabbits multiplied quickly. By the second decade of the 1900s the rabbits had become so abundant that they had virtually demolished the plant life on Laysan. The rabbits' appetite destroyed the only habitat of the Laysan millerbird (*Acrocephalus familiaris*) and the Laysan

LAYSAN FINCH
Hawaiian Islands

NIHOA FINCH
Hawaiian Islands

honeycreeper (*Himatione sanguinea*). The habitat of the Laysan finch and the Laysan rail were damaged, too. The rabbits that did not starve were eradicated but not before the millerbird and the honeycreeper slipped into extinction. Only three Laysan honeycreepers were found on the island during an expedition there in 1923. A gale buffeted the island for three days. When the storm passed, the honeycreepers were gone forever.

One species gone

Once the rabbits were gone, Laysan's plants began to recover. The finch population also began to grow, but the rail's did not. One estimate was 2,000 in 1915, but ornithologists on the 1923 expedition found only two. The rails were known to eat insects, carrion, and bird eggs. Ironically, so does the Laysan finch. Some ornithologists suspect that the growing Laysan finch population may have fed on rail eggs to try to compensate for the loss of other foods. By 1944 the Laysan rail was extinct.

The Laysan finch population grew to somewhere over 10,000 birds by 1990. The Bureau of Sport Fisheries and Wildlife (now the U.S. Fish and Wildlife Service) moved 110 birds to Pearl and Hermes Reef in 1967. The birds survived, reproduced, and spread to various islands in the reef. Today, the population approaches 1,000 birds. Laysan itself now has about 10,000 birds. Laysan covers only 993 acres (397 hectares), of which only half offers any finch habitat. Pearl and Hermes Reef covers only 141 acres (56.2 hectares), with only half of that well suited for the finches. By having two discrete populations, the Laysan finch should have a better chance of surviving cataclysmic weather or natural disasters of other kinds. A single population on a small island is extremely vulnerable to any changes. Laysan Island was designated as a research natural area in 1967 and is now part of the Northwest Hawaiian Islands National Wildlife Refuge. The refuge is administered by the U.S. Fish and Wildlife Service. Access to the island is now allowed only through a permitting process for scientists with a valid purpose for visiting Laysan. The regulation protects the birds from harassment, but more importantly, helps prevent accidental introductions of rats or other harmful exotic species onto the island.

Nihoa Finch
(*Telespiza ultima*)

ESA: Endangered

IUCN: Vulnerable

Length: 6½in. (16.5 cm)
Weight: ¾ oz. (22 g)
Clutch size: 3 eggs
Incubation: 14–16 days
Diet: Seeds, leaves, stems, flowers, insects, bird eggs, carrion
Habitat: Rocky outcroppings
Range: Nihoa, Hawaiian Islands

THE NIHOA FINCH "rides" an island adrift in the Pacific Ocean. Geologists believe that large plates make up the Earth's crust. These plates float on the earth's inner mantle, which is hot and more plastic than liquid. Holes penetrating to the mantle create "hot spots" as the crust drifts over them. The oozing of magma (molten rock material) through these hot spots eventually leads to the formation of mountains. When they get tall enough, the mountains protrude above the ocean as volcanic islands. As the plates continue to move, the mountains drift past the hot spots and the volcanoes become extinct. Eventually, new mountains form and rise above the ocean. This process has created the Hawaiian Islands.

Nihoa was an active volcano some millions of years ago. It eventually drifted past the hot spot in the ocean floor and became dormant. Now a tiny speck of an island, it covers a mere 156 acres (62.4 hectares). It lies roughly 230 miles (368 kilometers) northwest of Honolulu on Oahu and rises substantially higher above the ocean than do the more distant islands to the northwest. Seabirds use its rocky slopes to make their nests, lay their eggs, and raise their young. Among these are birds such as shearwaters, petrels, tropicbirds, boobies, frigatebirds, terns, and noddies. The Nihoa finch has learned to take advantage of the larger and more abundant seabirds.

Given the chance, Nihoa finches peck open the eggs of the nesting seabirds. They have been seen to eat the egg contents, but captive birds have eaten the shell as well as the yolk. Being a small bird, the finch can only peck through the smaller eggs of smaller birds. But they have been seen to dislodge larger eggs that subsequently roll or drop and break open. An open egg is a feast for all. When nestlings, juveniles or even adult birds die, the finches scavenge them. They eat not only the carrion but also the insects attracted to the carcass.

Nihoa finches strongly resemble Laysan finches but are a little smaller. Their beak is not so large and lacks the hooked tip. The male has a yellow head, face, chin, and throat contrasting with a whitish to grayish belly. The back has a gray band below the nape, a golden green middle back, a gray lower back, and a gray-green rump. The wing and tail are dark with some pale feather edgings. The female is heavily striped in black, appearing darker than the female Laysan finch.

The Nihoa finch was first described in 1917 by W.A. Bryan. He assigned it the Latin name *ultima* because he thought it would "ultimately" be the last of the Hawaiian honeycreepers. He was wrong. At least one other living species was discovered, and some remains of recently extinct species were found. The Nihoa finch itself has been the subject of debate, with some experts believing it to be a subspecies of the Laysan finch and others believing it to be a distinct species of its own.

Ornithologists estimated that there were as many as 2,300 Nihoa finches in the early 1970s. That figure has not changed much as the population is now estimated to number more than 2,000. The island of Nihoa is too small and too remote from the main cluster of Hawaiian Islands to be useful to people. Consequently, it has not been as thoroughly damaged as have many islands. It is now part of the Northwestern Hawaiian Islands National Wildlife Refuge. The U.S. Fish and Wildlife Service regulates access to the island, partly to protect the birds from humans and partly to guard against the unintentional spread of rats or other animals that could jeopardize the Nihoa finch. Although it seems stable, this finch will always suffer from vulnerability to severe weather and to the presence of rats.

People can prevent problems associated with rats, goats, and rabbits. But people can neither control the weather nor can they stop the drift of Nihoa Island. It is a fact that, as the millennia pass, the island will shrink back into the sea and *Telespyza ultima* will ultimately disappear.

Kevin Cook

Masked Finfoot
(*Heliopais personata*)

IUCN: Vulnerable

Class: Aves
Order: Gruiformes
Family: Heliornithidae
Length: 21 in. (53 cm)
Weight: Unknown
Clutch size: 3-5 eggs
Incubation: Unknown
Diet: Worms, various insects, crustaceans, snails, small amphibians such as frogs, and possibly fish
Habitat: Open water in forests; swamps; mangrove in winter
Range: From India to Burma; winters in Southeast Asia, Malaysia southward to Indonesia

IMAGINE A BIRD that is a little like a duck, a grebe, a rail, and a cormorant. The masked finfoot is such a bird. The masked finfoot belongs to a family composed of just three species. Known collectively as the sun grebes, this family also includes the sun grebe (*Heliornis fulica*) of Central America and northern South America and the African finfoot (*Podica senegalensis*). The masked finfoot is the rarest.

The masked finfoot was probably never abundant, which is one reason so little is known about this bird. It is not just shy; it inhabits places that are difficult for people to explore. The masked finfoot uses pools and other open water in dense forests, but it probably prefers swamps choked and tangled almost beyond use. In winter it inhabits mangrove. It can swim but prefers to scramble about the flotsam and tangles that are so common in a swamp habitat. The finfoot rides low in the water and swims by paddling duck-style, but the three front toes lack the connecting webs common to ducks and many other aquatic birds. Instead, the finfoot has long, lobed toes much like a coot or a phalarope. The masked finfoot also pumps its head as it swims, much as a coot does. The long, slender neck, however, gives it the look of a grebe.

The finfoot's neck is long and slender; the male is mostly olive-brown on top, with white underneath and brownish sides. Its nape and the back of the head are gray, while the throat, chin, cheek, lore, forehead, and forecrown are black and resemble a

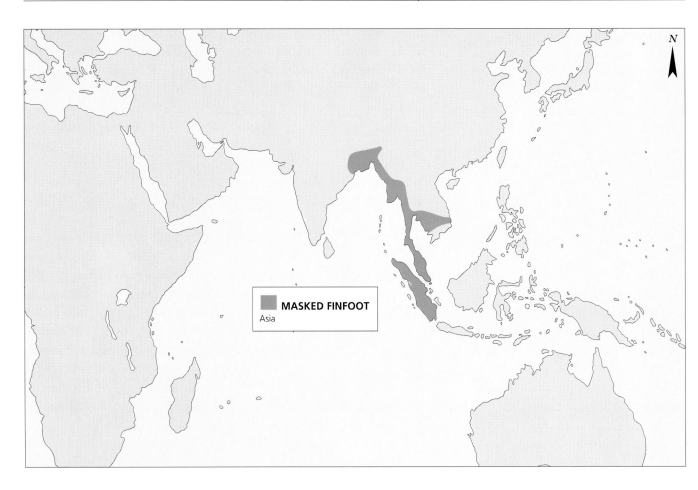

MASKED FINFOOT
Asia

bib. The female's plumage is similar to the male's but with a white patch inside the black bib.

The masked finfoot's forest habitat is exploited by humans for its lumber. The swamps are also drained for land development and agriculture. When the forests are replanted, the trees are aligned in neat plantation rows that offer no habitat for the finfoot. Drained swamps converted to grazing pasture, rice paddies, or other cropland leave no place for the finfoot to live. The status of the masked finfoot is unclear. It is no longer found in some areas of its original range, because habitat no longer exists. Scientists presume that the masked finfoot's population is declining as its habitat is reduced.

With so many things unknown about the masked finfoot, no meaningful protective action can be taken on its behalf. Until more is known about its natural history, population size, and present distribution, the best protective measures are probably to attempt to preserve the remaining dense forest and swamps where the species still occurs.

Kevin Cook

The masked finfoot has a thin white line that runs from behind the eye down the side of head and neck onto the breast. The foot and toe are bright green, and its stout beak is yellow.

Crested Fireback

(Lophura ignita)

IUCN: Vulnerable

Class: Aves
Order: Galliformes
Family: Phasianidae
Subfamily: Phasianinae
Tribe: Phasianini
Length: 22–27½ in. (56–70 cm)
Weight: Unknown
Clutch size: 4–8 eggs
Incubation: 24–25 days
Diet: Fruits, seeds, leaves, buds, insects
Habitat: Mature lowland forests
Range: Malay Peninsula, Sumatra, Borneo, Myanmar, and Thailand

THE CRESTED FIREBACK can be detected by the whirring sound it produced which drifts through the jungle. Like most pheasants, firebacks drum their wings to produce this whirring. The noise simultaneously attracts females and warns off other males. Usually, the males punctuate these whirring sounds with a distinctive vocal clucking. These are natural sounds that blend with the other jungle noises, but they are also sounds that are disappearing with the vanishing tropical forests.

The name fireback comes from this bird's dazzling plumage. The coppery red plumage on its lower back fades to a purplish maroon rump. These colors contrast with the overall shiny deep blue body plumage. The crown is adorned with a tight, compact tuft of feathers that stands erect. The Borneo and Sumatra populations recog-nized as two subspecies, have a dull, flesh-colored, or grayish white foot and toe. The leg of the subspecies on peninsular Malaysia and Thailand is bright red.

A tropical pheasant

The crested fireback is just one of many pheasants that live in Southeast Asia. Just as quails are the most diverse in Central and northern South America, and francolins are the most diverse in Africa, the greatest diversity of pheasants is found in southern Asia. Historically, the crested fireback occurred from extreme southern Myanmar, Thailand, and Malaysia southward into Sumatra and Borneo. But only one sighting of a crested fireback has been recorded in Sumatra since 1950. Ornithologists are not sure whether the species still exists there or is extinct.

Even though they live in mature forests, crested firebacks are not arboreal. As with typical pheasants, they are terrestrial or ground birds. As a result, they have a thick and strong leg, foot, and toe. This suits the bird for scratching among leaf debris, where it finds much of its food. They also make the fireback a swift runner. When danger appears, a fireback will often escape by dashing into thick vegetation, particularly bamboo thickets along streams.

Firebacks can also fly. They have a short, broad wing with stiff, strongly curved flight feathers. This wing structure gives them quick speed. Despite these defenses, however, a few crested firebacks inevitably fall prey to snakes and other predators. Chicks and juveniles are particularly vulnerable. Crested firebacks are also vulnerable to the effects that humans are having on their environment.

The forests of Southeast Asia where crested firebacks live are highly prized because they yield good lumber in high quantities. Desirable trees that are simple to cut are the first to go when cutting begins. The crested fireback depends only indirectly on the trees. Trees shade the ground,

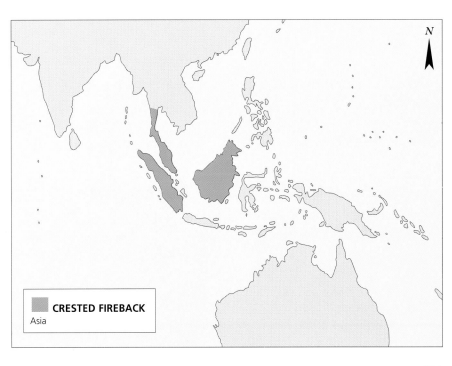

CRESTED FIREBACK
Asia

deflect wind and rain, harbor other animals that eat fruits, and distribute seeds. Collectively trees determine the character of a forest, right down to the types of undergrowth on the forest floor, which is where the crested fireback lives. More cutting of trees means that more sunlight and rain reach the forest floor. Plants of the forest floor change.

Many animals are able to adapt to such changes, but those animals with more specialized lifestyles usually cannot adapt and simply disappear.

Habitat invasion

Since the 1960s, the Indonesian government has pursued a national policy called "transmigration." This policy involves resettling people from areas of high human density to areas of low density. This is bad for rare and endangered birds. The policy causes remaining tracts of native forests to be cut as settlers create cropland, and space to live.

Firebacks do breed well in captivity, despite early failures. Chicks succumbed to diseases a few months after hatching. But improved housing techniques and veterinary care now virtually guarantee that crested firebacks can be maintained in captivity. The fireback still survives in scattered populations around Borneo.

Less is known about its populations on the Malay Peninsula. In any case, no effective measures have been taken to preserve the native habitat for crested firebacks.

Kevin Cook

The crested fireback does not adapt to forests severely changed by human activities and shows no willingness to occupy plantation habitats.

Juan Fernandez Firecrown

(Sephanoides fernandensis)

IUCN: Critically endangered

Class: Aves
Order: Apodiformes
Family: Trochilidae
Length: 5 in. (12.7 cm)
Weight: Male, ½ oz. (11 g); female, ¼ oz. (7 g)
Diet: Nectar
Habitat: All island habitats
Range: Juan Fernandez Islands in the Pacific Ocean off Chile

THE JUAN FERNANDEZ firecrown is a tiny hummingbird that inhabits the remote Juan Fernandez Islands in the Pacific Ocean.

It is on one of these island that the Scotsman Alexander Selkirk was marooned. Four years and four months passed before he was rescued. The writer Daniel Defoe based his book *Robinson Crusoe* upon Selkirk's experiences. How a sailor comes to an island can be easily understood, but explaining how a tiny bird, that weighs less than half an ounce, crossed 417 miles of open ocean is not as easy. Although several hummingbird species live on coastal islands, the firecrowns are the only hummingbirds to inhabit oceanic islands. Ornithologists have yet to resolve the mystery of the firecrowns. There are only two possibilities: either the Juan Fernandez firecrown emerged as a species on the South American continent and flew to Juan Fernandez Islands before becoming extinct on the continent, or it developed as a species after some ancestors found the islands. Only two species form the firecrown genus *Sephanoides*. The Juan Fernandez firecrown inhabits only the Juan Fernandez islands, while the green-backed firecrown *(Sephanoides sephanoides)* inhabits both islands and mainland. The green-backed firecrown inhabits portions of western Argentina and Chile as far south as Tierra del Fuego, the tip of the continent near Antarctica. This range makes the green-backed firecrown the most southerly of all hummingbirds. Breeding at 55 degrees south latitude, the firecrown is rivaled only by the rufous hummingbird *(Selasphorus rufus)*, which breeds at or slightly above 60 degrees in the

Northern Hemisphere. The green-backed firecrown covers a broad area, where it lives in the margins between forests, meadows, and shrub lands. It survives in healthy numbers. The Juan Fernandez firecrown, however, suffered dramatically during the 1970s and 1980s.

The male has a unique reddish or coppery hue; the wing and tail are so brown as to appear black. The crown is a shiny golden red or coppery orange. The female upperparts are shiny blue green or turquoise green, the wing a dark gray-green, and the tail blue green, with white outer markings. The underparts are pure white, and the throat and side are patterned with turquoise green spots; the crown is a shiny, dark purplish blue.

Changing habitat

When island birds decline in numbers, the reason for their decline is usually because of a habitat problem. Either the habitat is destroyed outright, or else it is degraded to the point where it does not meet the needs of the birds that depend on it. Cutting all the trees in a forest or letting plant-eating mammals wander loose in an island forest cause plants and the wildlife they support to disappear. Or, large trees may be allowed to remain, but important undergrowth that provides food and cover may change. Quite often, plants from other parts of the world start growing on islands. These exotic plants can outgrow native plants and likewise alter habitat quality.

On the Juan Fernandez Islands, exotic plants and animals have taken hold. The Juan Fernandez firecrown appears to have accepted several exotic plants because their flowers offer a usable source of nectar for the ever-hungry hummers. Eucalyptus trees (*Eucalyptus* sp.) produce extravagant numbers of flowers rich in nectar, and the hummingbirds use them. Bramble (*Rubus ulmifolius*) also produces nectar but in smaller quantities. The Juan Fernandez firecrown perches while taking nectar, and several plants endemic to the Juan Fernandez Islands grow in a way that allows the hummingbird to perch for nectar feeding. The bramble flower structure, however, does not allow perching for nectar feeding. This means the Juan Fernandez firecrown has to hover more to feed for less nectar. The smaller green-backed firecrown thus enjoys a definite feeding advantage. Unfortunately for the Juan Fernandez firecrown, the bramble outcompetes endemic nectar-bearing plants more suited to the hummingbird.

The European rabbit (*Oryctolagus cuniculus*) was intentionally released on the islands in 1935. Without any constraints, the rabbit population grew rapidly and altered the native plant communities through its feeding habits. Goats were released on the islands in the late 1500s and have steadily over-eaten the island vegetation. Black rats (*Rattus rattus*) and Norway rats (*Rattus norvegicus*) also found their way onto the islands, as did cats and dogs. The cats and dogs have largely disappeared, but goats and rabbits continue to graze. Black rats, who eat eggs and nestlings, have declined, but they still remain on the islands.

Coatimundis (*Nasua nasua*), a relative of the raccoon, were introduced in either 1935 or 1940. They were supposed to help control the rat population, in which they may have succeeded. However, they are now suspected of raiding firecrown nests, taking both eggs and nestlings. The Juan Fernandez firecrown typically builds its nest low to the ground on the limbs of fern plants. The species had no natural predators for thousands of years, so it developed no instinct for escaping danger. Thus, it is extremely vulnerable to nocturnal predators such as the coatimundis and black rats.

The Juan Fernandez Islands have been designated a Chilean national park and an International Biosphere reserve, and a long term study of these birds has been underway since the late 1980s. Once numbering in the thousands, the species vanished altogether on Selkirk Island and dwindled to only 250 birds on Crusoe Island by the late 1980s. Survival will depend on eradicating brambles, and predators such as rats, and coatimundis, from at least one of the islands.

Kevin Cook

JUAN FERNANDEZ FIRECROWN
South America

Fringe-backed Fire-eye

(Pyriglena atra)

IUCN: Endangered

Class: Aves
Order: Passeriformes
Family: Formicariidae
Length: 6½ in. (16.5 cm)
Weight: Unknown
Clutch size: Unknown
Incubation: Unknown
Diet: Mostly insects
Habitat: Primary and secondary forest
Range: North of Salvador, Bahia, in southeastern Brazil

IN THE TROPICAL forests of South America, ants have found a way to occupy almost every conceivable nook and cranny. There are ants that live in trees, ants that live in the soil, ants that swarm over the ground, ants that farm, and ants that hunt. Birds such as the fringe-backed fire-eye have found these communities of ants.

The fire-eyes are a group of three species in the antbird family. Antbirds form one of the largest families of songbirds in the world. Many of them have acquired specialized body forms that suggest other bird families. The names *anthrush* and *antshrike* reflect these similarities. The fire-eyes derive their name not from any resemblance to other birds but from the brilliant red iris of their eyes.

Range

The fringe-backed fire-eye occurs naturally only in a small forested area in the state of Bahia, Brazil. The state of Bahia has become an enormously important agricultural area for Brazil. Forests are cleared for lumber products as well as to make space for other land uses. Cattle grazing usually moves into cleared forest land. The plants and animals that depend on those forests have nowhere else to go, and often they simply disappear. The fringe-backed fire-eye depends less on primary forests than do some other species; it actually adapts fairly well to secondary forest. Unfortunately, even secondary forests in its range have been heavily grazed, cut over, or converted to plantations.

Beyond its general habitat preference, little else is known about the fringe-backed fire-eye species. Details of its breeding habits, territorial needs, association with other species, and other basic information about its natural history are lacking.

Appearance

The male fringe-backed fire-eye wears shiny black plumage except for a patch on the back. Each feather of this patch is edged in white, giving this bird its name. The female's coloration is cinnamon brown above and dingy white below, and it also displays the back patch. This appearance is common to the other fire-eyes as well.

Diet

Antbird species either follow ant swarms or they ignore ants altogether. Army ants (*Eciton burchelli* and *Labidus praedator*) often form large swarms, which some antbirds actively follow. Others only follow them if the ants scare up food. As the ants move about, other insects such as spiders, small reptiles, and amphibians scurry out of the ants' way. Antbirds follow the ant swarms to watch for these flushed animals. Some antbirds are large enough to handle small lizards and frogs. Other antbirds eat only insects. Few, if any, antbirds actually eat ants, except perhaps coincidentally when capturing other prey.

The future

Recommendations have been made for protecting what little primary forest and natural habitat remains in Bahia. A proposed sanctuary would help other species in addition to the fringe-backed fire-eye. However, Bahia is an important food-producing state in which agricultural interests strongly influence the political decisions that govern natural resources. As of 1990, no action had been taken to establish a sanctuary. With only two small populations still known to exist, delays could ultimately doom the fringe-backed fire-eye.

Kevin Cook

FRINGE-BACKED FIRE-EYE
South America

Fissi

(Sarotherodon caroli)

IUCN: Critically endangered

Class: Actinopterygii
Order: Perciformes
Family: Cichlidae
Length: 7 in. (18 cm)
Reproduction: Egg layer
Habitat: Near shore and open-water areas
Range: Lake Barombi-Mbo, Cameroon

THE FISSI IS A member of the family of warm water fishes called Cichlidae, a group that includes about 250 endangered fishes in Africa's Lake Victoria. This family contains a large number of fishes, and within the Cichlidae there is a subfamily called Tilapiinae (tilapias), which includes many of today's threatened and endangered fishes.

As with the cichlids of Lake Victoria, the only home for the fissi is a single lake: Lake Barombi-Mbo in western Cameroon. Unlike other tilapias in the same genus, the fissi is totally reliant on the continued stability of this lake's ecosystem. Its relatively small range is the principal reason for concern over its survival. Any natural or human-made catastrophes could quickly cause the extinction of the fissi. Introduction of larger and more aggressive predators or overfishing must also be considered potential threats.

Despite their seemingly endless physical and behavioral differences, cichlids possess many similar physical characteristics. All cichlids present a fairly flattened and rounder appearance (like a plate on edge) than other streamlined and torpedo-like fishes. Most have broad, hardened mouth parts that are used to scrape algae from surfaces or to crush hard food items. In addition to teeth on the jaws, the mouth contains hundreds of teeth on a plate-like bone at the base of the mouth and throat. These teeth hold food within the throat and are called pharyngeal teeth. After food is swallowed, the cichlid's long gut absorbs the nutrients. The length of the gut is often more than two and a half times the length of the fish.

A distinctive characteristic of the fissi as well as of all other cichlids is the long, spiny dorsal fin on the back that may extend from just behind the head all the way to the tail section of the body. The segment near the tail usually is longer than the segment near the head. In addition to a longer dorsal fin, the pectoral fins on both sides of the body, just behind the gills, are long and pointed. This trait gives the subfamily of cichlids great lateral mobility as they search for food.

Mouthbrooding

Most cichlids build nests in vegetation or dig holes in bottom sediment in which to lay their eggs. The fissi, however, does not build a nest but engages in an activity called mouthbrooding.

After eggs are laid by a female and fertilized by a male, one of the parents (depending on the species) picks up the eggs with the mouth and guards them in a chamber in the mouth cavity. The parent then incubates the eggs until they hatch after a period of one to two weeks.

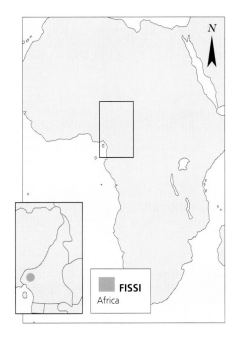

FISSI
Africa

Armored

Several physical traits make the fissi stand out from other tilapias. It has an unusually large, long head and large eyes to effectively find and eat prey.

The teeth of the jaws and mouth cavity are quite small. The fissi is well-armed against predators, with 16 or 17 spines on the dorsal fin to ward off attacks.

The overall coloration of the fissi is a dull gray with a hint of green in breeding males. In males this coloration underlies several irregular dark blotches on the lower head and body.

The preferred food of the adult fissi, like many cichlids, is microscopic plant material, called phytoplankton, and some algae. The fissi obtains these small plants from the water using small adhesive "threads" in the throat. When young, the fissi is omnivorous and will eat whatever might be available, even other fishes.

William E. Manci

See also Cichlids, Lake Victoria; Dikume; Kululu; Leka Keppe; Tilapia, Otjikota; and Unga.

FLORICANS

Class: Aves

Order: Gruiformes

Family: Otididae

Floricans belong to the bustard family. This family is typically patterned in gray and brown hues accented with black and white. Many species display the hues in subtle patterns of small, alternating bands. This pattern, called cryptic coloration, makes their plumage resemble vegetation and plant debris. Such coloration helps them hide in the prairies—their favored habitat. Bustards look like perfect crosses between pheasants and rails. Some species have a moderately long, narrow, slightly decurved beak that is similar to a rail's, but other species have beaks suggestive of a pheasant's. Their legs and feet are long and powerfully built, which suits them well for a terrestrial lifestyle. They also have a long, slender neck. The long foot, leg, and neck contribute to the bustard's tall stature. Their height probably allows them to see over prairie vegetation so that they may spot predators and competitors.

Bustards often sport plumes that originate from the crown, nape, cheek, or throat. These plumes probably help females to recognize males of their respective species during courtship. Bustards typically go through elaborate courtship displays in which males inflate special air sacs and fan their wings and tails. The males establish territories that they defend against other males, where they do their strutting and displaying to attract females. Their behavior closely parallels the courting rituals of many pheasants and grouses.

Ornithologists recognize between 22 and 25 bustard species. One species occurs only in Australia and New Guinea; three species occur either primarily or exclusively in India; two species occur in Asia and Europe; one species occurs through much of Asia, extreme southeastern Europe, and northern Africa (see Houbara Bustard); and the remaining species all inhabit portions of Africa. No bustards live naturally anywhere in the New World.

Bengal Florican

(Eupodotis bengalensis)

IUCN: Endangered

Length: Male 27 in. (68.6 cm); female slightly larger

Weight: 4–5 lb. (1.8–2.25 kg)

Clutch size: 2 eggs

Incubation: 30 days

Diet: Omnivorous

Habitat: Tall grasses and wet grasslands

Range: Northeastern India, Nepal, and Vietnam

THE WORLD AWAKENS to a peculiar rattling that rises above the morning song of birds and insects. As the sun rises across the plains, the rattle comes and goes, starts and stops, first here and then there. Dawn has returned to the prairies of northeastern India, and the Bengal floricans are courting.

The male has a black head, neck, breast, and belly; his back is also black but finely patterned with buff and tan, and the wing is white with some black in the outer flight feathers. The female is patterned overall in black, tan, and buff, and her wings are dark with no white.

Modified feathers grow in each wing of the male Bengal florican. These feathers cause the wings to clap noisily when the bird flies. During the breeding season, males perform dramatic courtship displays. They leap six to ten feet (two to three meters) in the air, fluff out their feathers, arch their wings, and glide erratically back to the ground. This astonishing performance probably wards off competing males from defended territory while simultaneously attracting females ready to breed.

Males usually choose their territories carefully. They prefer to leap and display in areas where the grass is short, to improve their visibility to females. However, floricans also need tall grass nearby where they can hide during midday. As afternoon fades into evening, they emerge to start the ritual all over again.

Noisy flight and leaping about attracts more than mates. Such displays also attract predators. Ordinarily, floricans are wary birds. They escape danger by running away to hide in thick grass or by crouching and sitting still, but hunters soon learned the Bengal florican's courtship habits and were able to shoot them in great numbers. Besides being a target for recreational hunting, the Bengal florican provided gourmet table fare. An old Latin name for the species was *deliciosa*. Hunters undoubtedly played a major role in the florican's disappearance from much of its former range. Excessive hunting, however, was not the species' only problem.

The Bengal florican's need for good grass cover is another key factor in its decline. The people of India have treated their grasslands with no better care or reverence than have people on other continents. People all over the world have abused the planet's prairies by burning them, plowing them, and covering them with cities and towns. Now birds such as the Bengal florican are disappearing as natural prairies dwindle away.

In India the native grasses are mowed for hay and are heavily grazed by cattle and other livestock. Many prairies have been converted to croplands to feed India's enormous human population. Cultural changes have affected the prairie, too. As once nomadic peoples have ceased to wander and have settled instead into one area, the impact on native plant communities has often been devastating. In many areas the prairies are burned, which destroys florican nests. Many prairies have been plowed so that grasses favorable to game animals such as swamp deer (*Cervus duvauceli*) can be planted.

One consequence of prairie destruction has been severe erosion. When soil becomes too badly damaged by erosion, native plant communities can be nearly impossible to restore. This means that florican habitat can never be recovered in such places.

Call to action

In 1980 an international symposium on bustards was convened. Surprisingly, the Bengal florican and the lesser florican were not discussed because no one knew enough about them or their status to offer any remarks. As a result, in 1982 the International Council for Bird Preservation (ICBP) organized field studies to collect more information about the floricans. Less than 100 Bengal floricans survive in Nepal. Nearly all the grasslands in eastern Nepal have been converted to croplands. The status of Bengal floricans in Vietnam remains uncertain, and some ornithologists have questioned the accuracy of the counts of Bengal floricans in other areas. Surveys conducted in 1984 and 1985 found 49 Bengal floricans in India, all found in Uttar Pradesh, West Bengal, and Assam, but experts suspected that in the late 1980s perhaps 100 to 300 Bengal floricans were still living in India. The greatest numbers live in Kaziranga National Park, and the wildlife sanctuaries of Manas, Orang, and Sonai Rupa, all in Assam.

Hope for the future

Saving the Bengal florican depends upon protecting what is left of its prairie habitat. Most of India's wildlife sanctuaries are in the mountains and consist of forests. More attention needs to be directed toward the prairies, especially the wet grasslands where the Bengal floricans live. There is a need to locate and evaluate all the remaining prairies in India, map the distribution of prairie animal species, investigate the effects of overgrazing by livestock, and document the effects of forest destruction on prairies. Another vital task is to find out whether Bengal floricans migrate or remain on breeding grounds all year. If they do not migrate, the potential for maintaining a healthy gene pool diminishes. As populations become smaller, the possibility of inbreeding grows larger, and inbred populations are less healthy.

The Bengal florican is one of the most threatened birds on the Indian subcontinent. Unless deliberate protective action is taken soon, India's prairies will disappear and the Bengal florican will disappear with them. The bird's peculiar courting noises at dawn may be missed as well.

Lesser Florican
(Sypheotides indica)

IUCN: Critically endangered

Length: Male 18 in. (46 cm); female 20 in. (51 cm)
Weight: 18–26½ oz. (504–740 g)
Clutch size: Usually 3–4 eggs
Incubation: Probably 22 days
Diet: Omnivorous
Habitat: Grasslands
Range: Gujarat, western Madhya Pradesh, and eastern Rajasthan in India

FROM THE SOUTHWEST come the winds. They are the monsoons of the Arabian Sea. Blowing early in the year from the northeast, they drag dry, continental air across India and out to sea. When the direction changes in May, the winds carry rains inland from the Arabian Sea. The rains initiate the growing season and the return of the lesser floricans.

The smallest of India's three bustard species, the lesser florican differs from its two relatives by migrating. No one knows exactly where the lesser floricans

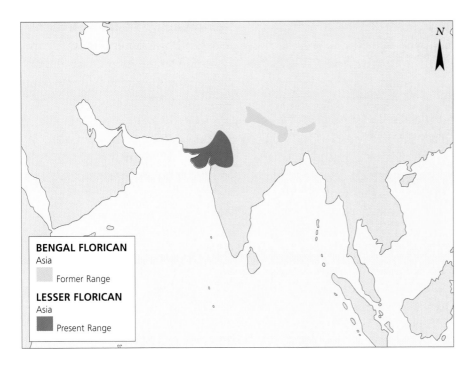

BENGAL FLORICAN
Asia
Former Range

LESSER FLORICAN
Asia
Present Range

spend their time when not breeding, but they do leave their breeding grounds in western India. They are secretive and wary birds. The females, in fact, are seldom seen.

This florican has long legs and a long thin neck that give it a heronlike look, but the beak is more like that of a rail. The male has a black head, neck, breast, belly, and undertail. There is some white on the chin and a white horseshoe pattern extending forward from the tip of each wing, curving up and over the upper back at the base of neck. The back is patterned in light and dark gray. Thin, wiry plumes with broad tips arise from the back of the head and curve forward. The female is without head plumes. She has what is called a "dead leaf" pattern of tan, buff, brown, black, and white arranged in alternating bands and small patches on individual feathers. The male is conspicuous during breeding season because of his habits. The male leaps and leaps, jumping about three feet (one meter) above the grass, flashing the white in his wings, and rattling loudly. He throws his head back and pulls his feet up as he leaps. Then he glides back to ground on partially spread wings and leaps again. When a male sees a female, he leaps ceaselessly to attract attention. Each male lesser florican may leap more than 400 times a day when the breeding season peaks. The females that are impressed enough to approach are then courted. The male struts up to her with his feathers fluffed out and his head and neck stretched forward. Suddenly, he jerks his neck backward so his head rests on his back. He repeats the dance again and again, so long as females remain present.

Hunted by humans

As obvious as the males make themselves, they are too wary and quick for most predators, so their survival under natural conditions is high. However, they have also been hunted by humans. Lesser floricans were hunted heavily for years, but this toll by itself cannot explain the species' decline.

For many years, Indian people depended on other countries to provide food, but a national strategy for food independence has encouraged the expansion of agriculture. As people have plowed the grasslands, lesser floricans have found fewer places to nest and probably fewer places to rest between breeding seasons. They have been seen in fields of cotton and millet, where males have performed their leaping displays. However, it is not known how successfully the lesser florican has adapted to croplands, and the declining population and complete disappearance of floricans from many traditional areas suggest the bird cannot thrive in altered habitat.

Some prairies have been protected from plowing and crop planting, but they are still cut for hay. Cutting can destroy nests and ruin essential cover needed by females with chicks.

Several areas have been specifically preserved for the lesser florican, but they are not well managed. Surveys in 1982 estimated that there were only 362 lesser floricans in the Rajkot, Jamnagar, and Junagadh districts in the state of Gujarat. A 1984 survey of Ratlam, Dhar, and Jhabua districts in the state of Madhya Pradesh estimated 150 birds. Other birds undoubtedly survive elsewhere, but where and how many are unknown. If the lesser florican is to survive extinction, the remaining native prairies must be preserved and appropriately managed for grassland birds.

Kevin Cook

See also Houbara Bustard.

FLYCATCHERS

Class: Aves

Order: Passeriformes

Family: Muscicapidae

Flycatchers belong to several different families in the songbird order Passeriformes. The relationship of these families continues to be revised by ornithologists, and the perfect classification system may never be achieved.

Flycatchers earn their name from their feeding habit. They sit on an exposed perch and watch for flying insects. When they see one, they fly out from the perch and snatch it. To help them catch flying insects, they usually have wide mouths and a tuft of bristle-like feathers around the mouth. Not all flycatchers use this technique, but they carry the name because of their relationship to those that do.

Ashy-breasted Flycatcher

(Muscicapa randi)

IUCN: Endangered

Class: Aves

Order: Passeriformes

Family: Muscicapidae

Subfamily: Muscicapinae

Length: About 5½ in. (14 cm)

Weight: Unknown

Clutch size: Unknown

Incubation: Unknown

Diet: Small insects

Habitat: Lowland tropical and partially degraded forest

Range: Philippine islands of Luzon, Negros, and possibly Samar

IN THE LOWLAND tropical forests north of Manila, in the Philippines, lives one of the rarest of birds—the ashy-breasted flycatcher. Here the forests are hot and humid. Deeply rutted dirt tracks cut through the dense vegetation, leading to clearings where the trees have been cut down, a reminder of the continuing destruction of prime habitats.

The ashy-breasted flycatcher typically sits on a snag about 30 feet (9 meters) above the ground, and looks for insects. The bird is slim, the size of a small sparrow, with a fine bill. It has no distinctive plumage features, being grayish-brown above with a gray breast and paler belly, but its shape and size, demeanor, and location single it out. Only declared a full species as recently as 1991, the ashy-breasted flycatcher is one of at least 107 species of Old World flycatcher in the family Muscicapidae. Until 1985 it was only known from five sites, but since then 14 birds have

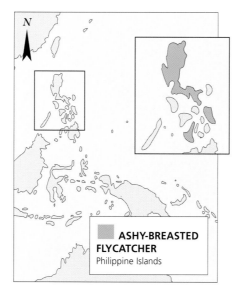

ASHY-BREASTED FLYCATCHER
Philippine Islands

been observed at eight locations in the Philippines, mainly on Luzon. It was also rediscovered on the smaller island of Negros in 1992, 115 years after the only previous record.

The ashy-breasted flycatcher is a bird of lowland and hill forest. It has never been seen higher than 3,800 feet (1,200 meters). The distribution of the few sightings present something of an enigma; it seems strange that these records should come from such a wide area, given the species' rarity. It was once suggested that the reason for this was that it was a rare vagrant, not a breeding bird, but this has been disproved. Two juvenile birds have been seen, and in May 1997 a pair of adults was seen taking food to young. An alternative suggestion is that its numbers are restricted by competition for food from other flycatcher species that winter in the Philippines.

It is important that its needs and distribution are better understood, and it is hoped that a mist-netting project will provide more information. Proposals have been made to extend the boundaries of the Northern Sierra Madre Natural Park, and to seek funding for conservation of other sites where it has been seen—Amiakan, Los Dos Cuernos, the Angat watershed, and Mount Talinis. According to the book *Threatened Birds of the Philippines*, currently being prepared by N. J. Collar and others, "Integrated forest conservation strategies should consider the distribution and requirements of this species and a suite of other threatened endemic, or near-endemic, birds on Luzon and Negros."

Tim Harris

Guam Flycatcher
(Myiagra freycineti)

IUCN: Extinct

Length: 5 in. (13 cm)
Weight: Unknown
Clutch size: 1 egg
Incubation: Unknown
Diet: Insects
Habitat: Woodlands and forests
Range: Guam, Mariana Islands

THE MALE GUAM flycatcher (subfamily Monarchinae) was slate-blue above, including its head, back, wing, and tail. The chin beneath its stubby beak was pure white. Its throat and upper breast were a golden buff color and it had a white belly and undertail. The female was not so blue above, with more golden tones. Both had the large head that is common to many flycatchers. They also had a whiskered appearance, due to the many hairlike bristles around the base of the beak.

The Guam flycatcher once inhabited almost all of the woodlands and forests of Guam. This island covers 209 square miles (543 square kilometers), with savanna, woodland, and forest mixed together, including mangrove swamps. In the late 1800s and early 1900s, observers said the bird was frequently seen. By the mid-1900s, ornithologists decided the bird was becoming uncommon. In 1990 the Guam flycatcher was deemed critically endangered.

No specific events explain the flycatcher's decline. Certainly deforestation on the island reduced its available habitat. The woodlands and forests were cleared to provide living space, cropland, and industrial sites for the people of Guam. These inhabitants grow a variety of fruits and vegetables, both for domestic consumption and for export. As an insectivore, the flycatcher could easily be affected by agricultural pesticides.

A further hazard to Guam flycatchers crept up on it in the night. The brown tree snake *(Boiga irregularis)* specializes in eating small birds and birds' eggs. A good climber of trees, and active at night, the brown tree snake is especially deadly for small birds such as the Guam flycatcher because they do not recognize or understand how to defend themselves against it. The brown tree snake is an exotic species on Guam. Its homeland is southeast Asia, where snakes and birds evolved together. In normal predator-prey relationships, prey species develop skills that allow them to avoid predators. The predators likewise develop special skills that allow them to foil enough of the prey's defenses to catch and eat them.

On Guam, the brown tree snake faces no predators of its own. It is free to multiply as long as its food supply lasts. Unfortunately, the Guam flycatcher did not evolve with snakes, much less a bird-eating snake, so it had no natural defenses against it. Because the flycatcher only laid a single egg per clutch, it was extremely vulnerable to heavy predation.

Island isolation

The Guam flycatcher suffered several disadvantages at the same time. It was unique to the island of Guam, so it could not escape to some other place or survive elsewhere. For the flycatcher, it was Guam or no place at all. The flycatcher's habitat declined so drastically that the island could support only a fraction of the flycatcher population it once did.

The modernization of agriculture may have brought enough pesticides to Guam to threaten or contaminate the flycatcher's habitat.

Not only was the habitat much reduced, but quite possibly the food supply was either reduced or contaminated. Finally, an exotic predator had unlimited access to the flycatcher's last habitat. Collectively, these factors made survival very difficult for this spirited little bird.

The U.S. Fish and Wildlife Service had an ongoing research program aimed at controlling brown tree snake populations and perhaps someday eradicating the snake from Guam. In addition, the Guam flycatcher population was carefully monitored. Even if steps had been taken to reforest the island, a decade or more would have been needed to restore the flycatcher. For the Guam flycatcher time just ran out.

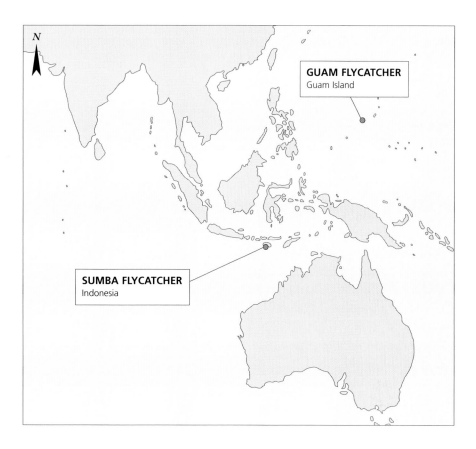

Sumba Flycatcher

(Ficedula harterti)

IUCN: Lower risk

Length: Probably 4½–5 in. (11–12.7 cm)
Weight: Unknown
Clutch size: Unknown
Incubation: Unknown
Diet: Insects
Habitat: Forests
Range: Sumba Island, Indonesia

FOR MANY DECADES, Sumba was known as Sandalwood Island because of its trees. Sandalwood trees do not grow especially large in comparison to other trees, but their wood is highly prized and has been for centuries. When first cut, sandalwood is odorless. The valued aroma develops as the wood dries. After drying, the wood is fashioned into ornamental boxes and chests. Sandalwood also yields a fine oil that is used in manufacturing incense and certain perfumes.

The best known sandalwood comes from *Santalum album*, a tree native to India but planted in many tropical areas. Other sandalwood trees in the family Santalaceae grow elsewhere in the world, including Hawaii and portions of the southern United States.

All told, Sumba covers 4,306 square miles (11,196 square kilometers). One of thousands of Indonesian islands, it is part of the Lesser Sunda Islands of Indonesia. The island is somewhat mountainous, so most of its forests are montane. The narrow coastal plain has been largely developed for agriculture. For decades trees have been cut aggressively on Sumba with little regard to the consequences.

The little Sumba flycatcher (subfamily Muscicapinae) has not been well studied. Almost nothing is known of its basic natural history. It has been found in evergreen forests at about 1,640 feet (500 meters), but by itself this means very little. Without more knowledge, experts cannot determine whether these are vagrant birds in an unusual habitat or normal birds living in their ideal habitat. Basic research is still needed to determine the flycatcher's habitat requirements. Without such information, nothing effective can be done to protect this species.

No one knows the actual status of the Sumba flycatcher. But ornithologists guess that at present the bird is near threatened but at lower risk of becoming extinct.

Kevin Cook

Flying Foxes

(Pteropus sp.)

IUCN: Vulnerable to Critically endangered

Class: Mammalia
Order: Chiroptera
Family: Pteropodidae
Weight: 1½–56 oz. (45–1,600 g)
Head-body length: 6½–15¾ in. (170–406 mm)
Wingspan: 23¾–66½ in. (610–1,700 mm)
Diet: Fruit juices
Gestation period: Variable up to 140–150 days
Longevity: Up to 30 plus years
Habitat: Tropical and subtropical forest and swamp

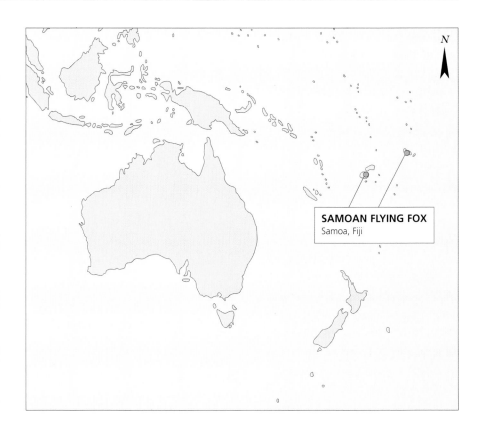

SAMOAN FLYING FOX
Samoa, Fiji

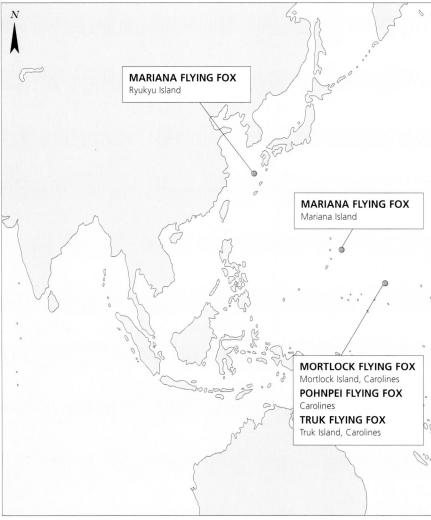

MARIANA FLYING FOX
Ryukyu Island

MARIANA FLYING FOX
Mariana Island

MORTLOCK FLYING FOX
Mortlock Island, Carolines
POHNPEI FLYING FOX
Carolines
TRUK FLYING FOX
Truk Island, Carolines

FLYING FOXES ARE part of a large family of mammals known as Old World fruit bats. They are called fruit bats because their diet is composed almost entirely of fruit juice. They obtain the juice by mashing up ripe fruit in their strong jaws, drinking the liquid, and spitting out the pulp and seeds onto the ground where they may germinate.

The 59 species that make up the genus *Pteropus* have the common name flying foxes because their larger size and long muzzle resemble that of a fox; they look less like a typical bat. Most species are a dull brown or black, often with a yellowish area between the shoulders.

Due to their habits of roosting in trees and feeding actively during the day, flying foxes are among the most easily observed bats. However, owing in part to their remote ranges and diminished numbers, this group has not been studied very extensively.

Early in the 20th century, flying fox groups were estimated to contain up to several hundred thousand individuals. Today, while some species are still seen in substantial numbers, many species are down to only a few hundred individuals and have been eliminated from some islands within their former range.

Always hanging out

Flying foxes are most frequently found in coastal forest areas on small islands. Occurring either singly or, more typically, in small or large groups, they spend most of their nonforaging time hanging upside down, roosting in typical bat fashion within trees. They have a high degree of loyalty to one roost site, with the same trees being used as roosts day after day for many years.

Eating out

Whether a particular species feeds during the day or at night, their behavior is similar. They depart the roosting site and fly some distance to a feeding site. That site can be on the same island or, in some cases, as far as 22 miles (36 kilometers) across open ocean on a different island. Once at a feeding site, the bats squabble over feeding locations, often resulting in only one individual per tree or branch.

Besides fruit juice, flying foxes are known to eat flowers occasionally. It is not known whether flowers are eaten for the energy contained in the nectar, or for the mineral nutrients contained in the pollen. Because a diet of fruit juice is low in minerals, this deficiency may explain why some flying fox species drink seawater, which is high in minerals.

The future of many flying fox species is in question. The Chamorro people of Guam have eaten fruit bats for more than 1,000 years. The switch from traditional hunting methods to firearms led to increased hunting and the extinction of one endemic species. Fruit bats are in demand as food throughout much of their range. In Southeast Asia, fruit bat meat is also used medicinally to treat asthma and kidney ailments. In Indonesia

After feeding, flying foxes often "hang out" at the feeding site, digesting their food prior to the flight back to their roost tree.

and Malaysia, the annual sales of a single vendor could exceed 10,000 bats.

Captive breeding

While population estimates for a few species of flying fox are uncertain, it is known that species such as the Comoro black and the Rodrigues flying fox number only in the hundreds. The Mariana flying fox is estimated to have about 1,000 surviving individuals. Some captive-breeding programs have been undertaken, including one for the Rodrigues flying fox. However, the most important issues at this time are the direct loss of individuals to hunting and the continuing loss of habitat to development. Unless an organized effort is undertaken to secure roosting and feeding areas and to convince local people to reduce hunting of the flying fox, there may be no future for many of the species.

Terry Tompkins

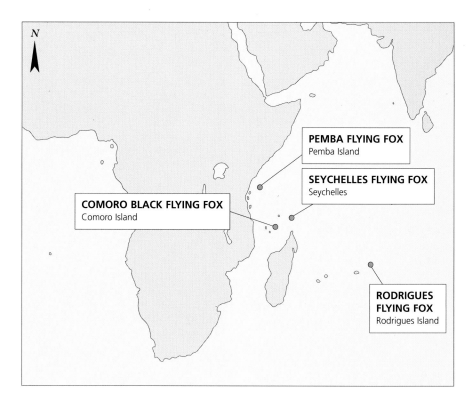

The following is a list of species in danger of extinction, along with their status and range.

COMORO BLACK FLYING FOX

(*P. livingstonii*)

IUCN: Critically endangered

Range: Comoro Islands between Africa and Madagascar

MARIANA FLYING FOX

(*P. mariannus*)

IUCN: Endangered

Range: Several islands in the western Pacific Ocean

MORTLOCK FLYING FOX

(*P. phaeocephalus*)

IUCN: Critically endangered

Range: Mortlock Island and the Caroline Islands, western Pacific Ocean

PEMBA FLYING FOX

(*P. voeltzkowi*)

IUCN: Critically endangered

Range: Pemba Island, northeast of Tanzania

POHNPEI FLYING FOX

(*P. molossinus*)

IUCN: Critically endangered

Range: Caroline Islands, western Pacific

RODRIGUES FLYING FOX

(*P. rodricensis*)

ESA: Endangered
IUCN: Critically endangered

Range: Rodrigues Island, Indian Ocean

SAMOAN FLYING FOX

(*P. samoensis*)

IUCN: Vulnerable

Range: Samoa and Fiji islands, South Pacific

SEYCHELLES FLYING FOX

(*P. seychellensis*)

IUCN: Not evaluated

Range: Aldabra Island, Seychelles, western Indian Ocean

TRUK FLYING FOX

(*P. insularis*)

IUCN: Critically endangered

Range: Truk and Uala islands, the Caroline Islands, western Pacific Ocean

FODIES

Class: Aves

Order: Passeriformes

Family: Ploceidae

Subfamily: Ploceinae

Fodies sport brilliant plumages of red or orange red that brighten the forests where they live. They belong to the weaver family, as does the house sparrow (*Passer domesticus*), which they resemble in physique and body size. Whereas house sparrows have found their way all around the world, the fodies are restricted to islands in the Indian Ocean. Four species of fody are listed by IUCN–The World Conservation Union, one of which, the Réunion fody, (*Foudia* sp.) is listed as extinct. The Madagascar fody (*Foudia madagascariensis*) is often called "cardinal." It has been introduced to many different islands and, as an exotic species, may compete with native species. Of the two Mascarene fodies, one occurs on Mauritius and the other on Rodrigues. Both are in danger of extinction.

Mauritius Fody

(Foudia rubra)

ESA: Endangered

IUCN: Critically endangered

Length: 5–5½ in. (12.9–14 cm)

Weight: ½–¾ oz. (16–20 g)

Clutch size: 3 eggs

Incubation: Unknown

Diet: Insects and nectar

Habitat: Native forest

Range: Mauritius Island, Indian Ocean

A LITTLE RED and green bird once flourished in the forests that covered the island of Mauritius. For the greater part of the species' existence, it had no name. When people eventually found the bird's island, they also discovered the bird. Eventually people came to know the little bird as the Mauritius fody.

Clinging to tree bark, it picked and poked into crevices where it would find hidden insects. Pecking away at rotten wood, the fody would find more insects. When flowers bloomed on the island of Mauritius, the fody would visit them. With its brushy tongue it would find the nectar hidden inside the blossoms. As the bird moved from flower to flower, it undoubtedly carried a little pollen on its face. Some of that pollen would rub off on other flowers, helping them to pollinate. For the cost of a little nectar, a plant was able to set another crop of seeds. For thousands of years, flowers, birds, insects, and forests all thrived on the island of Mauritius.

In 1507 the island began to change. Portuguese sailors, by some accounts, discovered the island in that year. Arabic sailors reportedly knew of the island long before, but records from that era are difficult to interpret. The Portuguese probably visited the island from time to time until the Dutch claimed it in 1598. They started a colony there in 1638 and converted it to a prison colony in 1644. France took control of Mauritius in 1721, and British rule followed from 1810 to 1968. The first major event on Mauritius was the extinction of the dodo. The last live one was seen in 1680.

An island ravaged

Forest covered much of Mauritius when sailors first dropped anchor at this remote spot in the Indian Ocean. Dutch settlers cleared some forest for living space and for building materials. They also cut ebony (*Diospyros tesselaria*), a valuable lumber tree, for export. A small colony with relatively few people, the Dutch caused only localized forest loss on Mauritius. They did, however, open up the island and are credited by some with introducing sugarcane. By 1990 the island's 747 square miles (2,046 square kilometers) hosted a human population that surpassed one million. On Mauritius the effect has been the loss of its once great forests. Plantations of sugarcane and trees imported from other lands now grow there, and those plantations cannot support the same complex variety of wildlife that the native forests did.

The Mauritius fody probably became known to ornithologists in the early 1700s. By the late 1800s the species, which can be extremely difficult to find, was already becoming rare. The male fody has a red or orange-red head, nape, chin, and throat that gives it a hooded look. Black eyes, lore, and beak create a mask that contrasts with the red. The belly is olive green. The back is also olive green with darker green stripes and a red rump. The wing and tail are darker green. The female resembles the male but lacks any red coloration.

The fody prefers native forests that receive about 78 inches (200 centimeters) of rain each year and where summer temperatures do not rise much above 75 degrees Fahrenheit (24 degrees Celsius). In these humid but cool forests, wood rots quickly. Decaying wood attracts insects that the fodies eat. The native trees also host many smaller plants, known as epiphytes, that grow piggyback on the trees. The fodies search these epiphytes for insects too.

Exotic trees such as those grown on plantations for fruit or for lumber crops do not harbor enough of the right insects to support a fody population. Nor do they grow epiphytes.

Fodies will, however, eat small fruits from exotic trees. In a style that seems to be unique to this species, the birds eat the fruit pulp but leave the seeds and stem still attached to its twig.

The fody has dwindled along with its habitat. By the 1970s it was found only in a few tracts of remaining native forest in southwestern Mauritius. It usually stays at or above 1,500 feet (457 meters), but it has been seen as low as 1,000 feet (305 meters) in the Bel Ombre Reserve. Normally a solitary bird, the fody occasionally moves about in flocks of Mauritius gray white-eyes (*Zosterops borbonicus*). Strictly arboreal, it remains in the trees from ground level into the canopy. Its most significant predator is the crab-eating macaque (*Macaca fascicularis*), a species native to Java. The Dutch probably introduced the macaque onto Mauritius in the 1600s. The macaques move about the trees quite easily and are known to destroy birds' nests while taking eggs and nestlings. Between habitat loss from cutting of forests and habitat degradation from the introduction of exotic plants and animals, the Mauritius fody has declined drastically.

Ornithologists estimated that 250 pairs survived in the mid-1970s, but at least 47 of those were living in areas immediately threatened by forest-cutting activities. At that time the fodies were widely distributed but with few birds in any one area. Where they did occur, they maintained their usual small territories as if more fodies were still around. This has been interpreted as evidence that Mauritius does not have enough fodies to occupy all the remaining available habitat. Further, poor nesting success prevents the fody population from growing.

Unsuccessful move

An attempt was made in the 1970s to move Mauritius fodies to Réunion Island. The fody native to that island has not been seen since the 1600s and is presumed extinct. More native forest survives on Réunion than on Mauritius, and no crab-eating macaques live there. Three birds were moved to the island in 1975 before a severe cyclone and other occurrences ended the project. No fodies have been seen on Réunion since then. Three fodies were also moved to other parts of Mauritius but apparently with no enduring success. Another course for helping the Mauritius fody was suggested in the 1970s. The idea was to mix species of plantation trees in a way that would still provide commercially valuable products but would also provide better habitat for the fodies. Some steps have been taken to

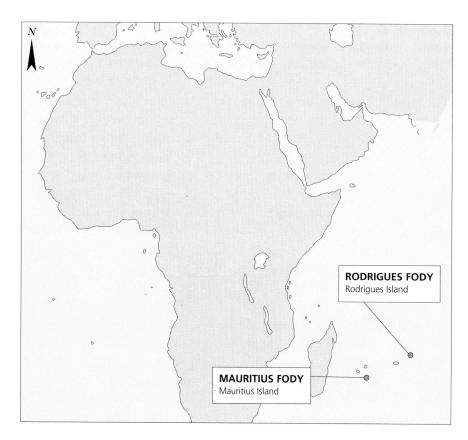

RODRIGUES FODY
Rodrigues Island

MAURITIUS FODY
Mauritius Island

protect remaining forest on Mauritius through reserves and parks, but more aggressive work is needed. Macaques must be eliminated and forests regenerated to recover the Mauritius fody. In 1990, there were an estimated 81–102 pairs, however, this number has more than likely declined.

Rodrigues Fody
(Foudia flavicans)

ESA: Endangered

IUCN: Vulnerable

Length: 5–5½ in. (12.9–14 cm)
Weight: ½–¾ oz. (14.7–17 g)
Clutch size: 3 eggs
Incubation: Unknown
Diet: Insects and nectar, some small seeds
Habitat: Forests and woody shrublands
Range: Rodrigues Island

THE RODRIGUES FODY demonstrates how degraded habitat quality eventually leads to habitat destruction and ultimately to the decline of a species. A bird species can be destroyed one of two ways. First, it can be directly killed. Second, its habitat can be eliminated. With no place to live, a species disappears quickly. Both of these factors have affected the Rodrigues fody.

In appearance, the male Rodrigues fody has a yellow head with a red face and a black beak. The breast and undertail are also yellow, with a white belly separating them. Its back, wing, and tail are a yellowish gray brown, somewhat golden, and occasionally accented by a yellowish rump. The female is much plainer. She lacks the yellow and red hues of the male.

Hungry, forceful eaters
Arboreal birds, they spend more time in the crowns of trees than on the trunks. They search leaves and twigs for the insects they eat. They also have a taste for nectar. They have the brushy tongue commonly found in nectar-feeding birds, but they are seemingly impatient creatures. Rather than contenting themselves with lapping nectar from the blossoms, they hold a flower down with one foot and peck a hole through its base. They then lap the flower through the hole. Often, they simply pluck the petals from a flower and gain easier access to the sweet juice. This behavior may allow them to reach nectar that would otherwise be unavailable to them. They also consume small seeds.

Rodrigues fodies remain in their home territories all year. They travel through the territory as individuals, as pairs, or as family groups after chicks fledge. The males have developed a wing-spreading display that they employ for a dual purpose: to attract females and to intimidate intruding males of the same species. How the wing-spreading display may affect the relationship between the native Rodrigues fody and the exotic Madagascar fody (*Foudia madagascariensis*) has not been studied. The Madagascar fody is exotic to Rodrigues Island, because it did not occur there naturally but was imported and released on the island by people. The Madagascar fody may compete with the Rodrigues fody. Apparently the Madagascar fody depends more on grass seeds than does the Rodrigues fody. Some observers believe that this acts to keep the Rodrigues fody more in the forests. However, forests are the native fody's original habitat.

Small island
Smallest of the three Mascarene Islands, Rodrigues covers only 43 square miles (112 square kilometers). At 1,000 miles (1,600 kilometers) east of Madagascar, Rodrigues also lies farther out in the Indian Ocean than either Mauritius or Réunion. When first discovered, it was densely forested and the Rodrigues fody was apparently abundant. When European sailors began stopping on Rodrigues, they brought livestock, pets, and vermin. Goats,

Like any island species, the Rodrigues fody is susceptible to changes in its environment. Its habitat has been seriously altered, and the bird is threatened as a consequence.

cattle, and pigs were the usual livestock; cats and dogs the usual pets, although birds and monkeys were also common; and rats constituted the vermin.

Settlers also brought crops for agriculture. The collective effect of exotic plants and animals was change in habitat character followed by an ever-quickening decline in habitat quality for native wildlife. Trees were cut to provide grassy openings for cattle grazing. Goats and pigs ate what they could find in the forests. As they multiplied, they ate more. Eating fruits, seeds, and seedlings, they prevented trees from reproducing. As old trees died, no young trees grew to replace them. The pigs and goats had eliminated entire and consecutive generations of trees. The forest dwindled away. In its place

a savanna developed that does not provide the variety of food necessary for the Rodrigues fody.

Very little forest, limited to isolated fragments, remains on Rodrigues. The Rodrigues fody is adapted to a forest habitat and cannot survive in a savanna habitat. The destruction of forest on Rodrigues Island resulted in the slow deterioration of the fody population. By the 1970s fewer than 200 Rodrigues fodies were known. A 1983 estimate suggested only 60 pairs remained.

Although originally reduced by human activities, the fody also became threatened by natural causes. The Mascarene Islands are subjected to annual cyclones that can be very intense. The high winds and driving rains of these cyclones may kill fodies and destroy nests. Cyclones have

swept across Rodrigues for thousands of years. These storms unleashed a great destructive force on the fodies because the birds no longer had dense forests to buffer the rain and wind.

The pressures on this bird slowly began to diminish, however, when revised wildlife laws enacted in 1983 extended some legal protection to the Rodrigues fody. This was followed in the late 1980s with measures to improve and expand this bird's habitat. These actions have resulted in an increase in the fody population. In July 1989 there were estimated to be 190–230 birds.

A survey in April 1991 indicated that there were around 150 pairs, and by August 1991 the numbers had risen to 350–450 individuals.

Kevin Cook

FOXES

Class: Mammalia

Order: Carnivora

Family: Canidae

Few animals have inspired literature to the extent that the fox has. A character in countless poems, fairy tales, and myths, the fox even played a role in shaping the New World: the North American trade in fox furs and beaver pelts largely determined the locations of the earliest population settlements in Canada and Alaska. Unfortunately, the human race has rewarded the fox for its inspiration with relentless persecution.

There are approximately 21 species of fox, 14 in the Northern Hemisphere and 7 in the Southern Hemisphere. Foxes are characterized by pointed muzzles,

erect triangular ears, and long bushy tails. Foxes are relatives of the dog, but they have more flattened skulls, longer ears, and longer, much fuller tails. Most people regard the red fox as typical, although in fact it is only the biggest and most widespread species.

English colonists, who were eager to enjoy the traditional fox hunt in the New World, introduced the European red fox to New England, where it soon interbred with the North American red fox. The clearing of North American forests for agriculture apparently brought the red fox farther south from its habitually more northern range. It migrated into areas populated almost exclusively by the smaller gray fox. Over time the red fox has taken over the central plains of North America, an area that once probably belonged to the gray fox and the kit fox.

Small foxes have many enemies. In California, coyotes kill the smaller San Joaquin kit foxes, often without eating them. Wolves are also known to kill foxes—if only to eliminate them as competition for scarce food. Humans, however, have proved to be the most destructive enemy of this nocturnal, sometimes wily carnivore.

Because of its real or fabled weakness for chickens and eggs, the fox has paid dearly. Yet despite the enduring prejudice of some farmers, the fox does not live exclusively on filched hens and eggs—or even on the rabbits, prairie dogs, or rodents it hunts and relishes. Foxes have molar teeth that are also adapted for eating squash, melons, corn, cherries, rose hips, apples, and even sour grapes. Unlike their rivals the coyotes and wolves, foxes will often bury food and return to it later.

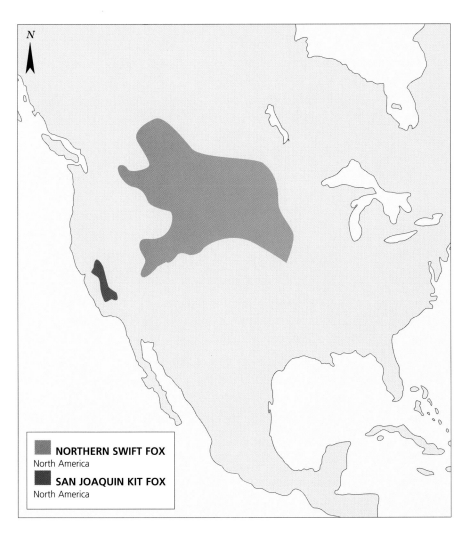

N

NORTHERN SWIFT FOX
North America

SAN JOAQUIN KIT FOX
North America

Northern Swift Fox

(Vulpes velox hebes)

ESA: Endangered

Weight: 4–6½ lb. (1.8–3 kg)
Head–body length: 14.8–20.7 in. (37½–52½ cm)
Tail length: 9–13¾ in. (22.5–35 cm)
Shoulder height: To 8 in. (20 cm)
Diet: Rodents, small birds, lagomorphs, insects, and fruit
Gestation period: About 50 days
Longevity: Up to 12 years
Habitat: Prairies; open grassy areas
Range: North American central and southern plains

COYOTES AND WOLVES more frequently hunt in pairs or packs and, therefore, gorge on as much meat as they can hold knowing that others will leave no scrap for a second meal. Although foxes usually hunt alone, they are profoundly social animals. Scientists have noted 22 play signals—invitations to frolic. Why they need so many signals is not known.

Because of its vulnerability to rabies, the fox has long been feared and routinely killed as a potential carrier of the disease. It has been hunted with horses and hounds for sport, trapped and poisoned for bounty money, and flushed and shot by American bird hunters eager to protect their own predatory game interests, notably the pheasant.

Despite this treatment, some species of fox have managed to survive and even flourish.

Over the years there have been many organizations in the United States dedicated to the reduction or elimination of the fox. During the 1970s, one organization called Pheasants Unlimited claimed to have killed more than 150,000 foxes.

Apart from such systematic attempts to control animal populations, foxes and coyotes have generally learned to adapt to the ways of people. Many coyotes and foxes have learned to survive in urban and suburban environments. This is not the case, however, with either the endangered northern swift fox or the San Joaquin kit fox.

COYOTES TRADITIONALLY hunt and run down jackrabbits as a pack, flanking the victim on all sides until there is no escape. With a good jump the swift fox, on the other hand, can sprint and overtake a jackrabbit on a dead run. While the name swift is appropriate, this fox does not have the caution and wary intelligence of many of its kind. This smallest of all North American foxes once roamed the Great Plains from Alberta to Texas. Preferring a grassy, open habitat, the swift fox has been all but eliminated from many areas by habitat loss to farming and by extermination. Although showing signs of a comeback, it is now reduced to isolated pockets and a few protected areas.

In the 19th century, farmers and ranchers in the midwest and western states began an all-out

569

war on predators. Any animal likely to kill livestock was poisoned or shot. When the buffalo vanished and could no longer be used to poison other animals, other toxic meat was left out for consumption. While coyotes and other carnivores seemed slower to take the bad meat, wolves and swift foxes proved much easier to eliminate by this method.

At the same time, the fox had another enemy: the Hudson's Bay Fur Company, which was buying up even the comparatively nonvalued swift fox pelts by the tens of thousands per year.

The gradual disappearance of the wolves that shared its plains habitat was not good news for the swift fox either. With the wolves all but gone, the red fox and the coyote moved into their habitat. But where the wolves were generally tolerant of the smaller foxes, the red fox and the coyote were decidedly hostile.

Competition for prey

This is because foxes and coyotes are closer in size than they are to wolves, so they are often competing for the same prey. The fox—the smaller of the two carnivores—is usually the loser in such competitions. Bobcats, golden eagles, and great horned owls are always on the prowl for fox pups.

The swift fox is yellowish gray in color, with a conspicuous black tip on its tail and orange-tinted flanks. In winter its coat

The northern swift fox was less valued for its fur than other species, but this did not stop the Hudson's Bay Fur Company from selling tens of thousands of pelts per year during the 19th century.

becomes thicker, softer, and also much lighter in color.

Although it sometimes emerges to sun itself during the day, the swift fox is basically nocturnal, coming out at night to hunt. The swift fox digs its own burrows or modifies and enlarges the burrows of other animals. It preys on rodents, small birds, prairie dogs, rabbits, and insects. When hunting mice, it stands motionless, listens intensely, and then leaps suddenly, using its forelegs to pin down its prey. Rabbits are

The San Joaquin kit fox may be small, but it is far from slow. Over short distances, it is known to reach speeds of 25 miles (40 kilometers) per hour.

stalked and overtaken with a rapid sprint.

Sexual maturity occurs at about ten months. Males may fight one another during the December through February breeding season, and the female may mate with several males.

However, for a period just before and after the birth of three to six pups, the female allies herself with a single male. The male hunts food and deposits it outside the den.

Strong family bond

The pups emerge from the underground den at about three weeks of age and later begin receiving hunting lessons. The family bond seems strong, for if the female dies, the male will raise the young alone. The young stay with their parents until the fall, when they are ready to live on their own. Although a fox may live as long as 12 years, few individuals live more than four or five years in areas where the animals are extensively hunted or trapped.

Some experts insist that the swift and kit foxes are one and the same, but it is more generally accepted that the smaller ears, broader skull, and grassland habitat of the swift fox sets it apart. There are indications that in Texas and New Mexico some hybridization may sometimes occur between the two species.

The northern swift fox has been intensely bred in captivity for about 15 years. Its survival may depend on reintroducing the animal in the wild.

San Joaquin Kit Fox

(Vulpes macrotis mutica)

ESA: Endangered

Weight: 4–7 lb. (1.8–3.1 kg)
Head-body length: 14¾–19¾ in. (37.5–50 cm)
Tail length: 9–13 in. (22.6–33 cm)
Shoulder height: To 8 in. (20 cm)
Diet: Rodents, small birds, lagomorphs, and fruit
Gestation period: About 50 days
Longevity: Up to 12 years
Habitat: Dry mountains, foothills, and deserts
Range: Southern and central California

LIKE ITS CLOSEST living relative, the swift fox, the San Joaquin kit fox is grayish with a yellowish tinge, becoming orange toward the flanks. A small fox, reaching up to 8 inches (20 centimeters) at the shoulder, the kit fox builds its den in loose desert soil and prefers the semi-arid hills and scrub of southern California to the open plains preferred by the swift fox. It digs its own den or modifies an existing den taken over from a badger or ground squirrel. For quick entry and safe escape, such dens have as many as seven entrances. With its many enemies and its precarious future, however, the San Joaquin kit fox needs more protection than a secure burrow and a particularly acute sense of hearing.

Fast sprinters

Kit foxes rarely weigh more than 7 pounds (3.1 kilograms), but they can dash 25 miles (40 kilometers) an hour over short distances and overtake and bring down anything they can hunt. Eagles and coyotes prey on these small foxes while they roam the semidesert areas of southern California in search of mice, rats, ground squirrels, birds, lizards, snakes, insects, and rabbits. They will also eat fruit when it is available. They range in the Tehachapi Mountain foothills in the Mojave Desert, the foothills of the western San Joaquin Valley, into

The fox shown here is the desert kit fox (*Vulpes macrotis arsipus*). Other subspecies of the kit fox have fared better than those of the San Joaquin group. The California kit fox (*Vulpes macrotis macrotis*), however, has already met with extinction.

Byron and Contra Costa Counties, and on the eastern edge of the San Joaquin Valley.

As with the the kit fox, sexual maturity occurs at about ten months. Three to six pups are born after a gestation period of about 50 days. Pair bonding seems strong, and the young become independent each fall, after being taught to hunt by either or both parents. Several vocalizations are known, including a female's bark that warns its young of impending danger.

Its one-time neighbor and cousin, the California kit fox (*Vulpes macrotis macrotis*), has been extinct since the early 1900s. Both animals were once trapped for their fur, and both proved vulnerable to the poisoned meat that growers routinely put out for coyotes. Today the survival of the San Joaquin kit fox hangs by a thread.

Decline

There are many reasons for the animal's decline. Chief among them appears to be the concentrated farming of its preferred terrain. The conversion of rough, dry valley land to irrigated fields has left the San Joaquin fox with a shrinking habitat, marooning it in an altered environment to which it is not particularly well suited. By depriving the animal of natural ground cover and a networks of dens in which to hide and escape, modern agriculture has left the San Joaquin fox more vulnerable to the natural predation of coyotes, eagles, owls, and hawks. Many foxes and coyotes have learned to adapt to living in urban and suburban environments where they have thrived. This, however, is not true of the San Joaquin kit fox.

Secondary poisoning

These foxes too readily eat carrion and are therefore vulnerable to harm from pesticides and rodenticides. For example, attempts to control the proliferation of the Beechey ground squirrel (*Spermophilus beecheyi*) in the fox's range seem to have resulted in secondary fox poisonings.

Thanks to the efforts of the California Fish and Game Commission and the U.S. Fish and Wildlife Service, a San Joaquin Kit Fox Recovery Plan has been put into effect.

Among its goals is the transfer of foxes from areas of poor suitability to areas that may be more suited to its long-range survival.

Although total population estimates have been as low as 10,000, the California Department of Fish and Game believes that the animals are out of immediate danger for the time being. With continued monitoring, the San Joaquin kit fox will probably survive.

Renardo Barden

GLOSSARY

actinopterygii: the scientific name for bony fish

amphibia: the Latin scientific name for amphibians

apically: relating to, or situated at the apex

aves: the Latin scientific name for birds

biota: flora and fauna of a region

buff: in bird species, a yellow-white color used to describe the plumage

captive breeding: any method of bringing several animals of the same species into a zoo or other closed environment for the purpose of mating; if successful, these methods can increase the population of that species

carnivore: any flesh-eating animal

carnivorous: flesh eating

carrion: the decaying flesh of a dead organism

clutch, clutch size: the number of eggs laid during one nesting cycle

cyathium: a type of flower cluster consisting of several male flowers

decurved: curving downward; a bird's beak is decurved if it points toward the ground

defoliate: to strip trees and bushes of their leaves

deforestation: the process of removing trees from a particular area

dehisce: to expel seeds from a fruit such as a broom pod

diurnal: active during the day; some animals are diurnal, while others are active at night (see nocturnal)

dominance: the ability to overpower the behavior of other individuals; an animal is dominant if it affects others of its own species in a way that benefits itself; also, the trait of abundance that determines the character of a plant community: grasses dominate a prairie, and trees dominate a forest

dorsal: pertaining to or situated on the back of an organism; a dorsal fin is on the back of a fish

ecology: the study of the interrelationship between a living organism and its environment

ecosystem: a community of animals, plants, and bacteria and its interrelated physical and chemical environment

endemic: native to a particular geographic region

epipetric: attached to rocks

estrous: the time period when female mammals can become pregnant

exotic species: a plant or animal species that is not native to its habitat

forest: a plant community in which trees grow closely enough together that their crowns interlock to form a continuous overhead canopy

gametes: male and female cells capable of uniting to form a new fern embryo

herbivore: any plant-eating animal

herbivorous: plant eating

hibernate: to spend the winter season in a dormant or inactive state; some species hibernate to save energy during months when food is scarce

home range: the area normally traveled by an individual species during its lifespan

humus: organic portion of soil resulting from partial decomposition of plant or animal matter

hybrid: the offspring of two different species who mate; see interbreed

hybridization: the gradual decline of a species through continued breeding with another species; see interbreed

immature(s): a young bird that has not yet reached breeding maturity; it usually has plumage differing from an adult bird of the same species

in captivity: a species that exists in zoos, captive breeding programs, or in private collections, perhaps because the species can no longer be found in the wild

incubation: the period when an egg is kept warm until the embryo develops and hatches

indigenous species: any species native to its habitat

indusium: a flap of membranous tissue in a fern or fungus

insecta: the Latin scientific name for insects

insular species: a species isolated on an island or islands

interbreed: when two separate species mate and produce offspring; see hybrid

invertebrate(s): any organism without a backbone (spinal column)

juvenal: a bird with an intermediate set of feathers after its young downy plumage molts and before growing hard, adult feathers

juvenile(s): a young bird or other animal not yet mature

lore(s): the irregularly shaped facial area of a bird between the eye and the base of the beak

migrate, migratory: to move from one range to another, particularly with the change of seasons; many species are migratory

milt: the reproductive glands of male fishes; also, the breeding behavior of male fishes

mollusca: the Latin scientific name for mussels, clams, and snails

montane forest: a forest found in mountainous regions

nocturnal: active at night; some animals are nocturnal, while others are active by day (see diurnal)

omnivore: any species that eats both plants and animals

ornithologist(s): a scientist who studies birds

pelage: the hairy covering of a mammal

pelagic: related to the oceans or open sea; pelagic birds rarely roost on land

perennial: persisting for several years

pinnae: leaf divisions

pinnules: small leaflets

plumage: the feathers that cover a bird

prairie: a plant community without trees and dominated by grasses; a grassland; often incorrectly used synonymously with plain or plains, which is a landform feature and not a plant community

predation: the act of one species hunting another

predator: a species that preys upon other species

primary forest: a forest of native trees that results from natural processes, often called virgin forest

primate(s): a biological ranking of species in the same order, including gorillas, chimpanzees, monkeys, and human beings (*Homo sapiens*)

pteridophyte: plant such as a fern that has roots, stems and leaves but no flowers or seeds

range: the geographic area where a species roams

rare: any animal with a small worldwide population (or local population) that is at risk but not yet threatened or endangered

recovery plan(s): any document that outlines a public or private program for assisting an endangered or threatened species

reptilia: the Latin scientific name for reptiles

rhizome: horizontal root that possesses buds, nodes, and sometimes scalelike leaves

riffle(s): a shallow rapid stretch of water caused by a rocky outcropping or obstruction in a stream

riparian: relating to plants and animals close to and influenced by rivers

roe: fish eggs

rufous: in bird species, plumage that is orange-brown and pink

secondary forest: a forest that has grown back after cutting, forest fire, or other deforestation; secondary forests may or may not contain exotic tree species, but they almost always differ in character from primary forests

sedentary species: one that does not migrate

serpentine: mineral rock consisting of hydrous magnesium silicate. It is usually a dull green color, and looks mottled

sessile: plants without stalks, with leaves attached to the base

siltation: the process of sediment clouding and obstructing a body of water

sori: clusters of spore-producing structures

species: a distinct kind of plant or animal; the biological ranking below genus; a subspecies is an isolated population that varies from its own species

sporangia: structures that make spores

spore: a reproductive structure of a fern

sporophylls: fertile, spore-bearing leaves of a plant

sporophyte: new fern

succulent: able to hold water in leaves, roots or stems

terrarium: transparent enclosure for raising plants

territory: the area occupied more or less exclusively by an organism or group, usually defended by aggressive displays and physical combat

tubercle: a prominent bump on a fish's body connected to a spine

vascular plant: all plants except algae and fungi

veld: a grassland region with some scattered bushes and virtually no trees; other terms are *steppe*, *pampas*, and *prairie*

ventral: on or near the belly; the ventral fin is located on the underside of a fish and corresponds with the hind limbs of other vertebrates

vertebrates: any organism that has a backbone (spinal column)

woodland: a plant community in which trees grow abundantly but far enough apart that their crowns do not intermingle, so no overhead canopy is formed

INDEX

The scientific name of a plant or animal is entered in *italics*; its common name is in roman type. Page numbers in *italics* refer to picture captions.